Sermons Which Have Won Souls

SERMONS WHICH HAVE WON SOULS

By

Rev. LOUIS ALBERT BANKS, D.D.

Pastor Trinity Methodist Episcopal Church
Denver, Colorado

Author of
"Christ and His Friends," "Paul and His Friends," "David and His
Friends," etc.

GEN. THEO. SEMINARY
LIBRARY
NEW YORK

FUNK & WAGNALLS COMPANY
NEW YORK AND LONDON
1908

252 Q
B226

108754

Copyright, 1908, by
FUNK & WAGNALLS COMPANY
Printed in the United States of America
Published, June, 1908

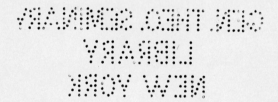
UNION THEO. SEMINARY
LIBRARY
NEW YORK

To
the Members of
Trinity Methodist Episcopal Church
of Denver, Colorado
This Volume Is Gratefully and Affectionately
Dedicated by the Author

CONTENTS

CONTENTS—*Continued*

Introductory Chapter
THE PASTOR
AS A PERSONAL
SOUL WINNER

THE PASTOR AS A PERSONAL SOUL WINNER

ANY clear-headed pastor will agree with me that, however desirable the occasional revival with its winning of souls to Christ may be (and I hold it to be desirable in every church), it is still more important that there be a steady evangelistic movement which secures the salvation of souls through the regular services of the church every week. It is this steady work which counts most for the power of the Christian church in the community.

Now I do not believe there is so fearful a waste anywhere as in the average Christian church to-day, where the Gospel is preached and men and women are awakened to conviction in their hearts and minds, have their consciences stirred as to their duty, and yet are not brought to intelligent decision and action concerning the truth of which they are convinced.

The church is not a club existing for the culture and entertainment of its members only. The Christian church exists first to preach the Gospel to sinners, to keep childhood in the way of truth, and to cultivate and develop Christian character; and its weakest point to-day is in the lack of the kind of personal following up of the Gospel preached in the church service that accomplishes the conversion of the people who hear. Of all men in the church the pastor has the best opportunity to do this work, and the pastor who is able to bring the largest number of other people into personal work of this character will be the most powerful and effective. The cultivation of this class of workers should be ever on his mind and heart. Every earnest worker of this type will mean the salvation of a great many souls every year. I was once able to win a young grocery clerk to Christ and to instil into his heart the desire to win some one else, and in the first six months after his conversion that young fellow, with only an average amount of intelligence and cultivation, and working all the time long hours, six days in the week, in a grocery store, was successful in bringing to the church twenty-five men whose conversion he secured and all of whom became members with him in the church. Many churches in that same city that year did not win as many men to Christ.

But, after all, the laboring oar is in the hands of the pastor, and unless he uses it, not a great deal of that kind of work will be done in the average church. Of late years I have come to the conclusion in my own ministry that it is a mistake to expect direct results in the salvation of souls from the Sunday evening service only. I have found that there are large numbers of men and women among the unconverted who only attend church on Sunday morning, and if they are to be reached they must be reached in the morning sermon. This has led me to the determination to so build my morning sermon that while it shall have in it truths that will develop Christian character and comfort those who are in trial, it will also never fail to have a message to the people who are without, and I seek to follow up the message by private conversation and appeal in their homes, or, where it is advisable, at their places of business, during the week. In order to do this I make the Sunday services yield me a large number of addresses of people who offer opportunities for such visitation. Every Sunday morning and every Sunday evening I am at the main entrance of the church when the doors are thrown open, half an hour before the service begins. I shake hands with the people as they come in. The first fifteen or twenty minutes, even in a very large congregation, the people gather rather slowly, and in a big city church, with an average congregation of from fourteen hundred to sixteen hundred people, there will be a large percentage of strangers during these early moments. I find out the names of these people, find out whether they are Christians, and if they have any church affiliation. If they are not Christians, I get by tactful questioning as much insight as possible unto their mental attitude toward Christianity. I go up to the sermon with my hands full of memoranda of names and addresses. Oftentimes I have in this way made discoveries that have been very stimulating to me in the sermon which followed, and the fact that I have had the friendly talk at the door makes the sermon far more effective to many people.

At the close of the sermon I say to the people that I shall remain for a while at the altar of the church, and shall be very glad to shake hands with any who would like to meet me and grateful if strangers who come occasionally will wait long enough for me to meet them. This brings to me many people from those who have come in late, after the sermon opened. It also brings, nearly every Sunday, some people to whom the sermon has been a message from God, and who give me a glimpse into their hearts, and put me on the trail of a possible convert. Again I have my pencil and memorandum book and gather still more addresses. The same thing goes on in the evening, and all through the year, every Sunday, rain or shine, when I am at home with my church.

Now on Monday morning I have this pile of addresses. With some of them I have made definite engagements for a certain time of the day and for certain days in the week. For some people who are busy during the day I have made definite engagements for certain evenings, and sometimes Monday morning finds me with every evening in the week booked full of this class of engagements, with the exception of the evenings upon which I have regular church services. This gives me a chance to follow up the message of the sermon before it has been forgotten, and ere its influence has been lost. The result is very remarkable. Scarcely a week has passed during the last two years that there have not been from one to a dozen who have been brought to a definite decision to seek Christ and to unite with his church through these personal interviews in the week following the sermon. I bring all these people into a class and meet them one evening in the week to study the simple beginnings of Christian life and character.

Many people are just waiting for some earnest Christian personality to lead them into the king-

dom of God. In the great congregation they are
held in bondage by their timidity and the lethargy
of the situation; but the moment an earnest Christian man comes personally to them they yield with
gladness. There are many other people who go
frequently to church and who are not far from
the kingdom, but who are kept out of it by seeming difficulties that vanish away like morning mist
when once brought up and clearly and intelligently
discust. Many other people are held away from
God by sins which never can be uncovered without
that sort of personal magnetic fellowship which
comes in the private interview with a man determined to bring a soul to Christ.

I shall never forget a dark lowering morning
when I went up into the pulpit much deprest by
the unusual gloom of the day. But when I looked
out on the congregation I was immediately interested in the striking-looking face of a man who had
come in after I left the door. He was a stranger
to me, but in the sermon which followed I was sure
that he winced under the application of the truth
to himself. I determined to get at him at the close
of the service, but he slipped away too quickly
for me. I found out a little later in the day that
he was one of the wealthiest business men in the
city, a man of reserved temperament, who lived in

a great mansion in one of the most fashionable suburbs. I confess I was greatly disappointed to hear all this. As a matter of theory I believed that God was as interested in rich men as in poor ones, and that Jesus Christ was as able to save this man as he would be if he were some struggling lawyer or clerk; but as a matter of fact I had had a good deal more experience with the other class, and my optimism and enthusiasm as to my ability to follow up my message for the man's help and comfort had received a great check.

All that afternoon and night, again and again. that man's face came back to me, and I was greatly worried as to what I ought to do. The result of it all was that Monday afternoon, in a pouring rain, I hired a closed carriage and drove three miles into the country suburb where stood the mansion of the man who had been to hear me preach the morning before. I never did anything more diffidently in my life. I fairly trembled as I went up the walk. I rang the bell in fear.

A servant came and ushered me into the parlor. A little later the door opened at the far end of the room and through it came my stranger of yesterday. When he saw me a startled look went over his face. He came forward and took my hand in a firm long grasp as he said, "This is a strange thing.

I have been thinking of you ever since I heard you preach yesterday morning. I thought of driving in again last night, but I have not been well, and my wife feared for me to do it. To-day I have thought of going to see you, but the storm kept me back. How did you happen to come to see me through all this rain?''

Then I just opened my heart to him and told him the whole story which I have told you—of how he had interested me during the sermon and how I had been worried about him and had prayed about him ever since; only in this case we were two men sitting close together with our eyes on each other's faces and our hearts greatly moved.

He told me that the sermon the day before had seemed to be God's message to him, and that he felt greatly condemned to have so long neglected making an open surrender of himself to Christ.

After we had talked a while, I asked him if I might pray with him, and he said it would be a great comfort to him and he would like his wife to be present. He went out and brought her in and introduced her, repeated to her something of the conversation, and then I prayed with them. The Holy Spirit was present in that room during that prayer. Our hearts were strangely warmed. When we arose from our knees I shall never forget the face or words of my new friend. His cheeks were bathed in tears; his eyes shone with a new light; he grasped me by the hand and exclaimed, "I thank you with all my heart. You are the first man in twenty-five years who has asked me about my soul or asked permission to pray in my house."

That prayer and conversation marked the beginning of a new Christian life in that household. I could relate many such incidents.

The sermons in this volume are all Sunday morning sermons, selected from those preached during the last two years because of the fact that they have been peculiarly blest of God in arousing the consciences and awakening the hearts of men and women who through this personal following up have been won to Christ and to the church. Every one of these sermons has had that peculiar sanction of God that it has been the instrument of winning souls to Christ. I send forth this, as I have the many volumes which have preceded it, with the sincere and humble prayer that the blessing of God which has been on these sermons in their proclamation may abide with them on the printed page. To every winner of souls to whom they may bring inspiration I extend a brother's faithful hand.   LOUIS ALBERT BANKS.

Denver, Col., January 10, 1908.

THE SOUL'S QUEST

THE SOUL'S QUEST

"That I may know him, and the power of his resurrection, and the fellowship of his sufferings, being made conformable unto his death; if by any means I might attain unto the resurrection of the dead."—Philippians, III: 10, 11.

THE first and supreme thought which inspires Paul in writing this letter is evidently his determination to come into the closest possible intimacy with Jesus Christ. He counts it the highest of all knowledge that he may know Jesus. He is willing to count all things but loss for the excellency of the knowledge of Christ Jesus his Lord. It was not to know about Jesus simply, or to understand the great doctrines taught by Christ, which was the supreme quest of Paul's soul. All this was interesting to him, but there was something else of greater interest, and that was to know Christ as a personal friend and Savior.

I

Experience is always the truest test. It is by far the most satisfactory test to which anything with which we have to do may be put. A man who

23

has traveled in a country, looked upon its cities, climbed its mountains, and crossed its rivers, knows a great deal more about it than a man who has only seen a map of it. A man who reads that honey is sweet has a very superficial knowledge of its characteristics compared with the man who has tasted it. You may tell a child that fire is hot, but such knowledge is not so convincing as a scorched finger. History tells us that the Gauls when they had once tasted the Italian grapes were determined to get into the country where they grew. Moses sent the spies into the promised land that they might bring the clusters of Canaan into the wilderness to convince Israel of the richness of the country.

And so in religion, as in other matters, experience only can give perfect satisfaction. The supreme quest of the soul of man is for personal acquaintance with Jesus. A man may know a great deal about the Bible—know it so well that he rejoices in its literature, is inspired by its splendid psalms, is exalted by its dreams of the triumph of goodness upon the earth, and may even know the story of Christ until, like a celebrated infidel, he gives to him the reverence of his tears—and yet have no satisfactory knowledge of Jesus. It is not knowing about Christ, but knowing Christ, that will give us inspiration and comfort and good cheer

in all the struggles of life. We often see much of
a man without knowing him. I once said to the
wife of a man whom I had known a great while,
"Your husband never seems to have the blues or to
suffer from changeableness of mood." "Ah," she
said, with a smile, "you do not know him as I do."
It made me think of what Christ said to Philip in
one of the last conversations he had with his disciples—"Have I been so long time with you, and
yet hast thou not known me?" Many people have
grown up in the Sunday-school and in the church,
and have heard a thousand sermons about Jesus,
and yet do not know him. I pray God that there
may possess our hearts this supreme ambition
which animated Paul to know Jesus. He is not
hard to get acquainted with. He wears his heart
on his sleeve. If with true purpose you are seeking to know him, to catch his spirit, to share his
life, you will find him ready with joyous and inspiring welcome to take you into the very secrets
of his soul. Never was there so charming a personality. It was once said of Garibaldi that he
charmed all who got into his society. But that
charm, which many a great man has had in small
degree, is only like candle light to the noonday sun
compared to the infinite charm in Jesus Christ. In
him are love, sympathy, gentleness, heroism, power,

forbearance, all at their perfection in a single personality.   To know Jesus, that is the supreme
knowledge and the supreme gladness of human
life.

II

We have also suggested in our theme the soul's
quest for power. In our text Paul says, "That I
may know him, and the power of his resurrection."
I am sure that Paul meant here more than the
resurrection of the body. From many of his utterances he makes it very clear to us that the resurrection of the body, in which he thoroughly believed, was to him a vivid and powerful illustration of the resurrection of the soul and its redemption from sin. In his letter to the Romans he says:
"Reckon ye, . . . yourselves to be dead indeed
unto sin, but alive unto God through Jesus Christ
our Lord. Let not sin therefore reign in your
mortal body, that ye should obey it in the lusts
thereof." And in his letter to the Colossians he
says: "If ye then be risen with Christ, seek those
things which are above, where Christ sitteth on
the right hand of God. Set your affection on things
above, not on things on the earth." And again,
Paul goes on to explain still more carefully what
he means by declaring that the Christian hath

"Put off the old man with his deeds; and hath put on the new man, which is renewed in knowledge after the image of him that created him."

These and other strong utterances of Paul give us authority to believe that in his mind the power of Christ's resurrection indicated in the strongest way the power to triumph over sin, to gain conquest over the human heart, and to live victoriously the Christ life amid the temptations and the sins of earth. In Jesus Christ alone can we find the power that can give us this victory. Dr. Watkinson, a popular English preacher now in this country, tells how he was recently reading a medical book on "The Sterilization of the Hands"—the importance of the medical man, the surgeon, having his hands clean for his operations. He tells us how he tried a great number of things to cleanse his hands, and in the end found it impossible. He came to the conclusion that there is no such thing as cleaning your hands; at least, they are surgically infective. The writer says that when he washed his hands in soap and water he found that they were more infected than they were before. The more he scrubbed the more the microbes multiplied. He gives reasons why this should be so, reasons that seem quite feasible. The more he scrubbed the more the microbes came to light.

Is not that exactly the case with the man who begins to deal with his sinful nature? What does Paul say? "When the law came, sin revived." It was fomented, stirred up, came to light, asserted itself. When the law came, when it came home, irrationality, passion, self-will, were stirred up and came to light. "Sin revived, and I died." Many people are living just there, with the painful consciousness of evil passions, of wicked affinities that appeal to them, and they have a gnawing, haunting consciousness of guilt that makes peace impossible. It is only the power of Christ's resurrection that can cleanse such a heart. In Isaiah we read of the wonderful times that are coming in this world when the kingdom of Jesus Christ shall come to full victory. He tells us that the wolf and the lamb, the leopard and kid, the lion and the ox, will all be brought into a marvelous harmony; the sucking child is to play on the hole of the asp, and the weaned child to put his hand on the cockatrice's den. That all seems very marvelous and very wonderful, but it is not so wonderful as when a sinful man by humility and prayer and self-surrender brings into his heart the resurrection power of Jesus Christ, and obtains the forgiveness of his sins, and finds his nature renewed in love and purity.

It is not only in the Bible that we learn it, but the most modern science tells us that a man's heart is by nature a dark forest, where wild beasts roam, and where they hiss and snarl and scream and bite. The scientists tell us that these beasts came out of the primeval forest in our ancestral days, and they are the survivals of the animality of our origin. We do not need to quarrel with the scientists. One thing we are sure of when we look into the human heart, and that is that the wild beasts are there— asp, cockatrice, wolf, leopard—all the wild passions are there; but, thank God, Jesus Christ has power to tame them, to take the drunkard and make him sober living, to take the sinner most wretched and tyrannized over and make him as peaceful and loving as the man out of whom he cast devils in Gadara. There is power in Jesus to soften and strengthen and harmonize in the human heart until what was a den of wild beasts becomes a garden of the Christian graces.

It is not only for our own salvation that this resurrection power of Jesus Christ should be sought after by us, but that with it bestowed upon us we may work the will of God in our own day and time. If we shall be worthy of this power it will be because we surrender ourselves completely to him and willingly give ourselves to do his work.

Some one sings who has known this experience:

My hands were filled with many things,
Which I did precious hold
As any treasure of a king's,
Silver, or gems, or gold.
The Master came and touched my hands,
      The scars were on his own.
And at his feet my treasures sweet
Fell shattered one by one;
"I must have empty hands," said he,
"Wherewith to work my works through thee."

My hands were stained with marks of toil,
Defiled with dust of earth,
And I my work did ofttimes soil,
And render little worth—
The Master came and touched my hands,
      And crimson were his own.
And when amazed, on mine I gazed,
Lo! every stain was gone.
"I must have cleansed hands," said he,
"Wherewith to work my works through thee."

My hands were growing feverish,
And cumbered with much care,
Trembling with haste and eagerness,
Nor folded oft in prayer.
The Master came and touched my hands,
      With healing in his own,
And calm and still to do his will
They grew, the fever gone.
"I must have quiet hands," said he,
"Wherewith to work my works through thee."

My hands were strong in fancied strength,
But not in power divine,

And bold to take up tasks at length,
That were not his, but mine.
The Master came and touched my hands,
    And might was in his own.
But mine, since then, have powerless been,
    Save his were laid thereon,
"And it is only thus," said he,
"That I can work my works through thee."

III

We have also, very earnestly set forth, Paul's
ambition to share the fellowship of Christ's sufferings. He does not put this first, he does not feel
that the fellowship of Christ's sufferings is the
first thing that the soul must seek. In Paul's writings, everywhere, life and not death is the key-note.
If ever a man was sane and healthy it was Paul.
He is ambitious to know Christ, to become acquainted with him personally, and he is determined
to attain the power of the risen Lord over sin;
but then he longs to share with Jesus to the full the
fellowship of his sufferings. A willingness to share
suffering is a test of true friendship. Casual ac-
quaintances do not feel it necessary to telegraph
us or write us if they are ill or in trouble, but old
friends with whom we have borne the burden and
the heat of the day, sharing their joy and their
power, do us honor when they call us to share with
them in their sufferings. And we cannot know

Jesus so as to receive the richest blessings from him unless we know the fellowship of his sufferings. Dr. Jowett commenting on this phrase recently said that we are apt to regard the table at which our Lord sits as only laden with delicate and dainty luxuries. But upon that table there is another cup which is very much nearer to the Master's hand. "Are ye able to drink of the cup that I drink of?" is Christ's question. Our intimacy with the Lord can best be estimated by our familiarity with the contents of that bitter cup. Our fellowship with the Lord can best be measured, not by our capacity for joy, but by our capacity for suffering. It is when deep calleth unto deep that we enter into the mystery of the Savior's cross.

This fellowship of Christ's sufferings will make us very sensitive to the approach of evil. It may be doubted if Jerusalem was as wicked a city as Denver, but the prevailing sin of the city hurt Jesus, and the closer we come into fellowship with Christ the more the sins of the city will hurt us, and the more we will share with Jesus in suffering over it, and that suffering will drive us to sacrifice in effort to stop the sin. Christians ought to be more sensitive and more easily shocked at the sins of the city than they are. See Christ when on one occasion they come to him and tell him a filthy story.

What does he do? He stoops down and writes on
the ground. What is he doing? He is blushing—
he is blushing. They tell him an impure story and
he hides his head for shame. But I fear many in
Christ's church to-day can listen to such stories
and not blush. Is it not true that we are often
fascinated by iniquity? We take up our morning
paper and follow its unclean track down column
after column of print when we ought to burn the
dirty sheet with consuming shame. Oh, disciples
of Jesus Christ, the sin of Denver ought to make
us smart. Does it?

The fellowship of Christ's sufferings must also
involve the power to enter into the sorrows of the
world. A servant girl came into her pastor's study
one day, and in the course of the talk said, "I only
get out one evening in two weeks, so I cannot do
much, but I will tell you what I do; an evening
paper comes into our house, and I am allowed to
look at it. I turn to the obituary column and to
the news about the homeless and starving, and I
pray over each name." Was not that sharing the
fellowship of his sufferings? What a strange pre-
scription for trouble Jesus gave when he said:
"Come unto me, all ye that labor and are heavy
laden. . . . take my yoke upon you." At first
glance it seems a strange way to find rest to add

one yoke to another. The secret of it is in the fellowship. In the doubling of the burden, the burden becomes light. When we add our grief to the grief of another, there is in the combined fire a third form, one like unto the Son of man.

The biographer of Charles Lamb tells us that when those awful periods of mental darkness threatened Mary Lamb, she and her brother Charles would go out in the early morning or late at night, speechless and weeping, treading their desolate way in silence. They went together hand in hand and weeping. I do not care what Charles Lamb's creed was; in his silent sympathy in those dread hours he was taking the awful goblet from the table of his Lord. He was sharing the fellowship of Christ's sufferings.

The great trouble with many of us is not that we are not sympathetic, but that we do not express it in service. We are moved, but we do not move. We are stirred by gracious impulse, but we do not stir. The impulse does not take on a practical form. We cry out, ''Lord, I will follow thee: I could do anything for thee; I will follow thee in a moment, suffer me first to go and bury,''— ''Let the dead bury their dead and follow me,'' is Christ's word. Do we not need to hear that voice to-day? Follow Christ at once in service and

sympathy, and in sharing the sufferings of your
fellow men with him, before the fire of sympathy
which has become kindled in your breast becomes
dead.

Dr. Jowett, from whom I have already quoted,
truly says that one of the greatest hindrances to
Christianity in our time is that while we share
Christ's fellowship to some extent we stop short
of the blood-letting. And yet it is precisely at the
point of blood-letting that our cause begins to win.
When our work becomes costly, it begins to pay.
Our life only becomes contagious when it becomes
sacrificial. The curse of our time in Christian
circles is that we are so comfortable. Good men
and good women are willing to allow their pastor
to stir them to generous emotions on a Sunday
morning, but would count it beyond their power
to come to a Sunday evening service, at the cost of
an extra nap, that sinners might be converted and
the lost sheep of Christ be brought home. It is
the laziness, the self-indulgence, the lack of willingness, the lack of real desire to share the sufferings of Jesus Christ in saving sinners, that makes
the church slow and stumbling in her course, when
she should march forth like an army "with ban-
ners." Oh, for a year of men like John Knox,
whose prayers a wicked queen feared more than an

army of soldiers! Oh, for a year of those Pente-
costal Christians who wrestled every man with his
neighbor until he surrendered to Jesus! Oh, for
a year of the early Methodists, whom stones could
not make timid, whom poverty could not shame,
who turned the world upside down by their fervor!
Oh, for a year of you, men and women sitting in
these pews, shaken out of your self-indulgence,
aroused to such gratitude to Christ for your salvation that you will cry out with Paul, and vie with
each other for an opportunity to share with Jesus
Christ in sympathy, and self-sacrifice, and suffering, that you may win the men and women of
Denver to salvation!

IV

We have another suggestion, or rather more than
a suggestion, for it is an essential part of the whole
quest of Paul's soul. That is, his determination to
know the immortality of Jesus. It suggests to us
the true quest of our souls after the immortal life.
Paul says, "That I may know him, and the power
of his resurrection, and the fellowship of his sufferings, being made conformable unto his death; if by
any means I might attain unto the resurrection of
the dead." If we live with Christ here; if we
know him in our own heart's experience through

prayer and song and blessed consciousness; if we
receive from him the resurrection power so that
we gain conquest over our own hearts, and in that
power live just and true lives; if we share in the
fellowship of his sufferings so that we are thrilled
and exalted as day by day we touch elbows with
him in a yoke-fellowship of service to help the
world, then we shall share his immortality. We
shall live and die without doubt concerning the
eternal life. No traveler to the heavenly world
has come back to tell us about it save Jesus only,
but since he is my friend, and my Savior, and has
honored me by calling me to share with him, I
may have no doubt that when I take that last
voyage into the mysteries of death I shall not only
meet my Pilot face to face when I have crossed the
bar, but I shall see a smile of welcome there, for I
shall see him as he is, and I shall be satisfied, for
I shall be like him.

Some of you who hear me are still in throes of
agonizing grief over the passing out from your
earthly company of those dear to you as your own
life. Your broken hearts are ready to exclaim
with Byron when he declares it to be: "A fearful
thing to see the human soul take wing." But if
we keep in close fellowship with Jesus we are never
far away from our loved ones who sleep in him,

and the promise of reunion becomes every day more real and comforting to us. The agonizing "good-by" is changed in our thought into the "good-night" of eager expectation. In such a hope we are able to say to our departing loved ones:

"Only good-night, beloved, not farewell,
A little while and all His saints shall dwell
In hallowed union indivisible,
          Good-night.

"Until we meet before His throne,
Clothed in the spotless robe He gives His own,
Until we know as we are known,
          Good-night."

THE ROYAL
KINSHIP
OF SERVICE

THE ROYAL KINSHIP OF SERVICE

"They dwelt with the king for his work."—I Chronicles
IV: 23.

WORK is the law of life, whether for king or
for peasant. The nearer a man gets to the
top the greater his responsibility and the more tax-
ing his work. These men doubtless counted it high
honor that they were engaged in the work of the
king. That they might serve him the better they
dwelt in the king's household and were always near
him. They were set apart entirely to his service.

Christ is our king, if we have chosen him with
whole-hearted acceptance. Christ never becomes
any man's king except through the loving choice
of the heart.

They tell us that once upon a time the old Repub-
lican city of Florence in Italy found herself greatly
indebted to one of her citizens. He had done Florence a great service and so the Florentines came
one day and said, "Ferrara, we owe to you everything, our lives, our liberty, our speech, and our

great city. Ferrara, we will make you king of the
kingdom.''

These people who boasted of their liberty were
willing to put their necks in the bondage of slavery
in token of gratitude to the man who had so sig-
nally served them.

Ferrara said, ''No, men of Florence, I cannot be
your king; but I will tell you of one who, if you let
him, will be king. Men of Florence, make Jesus
your king!''

And so it stood written on the books of the city,
for nine months, that Jesus was titular King of
Florence. And if you go there to-day you may
read over the door of the proud Palazzo Vecchio,
the headquarters of the city, this legend, ''Jesus
Christ, the King of kings and Lord of lords.''

But it would not do. They could, by no decree
of their city, make Jesus Christ king. Men under-
took it when Jesus was here in the flesh. They
were determined to make him king by force, but
you can never make Jesus Christ king by force,
either over a nation, or a city, or a single individual. Neither can you do it alone by signing
creeds or by any mere formal ceremony. The only
way to make Christ king is by the willing offering
of your love; by crowning him Lord over all in
your heart through your affectionate devotion.

If we have thus chosen Christ as our king or will now so choose him, we may find in our text a helpful theme. If we choose Christ as king it is for service, and we should consecrate ourselves first of all to be the loyal servants of Christ. Nothing must interfere with that.

The old German poet, Schiller, has a ballad which tells the story of the Count of Hapsburg. One day while hunting the antelope, and in full and wild swing of the chase, the Count heard the sound which told of the last sacrament being carried to the dying:

"He heard in the distance a bell tinkling clear,
    And a priest with the host, he saw, soon drawing near."

As the priest passed along his way, the Count saw that a brook, swollen by the rains, barred his steps with its current. Dismounting from his horse the Count placed the priest with his sacred burden on the saddle, enabling him to ride in safety over the stream and take "provision for the way" to the dying man.

"On the following morning, with grateful look,
    To the Count once again the charger he took;"

but the Count refused to take back for common use what had borne a burden so holy, and devoted the horse as a gift to the service of God in the monastery.

    " 'God forbid that in chase or battle,' then cried
      The Count in humility lowly,
    'The steed I henceforth should dare to bestride,
      That hath borne my Creator so holy.
    And if as a guerdon he may not be thine,
      He devoted shall be to the service divine.' "

So we should count ourselves sacred to the service of Jesus Christ. Anything that would dishonor him is out of character for us, since we belong to the King and hold ourselves responsible for his good name.

I

Service links men with kings. In the story of our text we find potters and gardeners and people who trimmed the hedge all associated with the king. They dwelt with him for his work. So Christian service links us with God and Christ. "We are workers together with God." If we are associated with Christ in service, then we catch his spirit, and the things which most interest him become of most importance to us. John Morley in his life of Gladstone says that Gladstone did some things because he was a Christian which no reasonable man could have expected him to do. One of the things he speaks of in that way is this: When Gladstone was at Oxford, he, a young man of high-souled integrity, with others, entered into

a covenant that all their life long, whatever their
avocation or calling, they would personally do
some Christian work; not merely patronize it, or
support it, but throw their whole energy into some
definite Christian work, as long as they lived. He
and Canon Hope Scott, noting the scarcity of such
workers, agreed that they would devote themselves
to the salvation of fallen women. Mr. Morley says
that one thing that greatly shocked him as a youth
was that a man, speaking strongly against Mr.
Gladstone, said: "You can see him any night,
after the house has risen, in the Strand or Picca-
dilly with these women." Mr. Morley remarks
that this kind of work got him into difficulty. "Of
course," Morley says, "it was very indiscreet and
very unwise. Everybody admits there was not a
scrap of worldly wisdom in it; but then, what are
people Christians for?" He leaves his question
unanswered, but gives his readers the impression
that he regards a man who professes to be a Christian as a man who does something beyond what
ordinary justice and ordinary prudence expect of
him, and that a man's religion is to go into his
business, not simply making him a just and moral,
but a holy man. The Christian's business life must
of necessity be mastered and controlled by Christ.
The presence of the King must dominate his busi-

ness as well as every other department of his life.

The Rev. Samuel Chadwick relates the interesting story of a man who came to his family physician one day not feeling very well. After a careful examination the doctor solemnly told him that he had a bad heart. He said, "At any time you may die suddenly, or you may live for years." The doctor and his patient were good friends, Christian brethren, and tho at first the man was greatly shocked, he did not after the first surprize seriously trouble about it. He said, "Well, shall I give up business?" The doctor said, "No, you would die the sooner probably for that; go on, but don't hurry and don't worry." On his way home from the doctor's office the man stopt at his place of business and called together the heads of the departments and told them where he had been and what the doctor had told him. "Now," he said, "I shall come to business, but I can't be everywhere; and I want you to understand that this business is to be run with the understanding and the expectation that Jesus Christ may come to the master at any minute, and when he comes I don't want him to find anything in this firm we would not like him to see."

That man under the shadow of death had the right spirit of consecrated service. But, my brother, do not wait until you get a bad heart, and a death warrant from your physician, before you hold yourself in strict accountability to carry on your business in harmony with the spirit of Christ.

If we are thus associated with Jesus, the burdens we carry for our fellow men will be made tender and loving ministries which will not gall or chafe us. Some poet sings:

"I met a slender, little maid, a rosy burden bearing;
'Is it not heavy, dear?' I said, as past me she was hurrying.
She looked at me with grave, sweet eyes, this fragile little
    mother.
And answered, as in swift surprize, 'Oh, no, sir; it's *my*
    brother.'

"We larger children toil and fret to help the old world
    onward;
Our eyes with tears are often wet, so slowly he moves
    sunward.
Yet did we all the secret seek of this dear little mother,
Unwearyingly we'd bear the weak, because he is *our*
    brother."

II

Fellowship with Christ strengthens us for service, rescues us from selfishness, and gives us the broader horizon. Selfishness is the most fruitful cause of discouragement and discontent. Some one says that it is when a church member begins to brood on himself, and remembers how much he has done for the church for which he never got credit, that he begins to feel badly treated, and to doubt the justice of God as well as of men. It is as tho a man had been given a magnifying glass to study the grandeur and beauty of the sunset on a mountain peak, and he changes the focus, and turns the lenses upon his sore finger, and wastes his time in mawkish sentiment over a scratch which he sees magnified into a fearful wound. In such a case a man's little finger is bigger than the world to him. It seems of more importance to him that he should live and escape suffering than that God should be glorified. When a man's life is the biggest thing in the world to him, he can neither be a good Christian, nor a good citizen, nor a good father, nor a humane man. The true remedy for this pitiful selfishness is fellowship with Jesus Christ in loyal service. We always have within our reach the key that will open the door into communion with him.

On one occasion, near the end of the life of Queen Victoria, she visited Sheffield to open the gates of the Town Hall of that city. She was so feeble that it was thought best she should not move from her carriage; so hidden electric wires were fastened to a golden key fitting into the lock, which she could turn as she sat in her carriage. By an act of faith she turned the golden key, and

as she did so, at some distance away, slowly, surely
the gates of the Town Hall opened. We have a
key like that which opens the door between us and
Christ. We cannot see the wires which connect the
golden key of prayer with Heaven's gate, but a
voice which we trust says to us, "Turn the key;
turn the golden key." "Ask, and ye shall receive;
seek, and ye shall find; knock, and it shall be
opened unto you"; and the history of the centuries
does not fail to prove that every one that asketh
receiveth, and to every one that knocks it is opened,
and every earnest seeker finds, unto the joy of salvation. It is this fellowship with Christ, this communion with him, and imitation of him, which is
the secret of the noblest service for humanity the
world has ever seen. St. Augustine says that the
essence of religion is to imitate Him whom you
worship. Not necessarily to understand Him, but
to imitate Him.

The most disagreeable and unpleasant tasks
which duty thrusts upon us, if entered upon with
a sincere love for Christ and a desire to help on his
kingdom and forward his cause, will be transfigured and ere long become beautiful to us, and be
to us a source of joy for their own sake. Do you
remember the old myth of "Beauty and the
Beast"? Beauty was a good daughter and a brave

woman. Her father lost his fortune, and she set herself to serve him. When he was captured by the Beast and forced to promise one of his daughters as a ransom, Beauty at once offered herself as the sacrifice. In the palace of the Beast, surrounded by every luxury, but not knowing what fate awaited her, she never forgot her old father, dreaming of him nightly, and at last begged leave to go to see him and return. Altho she was persuaded to stay a week beyond her leave, she came back loyally to the palace of the Beast. The poor creature was half dead with grief for what he believed to be her loss, and the sight of his pain and his delight gave her courage to avow her recognition of his noble qualities, her love for him, and her resolve to be his wife in spite of his hideous exterior. Instantly the Beast was transformed into a handsome young prince, freed from an evil charm by the devotion of the brave woman, and Beauty and the prince came into their just inheritance of joy and peace.

So, no doubt, some of you who hear me are confronted by duties which seem repulsive to you; but if in recognition of Christ's great love for you, and of the debt of gratitude which you owe to him, you would give yourself to this hard service, the very duty which seems so ugly would be transfigured by your love and devotion, and would ere long become your greatest joy and satisfaction.

III

It is only by dwelling with the King and sharing his service that we may be sure that at the end we shall have light and peace. The men or the women who give themselves up to the mere worldly pleasures which appeal to the senses and minister to their gratification are preparing for an old age which will be utterly empty and miserable when once the senses have lost their capacity to be stimulated into action. The man who thinks he will have peace because he has laid by great stores of wealth has his answer in the Rich Fool of Christ's gospel. He who gives himself to self-indulgence is hatching out a brood of scorpions that in the end will sting him with remorse.

George Frederick Watts was not only a great painter, but a great Christian as well. In the Tate Gallery in London are gathered many of his paintings, one of which is "The Prophet Jonah Denouncing the Sins of Nineveh." He stands with outstretched hands, with every finger outspread to the utmost, face worn and haggard, hair matted and wild, eyes fiery and rolling, muscles tense and

strained, mouth open and eloquent, as he denounces
the wickedness of the city.   Behind him are three
friezes illustrating drunkenness, gambling, and
horse-racing, while on the floor there are money-
bags and ugly figures crawling up to them.   It is a
representation not only of Jonah in Nineveh, but
of George Watts in the Babylon of the modern
city, denouncing the sins that with canker-like
voracity are eating away the vitals of our city life.
Watts regarded our excessive love of wealth and
our indecent haste to get rich as a menace and a
calamity.   On one occasion a friend said to him
that God owned all the wealth, and that the million-
aires were his money-bags and stewards.   "Then
I wish," said Watts, "that He would add to His
other duties the appointment of an auditor."   But
in his picture of Mammon he very clearly makes us
to understand that the auditor has been appointed,
and that he does his work with a tragic effective-
ness.   A grosser figure than Mammon it is difficult
to imagine.   A huge animal face, a neck with
creases and folds of sensuality, square jaws, thick
lips, bleared eyes, one hand dandling with his
money-bags, the other clutching by her hair a
maiden who has possibly married him for money,
or who has been induced to sell her womanhood
by the temptations of his gold.   With one of his

huge clumsy feet he tramples upon one of the young men in his employment. Behind him are two grinning skeleton-heads, and behind a curtain in the distance are the fires of hell. "His riches are corrupted, his gold and silver are cankered, the rust of them shall be witness against him, and shall eat his flesh as it were fire." There is no denunciation in the Old Testament more terrible than that. No Hebrew prophet ever denounced sin with the vehemence with which he denounces wealth ill-gotten and ill-used. In the same way, by the Minotaur, he sets forth the lustful man, a human being transformed into the form of an animal, crushing a frail bird with one of his hateful claws in wanton cruelty.

In these pictures the painter is true to life. Not only does the sinner, whether he be given over to drunkenness, or to greed, or to lust, or the mere giddy pursuit of indulgence, do infinite harm to others; but he ruins his own soul. There is no peace at eventime, there is no promised day-dawn of glory after life's sunset for such a soul.

Now the old eternal choice comes to every man and woman among us. At the bottom it is the choice between good and evil. It is the choice between Christ and his service or the world and self-indulgence. Which shall it be? We *must* choose.

"Ye cannot serve God and Mammon!" In that same gallery to which I have referred, Watts has two other pictures which represent these two choices. One sets forth the young ruler who came to Jesus inquiringly, and who made the great refusal. Watts paints him as a fine, well-built man drest in a gorgeous robe, his fingers glistening with rings, in the act of turning away from Christ. He turns away his face from the light because he has great possessions. But as he does so he casts down his head in desperation, as much as to say, "Now I have done it, I have lost my chance and wasted my life." Is any man or woman here tempted to such a choice to-day? Is any sin gripping your life with such a tiger-like clutch that it is causing you to turn your back on Christ, to your moral suicide? The other choice is represented by a picture called "Aspirations." It is the picture of a young soldier with bright hair and gleaming armor, facing the battle of life and looking across its plains. He hears the ringing call of duty, and his eyes are earnest with the weight of a great responsibility as he clutches the staff of his banner and determines to face the fray and play the man. He is the embodiment of the painter's great motto: "The utmost for the highest." His face is toward the dawn.

It is to this that I call you to-day. Young or old, you may take your stand beside the King, with your face toward the light, and in his fellowship tread the path that shall grow brighter and brighter unto the perfect day. Your whole career will be ennobled and transfigured if you thus dwell and toil with Christ.

> "If Christ be in the heart
> The wildest winter storm is full of solemn beauty.
> The midnight lightning flash but shows the path of duty:
> Each living creature tells some new and joyous story,
> The very trees and stones all catch a ray of glory,
> If Christ be in the heart."

THE POTTER
AND HIS
MARRED VESSEL

THE POTTER AND HIS MARRED VESSEL

"The word which came to Jeremiah from the Lord, saying, Arise, and go down to the potter's house, and there I will cause thee to hear my words. Then I went down to the potter's house, and, behold, he wrought his work on the wheels. And when the vessel that he made of the clay was marred in the hands of the potter, he made it again another vessel, as seemed good to the potter to make it. Then the word of the Lord came to me, saying, O house of Israel, cannot I do with you as this potter?"—Jeremiah XVIII: 1-6.

THIS incident, as well as its background, is exceedingly interesting and picturesque. Jeremiah was one of the most devoted of men. He gave himself unswervingly to the good of his people. One of the old Bible scholars, studying this picture, sees the prophet in his loose flowing robes, walking slowly and softly out of the temple where he has been pleading with God for Israel, and follows him as he passes away through the narrow streets of Jerusalem toward the Eastern Gate. Then, selecting his road, he wanders down the slopes into the Valley of Hinnom. The voice of God is in his ear. The Spirit is directing his steps. Listen! he is

reciting over the pathetic words of his great pre-
decessor, with almost as much pathos as Isaiah himself. "O that thou hadst hearkened to my commandments! Then had thy peace been as a river,
and thy righteousness as the waves of the sea."
The prophet had come forth from a night of sore
travail of spirit. The deep thought of his soul was
ever this, "How different might have been the
course of Israel, and the flow of their national life,
if only God's rule had been supreme." He had
chosen them to be a light to the Gentiles, but, alas!
they were darkness. In their evil choice and deeds
they had foiled the divine plan and frustrated the
divine purpose. Here is a father who loves his boy
dearly. He conceives a plan unto which to shape
his life. The boy is the one object for which he
lives; to carry out his ideal he saves his hard
earnings and seeks to inspire the lad to its lofty
attainment. But there is resistance, and the plan
is abortive. Again the father tries to shape the
boy's life according to another plan, only to result
in another failure. Still the father never despairs,
he will try again and again, until upon some noble
model he has shaped the career of his son. Now,
while Jeremiah was wandering on, he was thinking
something like that about Israel. Presently the
prophet reaches the base of the Valley of Hinnom,

and pauses in front of a potter's bench. Here he stands and observes. He sees the potter take the clay that is on his bench, knead it until it is soft and pliable to the touch. Then he sees him put it on the wheel and shape it into a vessel; and as he watches it, it becomes marred in his hand. But, to the astonishment of the prophet, the potter does not throw it away, but patiently he shapes it again and remakes it into another vessel. What seems to have made the deepest impression on the mind of the prophet is not the fact that the clay was marred in the hand of the potter, but that when the vessel was spoiled there was no sign of anger upon the face of the potter, but he set to work to do the next best thing that could be done with the clay.

Now, my friends, what God wants for nations he wants for individuals. As he deals with a people he deals with individual men and women. God is no respecter of persons. I am sure we may find in this picturesque and beautiful parable a revelation of the mind and heart of God toward each one of us.

I

I think we should have emphasized in our study, first of all, our individuality and our personal responsibility. We are living in a time and under certain conditions which make it hard to keep alive a keen sense of individual responsibility. It is a day when men do business in companies. It is the age of syndicates, and corporations, and trusts, and multiplied stockholders in great enterprises. Men will do as a part of a corporation what they would shrink from doing as an individual. Men are likely to lose in the atmosphere of such a time as ours a keen consciousness of the fact that in the sight of God we are not directors or stockholders, or partners to be judged in a mass, but we are an individual man or woman, held personally account- able to our God. Dr. Selbie, the English preacher, well says that there is no truer word in modern literature than the couplet of Kipling's, ''The sins men do by two and two, they shall pay for one by one.''

The clay lies in the hand of the potter to do with as he will; but Israel frustrated the grace of God. And the solemn reality faces us that in our freedom of will we too have the power to thwart God's plans for us. Walt Whitman drew a picture of the cow in the field. He says: ''Why am I not as the cow? It is not troubled with doubts and fears. It is not hopeless. It is not always whining about its sins, but seems content.'' And he goes on to paint an idyllic picture of the happiness he would have if he were as a cow chewing the cud in the field. It does not take us very far to answer why we cannot be as the cows. We have in us that "Spark that disturbs our clod," that divine something which lifts us above the beasts of the field and makes us infinitely more precious than they. As Robert Browning says: "Irks care the cropful-bird? Frets doubt the maw-crammed beast?" The beasts do not worry over their sins because the spark of divinity has not been imparted to them. But man is made in the image and likeness of God, and has been taught to look up in the face of his Creator and say, "Our Father, who art in heaven." So it becomes true that, as an earthly son may thwart the plan of his father, we may frustrate God's plan for us, and thus thwart his infinite love and wisdom exercised in our behalf.

II

Let us recognize anew in pursuing our theme that sin always mars and hurts and degrades our personality. It mars our very selves. It is not merely a stain that can be easily washed off. It is a marring of the vessel of our personality.

Stuart Holden tells how a friend of his, who was a collector of choice china, was once being shown through the works where most beautiful wares were made. As they passed along he saw a beautiful cup, and from his knowledge of the value of such things, he said to the one who was showing him around: "This must be a very expensive piece." The man looked at it and said: "Well, I believe you could get this for half-a-crown, if you like." "Why, surely it is worth more than that?" said the collector. "Ah," was the reply, "it was intended to be worth a great deal more than that; it is one out of a very choice set. But there is a flaw in it, and it has not been passed by the one whose duty it is to overlook and see that every piece which goes out is perfect." The gentleman looked at it and said: "I do not see any flaw." "No, you do not; but our master does. And he dare not send it out. That thing would not hold hot water." And so it was discarded and discredited. In such a manner it is that sin mars us. It may not be a sin easily discerned by the multitude. It may be a secret sin in the chambers of the imagination, nestling as yet in the secret purposes of the heart, hidden from the eye of the world; but if it is there, it mars the vessel of your personality and makes it impossible for God to use you for the very highest and noblest service for which you were planned. If we were wise, the deepest prayer of our souls would be for God to show us clearly the sin that keeps our personality from fitting into his noblest plans for us.

There is no personality so splendid or brilliant
as to be superior to this law. Some of the brightest
stars of our human race have been dragged from
the very gates of heaven down to the gates of hell
by sin. As Dwight Hillis says: "There is no Eden
that gifted men have not lost: There is no paradise the sons of genius have not destroyed." And
he goes on to illustrate it by the story of Rembrandt,
who was one of the supremely gifted painters. To-
day, one of his portraits would bring a hundred
thousand dollars in the market. But if you would
understand how a man can mar his very self by
sin, all you need to do is to study the two portraits of Rembrandt painted by himself. In the
first one he stands forth a gloriously handsome
youth. The lamps of love burn in his eyes. His
face shines like an alabaster vase with a lamp in
it. The whole man exhales strength, and there is
nothing for which he cannot hope. We know that
he has genius to create, and the imagination to
beautify the world.

Now look at Rembrandt's portrait of himself,
painted only twenty years later. The artist determined to deny himself no pleasure, he sought
out every delight, he became a sybarite, and one
by one the torches of his soul went out. Having
been untrue to himself, he lost faith in others, for

the penalty of dishonesty and impurity is the belief
that every one else is equally dishonest and impure. So in middle age we see the artist, shrunken,
an old rag around his throat, weakness in his chin,
the mark of the beast upon his brow, the eyes heavy
and dull, without vision, for the lights have gone
out. In his youth, Rembrandt lived for his ideals,
his dreams of love and country, of beauty and God.
Then he seems like some palace on a winter's night
when all the windows are ablaze with light, and
laughter and music and perfumed beauty fill the
halls, and happiness exhales like a cloud of incense
toward God. Oh, that glorious palace of sight
and sound, Man's Soul! But Rembrandt, after sin
has marred him, is to be compared to a mansion
deserted by these angelic guests. The lights have
gone out from his windows that once were full of
rich glass; the halls are empty; the spider's web
is woven over the key-hole of a closed door; the
weeds and thistles have grown up in the rocks;
the steps are rotten, the rose garden is a tangle of
thorns; all the foundations are noisome with mice
and vermin, and things that creep and crawl. Now
and then an old gibbering care-taker goes in and
out. The noble mansion is in ruins, given over to
darkness and decay. And the ruined mansion
is the house of Man's Soul. And yet every man

or woman of us who is yielding place to sin, even in the secret places of the heart, is daring just such a marred and despoiled and ruined personality.

III

The hope of the sinner is all in this, that the marred vessel is still in the hand of the potter, who has not thrown it away, but with patient love is able and willing to remake it. Some one studying this picture of the potter and his work repainted it in poetic lines:

"The Potter stooped—and took it in His hand,
    That vessel frail.
He turned it round, and gazed with wistful eyes
Upon its form, that told with silent words
    A hopeless tale.

"The Potter sighed—with sad grieved heart He marked
    The shapeless thing—
The gaping rents, the pattern spoiled and blurred,
The useless mouth. 'I meant thee,' low He said,
    'To serve a King.'

"The Potter wept—and while He held it close
    Within His hands,
He whispered to the heart that vessel shrined,
The broken heart within the broken life—
    'Love all demands.'

"The Potter cried—'Oh! foolish, foolish heart
    To fight 'gainst Me—
I, even I—I cannot mend the life
Thou thus hast marred, frustrating all My plans
    Thou couldst not see!'

"The Potter ceased. Then in the silence deep
        I heard His voice:
'To make thee, I must break—form thee again,
'Tis pain for thee, how much more 'tis for Me!
        I have no choice.'

"The Potter turned—and broke the useless thing—
        (It was not sweet!)
But from the shards a new form rose again,
His fingers molded, wrought another plan
        For service meet.

"The Potter smiled—the vase He held was fair,
        It pleased Him well.
Pure water could it hold for thirsty souls,
And recommend it by its loveliness—
        Draw—not repel."

The secret of the most splendid and beautiful
life for each one of us lies in our yielding submis-
sively to that divine love which has power to mold
us and fashion us into the best and holiest personality which God's infinite wisdom sees is still possible for us. It is not likely that the second vessel
which the potter made under the eye of Jeremiah
was as fine as the first, but it was the best that
still could be done with the clay. It is not probable that even the omnipotence and omniscience of
God can make of your life or mine the perfect
vessel that once was possible, but let us not despair
because of that. If we are still in the Potter's
hands, and yield ourselves to him, he will still fashion us into usefulness and beauty. In his loving

hands is the secret of the most beautiful life for
us.

Wayland Hoyt tells the story of a young Japanese who came into a pastor's study one morning
with the abrupt question, "Can you tell me where
I can find the Beautiful Life?" The puzzled pastor
asked him if he had ever read the Bible. "Yes,
somewhat," the young Japanese replied, "but I do
not care about the Bible; we have Japanese books
perhaps as good." What he wanted to find was
the "Beautiful Life." The pastor asked, "Have
you ever seen the 'Beautiful Life?'"

Then the story came out. The young Japanese
had come to this country to study in one of our
great American universities, but his main longing
was for a sight of the Life Beautiful. He thought
he had seen it once, where he first boarded in San
Francisco. The man illustrating it was not a
scholar, as was the Japanese himself; he was an old
man and a carpenter. But he seemed never to be
thinking about himself, always of others; was per-
petually doing service for others, and wore always
the happiest smile upon his face, as tho his
heart was held and shining in a strong peace. Since
then he had been searching in other places for the
Beautiful Life, but had only gotten glimpses of it.
Could the minister tell him where he could find it?

The minister read the Japanese student Paul's Hymn of Love in the thirteenth chapter of First Corinthians. "Was that it?" the pastor asked. "Something like it," the Japanese replied. Then the minister gave him a New Testament and charged him to study that.

Months passed away. Just before sailing to his native country, whither he had been called to an important post in the government, the young Japanese scholar burst in again upon the minister. With his face aglow, he exclaimed: "I have found the Beautiful Life, I have found Jesus!" My dear friends, it is there also that we must find the Beautiful Life. It is in his hands we must lose our sins, and be reshaped into usefulness and beauty.

IV

In the conclusion of our study we are forced back to the terrifying thought that our salvation for this world, and for all worlds, is here and now in our own hands. God will not violate your will. His spirit will brood over the sinner's heart. Christ will knock at the locked door of the soul. The gracious ministry of divine love will be offered. But it is for us to heed and answer the call. And it is a fearful truth that sin makes us dull of hearing. An English traveler tells how at Niagara Falls he descended into what is called the "Cave of the

Winds,'' where the great cataract comes sweeping
all round about, and those who are the beholders
are hidden, as it were, in a cleft of the rock. The
noise is absolutely deafening. You cannot hear the
voice of your companion unless he shouts at his
loudest in your ear. This traveler spoke to the
man who was guiding him, and who lives there all
the time; and he said to him, ''What a deafening
row you have to spend your life in!'' The guide
smiled, and said, ''Bless you, sir, I never hear it.''
''What do you mean?'' said the traveler. ''Well,''
he said, ''I was like you when I first took the job.
I thought I could not stand it because of the noise,
but now I never hear it.'' He had become familiar
with the constant repetition, the ceaseless repetition
of the sound, and it had become normal to him.
And so there is a terrible danger of our getting
into that condition with regard to the voice of God;
there is fearful peril of the atrophy of our faculty
of spiritual hearing. Oh, that God would arouse
every one of us to sensitiveness to the sound of his
voice.

I am sure there must be some who listen to me to
whom this might be—to whom this ought to be—
an epoch-making hour. It is a message which may
mean in the hands of God the recasting of your
whole personality into new and glorious fashion

under God's love in Jesus Christ. I pray God you shall not miss it through lethargy.

Joseph Medill, in his reminiscences of the great Lincoln and Douglas debate, says that one night he heard a great orator and a noble patriot who loved Douglas plead with him not to make the speech which was afterward his political ruin. Douglas would not be persuaded; but afterward, when Civil War flamed across the land, and Douglas saw his great blunder, shame and grief overwhelmed him and he fell ill with his last sickness. In his fever his biographer says he heard Douglas whispering, "I missed it! I missed it! I missed it!" God save any man or woman here from that cry when the shadows gather at the last!

THE MANI-
FESTATION
OF CHRIST

THE MANIFESTATION OF CHRIST

"I am the light of the world."—John VIII: 12.
"Ye are the light of the world."—Matthew V: 14.

CHRIST is the moral and spiritual luminary of the world. As the moon and the stars get their light from the sun and do all their shining with that borrowed light, so we get our light from Christ. He is the "Sun of righteousness," whose beams illuminate the whole moral universe. This declaration of Christ should shock into silence those who talk of Jesus as tho he were only a man, as we are. What other man in all history could have retained the respect of his fellows if he had made an utterance like this: "I am the light of the world." Yet it seems natural and appropriate to us falling, as it does, from the lips of Jesus.

There is in our theme also a glorious revelation of the nobility that is in us. The moon and the stars must have the power to receive and convey light, or the shining of the sun upon them would be worthless. Man must have in him some kinship to Christ, some divine capabilities, or the light from the Son of God falling on him would not create him in turn the "Light of the world." As Phillips Brooks said in commenting on this scripture, when the sun rose this morning it found the world here. It found the world in darkness, torpid and heavy and asleep; with powers all wrapt up in sluggishness; with life that was hardly better or more alive than death. The sun found this great sleeping world and woke it. It bade it be itself. It quickened every slow and sluggish faculty. It called to the dull streams, and said, "Be quick;" to the dull birds and bade them sing; to the dull fields and bade them grow; to the dull men and bade them talk and think and work. It flashed electric invitation to the whole mass of sleeping power which really was the world, and summoned it to action. It glorified, intensified, fulfilled the earth; so that with the sun's work incomplete, with part of the earth illuminated and the rest lying in the darkness still, we can easily conceive of the dark region looking drowsily over to the region which is flooded with light, and saying, "There is the true earth! That is the real planet. In light and not in darkness the earth truly is itself." So when Christ rises on the soul he quickens it through and through, and sounds the bugle of its true life in its ears. He inspires it to

be its true self. When the light from Christ falls
into a human heart, impulses which have seemed
hopeless are inspired with courage and spring into
mastery over the soul.

This brings us to see that Christianity is not
something foreign coming into our lives, but it is
something divinely natural which comes to complete our lives and bring us to our true manhood
and womanhood. "The fullest Christian experience is simply the fullest life. To enter into it
therefore is no wise strange. The wonder and the
unnaturalness is that any child of God should live
outside of this, and so in all his life should never
be himself. And yet how clear the Bible is about
it all! How clear Christ is! It is redemption and
fulfilment which he comes to bring to man. Those
are his words. There is a true humanity which is
to be restored, and all those unattained possibilities
are to be filled out. Let us see how all this is true
in various applications. Apply it first to the standards of character. We talk of Christian character
as if it were some separate and special thing un-
attempted, unsuggested, by the human soul until
it became aware of Christ. The Christian graces
are nothing but the natural virtues held up into
the light of Christ. They are made of the same
stuff; they are lifted along the same lines; but they

have found their pinnacle. They have caught the illumination which their souls desire. Manliness has not been changed into godliness; it has fulfilled itself in godliness. As soon as we understand all this, then what a great clear thing salvation becomes. Does this make smaller or less important that great power of God whereby the human life passes from the old condition to the new—the power of conversion? Certainly not! What task could be more worthy of the Father's power and love than this assertion and fulfilment of his child? Great is the power of a life which knows that its highest experiences are its truest experiences, that it is most itself when it is at its best. For it each high achievement, each splendid vision, is a sign and token of the whole nature's possibility. What a piece of the man was for that shining instant, it is the duty of the whole man to be always. When the hand has once touched the rock the heart cannot be satisfied until the whole frame has been drawn up out of the waves and stands firm on its two feet on the solid stone."

I

Our theme suggests to us beyond doubt that it is the supreme duty of the Christian to manifest Christ to the world about him. It is not only that being lighted up we are to light the world, but that being illuminated by the Lord Jesus we are to manifest the Christ who is the source of our light to those who are still in darkness. The great musician Gounod once said to a pupil: "You will soon think and speak of the great masters as I did. When I was your age I used to speak only of myself; at twenty I said 'I and Mozart,' at thirty-five 'Mozart and I.' Now I am content to say 'Mozart!'" It is like that with the sincere Christian who grows in the grace and service of his Lord. The first cry was: "What must I do to be saved?" And then if we attempted great things for God in the first flush of our enthusiastic joy we dwelt upon the "I," but if we prest forward sincerely devoted to Christ, his light ever shining upon us, we came to say like Paul: "Nevertheless I live, yet not I, but Christ liveth in me; and the life which I now live in the flesh, I live by the faith of the Son of God, who loved me and gave himself for me." And if we are pressing forward, still deeper humility will possess our souls, until the words of Paul will again find themselves on our lips: "I count not myself to have apprehended; but this one thing I do, forgetting those things which are behind, and reaching forth unto those things which are before, I press toward the mark for the prize of the high calling of God in Christ Jesus."

We come to realize more and more if we are faithful that the beginning and the end of our Christian life and Christian service must be in Christ. We must live in fellowship and in harmony with him if we are to manifest him.

A Swedish Christian poet has recently voiced this in simple but spiritual lines:

"Live for Jesus! All the gladness
    That may come from earthly things,
Equals not one hour's enjoyment
    Which his blessed service brings.

"Live for Jesus! for thus only
    Does our life deserve the name!
To thy heart, before all others,
    Jesus has a perfect claim.

"Live for Jesus! round his banner
    Gather souls while time doth last;
To his cross invite poor sinners,
    Soon the work-day will be past.

"Thousands of such wanderers round thee
    After peace and comfort sigh;
Tell them of the Friend who only
    Can their longings satisfy.

"Tell them simply of salvation
    Thou thyself in him hast found;
Of the grace and loving kindness
    Wherewith he thy life has crowned.

"Live for Jesus! Life's young springtide
    Give him, and thy summer's prime;
Live for him when fading autumn
    Speaks to thee of shortening time.

"Give thyself entirely to him;
  Thus he gave himself for thee,
When he lived on earth despisèd,
  When he died on Calvary.

"Give up all for him, well knowing
  Thus to lose is all to gain;
Live for Jesus, till with Jesus
  Thou for ever rest and reign."

II

Our theme makes very clear and unmistakable the great fact that the evangelistic element is to be dominant in Christianity. Every Christian is called to be a missionary and an evangelist. It is strange how far we get away from the old landmarks. How we see whole churches full of nice, high-motived people who live year after year without seeming to catch a glimpse of the supreme characteristic of Christianity. And yet there can be no mistaking it. Christ says, "I am the light of the world." Then he turns to his disciples and says, "Ye are the light of the world." We cannot make mistake. It is the purpose of Jesus Christ to shine through me, when I am illuminated, upon the man next to me, and I am traitor to that divine light unless I reflect it so truly that that man shall see Christ, and glorify Christ for the light he has had through me.

This is a great message, and God grant that it

may shake us out of our sluggishness, and our
lethargy, and awaken us to our duty. We are to
show Christ to men, and win them to him—that is
the mission to which every Christian is called. Are
we doing it? Is it the supreme thing in our lives?
If it is so you may be sure other people know it.
Dr. John G. Paton, the great missionary, tells of
John Sim, a dear little boy who was ill and near the
end of his earthly life. His child heart was filled
with joy at the thought that he was soon to see
Jesus. His simple prattle, mingled with deep ques-
tionings, arrested not only his young companions,
but pierced the hearts of some careless sinners who
heard him, and greatly refreshed the faith of Christians. It was the very pathos of song incarnated
to hear the weak quaver of his dying voice sing out,

> "I lay my sins on Jesus,
>   The spotless Lamb of God."

Shortly before his death he said to his parents,
"I am going soon to be with Jesus; but I sometimes fear that I may not see you there." "Why
so, my child?" said his weeping mother. "Because," he answered, "if you were set upon going
to heaven and seeing Jesus there, you would pray
about it, and sing about it; you would talk about
Jesus to others and tell them of that happy meeting with him in glory. All this my dear Sabbath

school teacher taught me, and she will meet me there. Now, why did not you, my father and mother, tell me all these things about Jesus, if you are going to meet him too?"

If we are to reveal Christ to men the spirit of his love must become dominant in us. That is the one thing that nothing can withstand. Some of you remember the old fable of the winds, how they competed in blowing upon a man going up hill, to see which would make him take off his coat: The North and East winds each blew fiercely, and the West wind brought rain, but the man only buttoned his coat closer. Then the South wind blew with a gentle breeze, when he first unbuttoned his coat, and then took it off. Love is like that. If all hate and anger and selfishness is burned out of our hearts in the light of Christ's nature, then we may manifest Jesus to others, and we will find something in every man and woman, however barren their natures seem to be, that will answer back to it. Some of you have read Victor Hugo's "Notre Dame." You will remember the dramatic chapter in which the brilliant writer describes the public flogging of the hideous dwarf who dwelt in the precincts of the great Cathedral. The half-witted creature raged like a wild beast, helpless in his bonds, while the wretched crowd roared and

shouted with delight at his pain, and pelted him
with missiles. The sufferer's clerical brother put
in an appearance for a moment, only to ride swiftly
away again for fear he should be associated in
some way with this poor victim of human justice.
The sufferer had seen him, however, and the sight
only added to his pain. He moaned for water, but
the crowd only mocked him. Both the desolation
and the mocking were exactly like that which
Jesus endured on Calvary. But could there be anything akin to Jesus in this misshapen and de-
graded dwarf? Victor Hugo shows us that there
was. A young girl pushed her way through the
crowd, and with one indignant word to his tor-
mentors held a flask of water to the lips of the sufferer. The miracle was effective in a moment.
What the warden's lash and the jeers of the mob
could not do, this simple action did. Into the
hideous face there came first a look of astonishment,
then of understanding, and then a tear coursed
slowly down the scarcely human cheek. The cup
of cold water had found the divine possibility in
the heart of the brute.

There is something like that in one of our more
recent creations of the novelist—one of the stories
of Anthony Hope. It is the story of a miser, the
story of a man who gradually lost his soul through

the accumulation of money. He had a great safe in his room. He was believed to be poor, because he lived so poorly; but in that safe the gradually piled up documents that entitled him to property here, there, and everywhere, and only one man knew how rich a man he was. Then there came into his home and into his life a young girl with a perfectly unselfish and disinterested soul, who was willing to give away everything that she possest in order that she might help another, and bless another, and gradually this radiant, Christlike influence broke him down with shame, melted his heart, until at last he began to propose to himself a veritable crucifixion, that he too should begin to give for the sake of others, that he too should take to the life of the Cross in order that he might be saved from his body of death and know the meaning of that life which is life indeed. He had everything, humanly speaking, that men seek for most. All power was his, and yet he had missed the secret of life because until love came into his very soul, and he saw the love of God and man, he did not realize what life means, and what life is given for. Then only did he learn Browning's truth that "Life is our chance of learning love."

Christ's love in your heart and mine cannot be long baffled in its influence on those about us.

"In the long run all love is paid by love;
    Tho undervalued by the hosts of earth,
The great eternal government above
    Keeps strict account, and will redeem its worth.
Give thy love freely; do not count its cost;
So beautiful a thing was never lost,
        In the long run."

We must not permit ourselves to fail to make
the application of our theme personally to our own
lives. This is the greatest thing that can pertain
to us as Christians. Christianity is not a luxury,
it is the water of life. The light of Christ does
not shine into our hearts to create us into a sort of
spiritual aristocracy, but to ennoble us, enlarge us,
make us splendid and gracious and skilful and
loving, so that we may lift men and women up into
the same light and courage. And it is not only to
the drunken and the brutal, the enslaved of sin in
shameful ways, that we must manifest Christ; but
to the many who are closer to us, and who are not
far from the kingdom, who have been born and
reared under such conditions that they have
already seen through a glass darkly the glory of
the Christ. If we only knew how many waiting souls
there are in our own homes, in the places where
we do business, among the people we meet socially,
whom we could introduce to Christ with a single
earnest consecrated effort, we would be amazed

at the white harvest all about us among which many are standing with folded hands.

The daughter of the Rev. Hugh Price Hughes in her recent biography of her father tells the striking story of the conversion of an Oxford Don, the head of one of the colleges. Mr. Hughes met him one day in the street and said, "Excuse me, but I am irresistibly led to ask you: 'What do you think of Jesus Christ? Do you know him as your Savior?'" The Don paused a moment and then said, with evident emotion, "Thank you, Mr. Hughes, for asking me that question. Do you know, I have been waiting for twenty years for some one to ask me that question. Will you come into my rooms?" Mr. Hughes readily responded, and had the joy of showing the Don the old, old way of salvation. I am sure that there are a thousand Christians here this morning who in the aggregate are living in close touch and influence with a thousand other people who do not know Jesus Christ as their personal Savior; but who could be won to him to-morrow or to-day by a definite effort such as that. O my friends, you have no other opportunity so great as this—to manifest Jesus Christ to another soul. Failing in that, you have made the great failure. Succeeding in that, whatever else happens, you have made the great success of life.

THE CHRISTIAN VISION TRANS-LATED INTO LIFE

THE CHRISTIAN VISION
TRANSLATED INTO LIFE

"Who art thou, Lord?"—Acts IX: 5.
"Lord, what wilt thou have me to do?"—Acts IX: 6.

VISIONS are always given as a prelude to life. Indeed, the life is born out of the vision. Peter, on the house top of Simon the tanner, has a great vision, and while he is perplexed and wondering about the new idea borne in upon his mind, and illustrated by the vision, a messenger comes, breaking in rudely upon his meditations, in a manner which I do not doubt was exceedingly annoying to Peter, as his mind was rapt in the ecstasy of the vision, and told him that there were three men waiting for him at the door. These men waited to lead him away to the house of Cornelius where his great vision of human equality before God was to be emphasized in his preaching the first sermon to the Gentiles, and his recognition that the Gospel of Jesus Christ was to all men. The vision had been given him to be translated into life. Visions are always given us for that purpose. God never

gives us visions simply to revel in. They are to
exalt us, to instruct us, to inspire us so that on
common days we may live by their power and
their wisdom. The Bible records many illustrations of this great truth. Paul has a vision on the
Mediterranean corn ship of an angel with gracious
words and promises of divine sympathy and help.
Translated into life it means the saving of all
on board and the preaching of the Gospel to a new
people. Paul has a vision at night of "A man of
Macedonia" appealing for help, and that form
seen in his vision leads him across land and sea to
strange towns and cities, and plants the Gospel in
many new regions. But the first great vision
granted to Paul was the one which transformed
him from Saul, the bigoted persecutor, into Paul,
the humble self-sacrificing apostle. It was that
day on the way to Damascus, when he was bent on
the destruction of the Christians, whom he believed
to be dangerous fanatics, that the heavenly light
shone above him and his company, and as they all
fell to the ground in dismay, the voice of Jesus
Christ spoke to him, saying, "Saul, Saul, why persecutest thou me? It is hard for thee to kick against
the pricks." Immediately Paul answered with the
inquiry, "Who art thou, Lord?" And back came
the answer, in tones that carried such convincing

weight that that keen-brained lawyer never doubted their truth, "I am Jesus, whom thou persecutest." Quick as a flash came back the answer of Paul with another inquiry: "Lord, what wilt thou have me to do?" Paul's mind was remarkably logical. By intuition he saw the relations between vision and duty. He knew that after this vision life could never be what it was before. It must be something entirely different. Having become convinced that Jesus was the Christ, he must now rise up into a new realm where Christ was Lord. And long years afterward, when Paul was getting to be an old man and stood a prisoner, with handcuffs upon his wrists, to plead his cause before King Agrippa, his supreme boast was this, "Whereupon, O King Agrippa, I was not disobedient unto the heavenly vision."

Now in these cases of Paul and Peter we have examples of the proper attitude toward the visions of Christ and of duty which come to all of us. Here is illustrated the right attitude of mind toward the visions which God gives us. Both Peter and Paul had been inclined to be narrow and bigoted and wrong-headed sort of men, but there was about each of them a certain genuine honesty of purpose to do right when they saw the right, that made it possible for them to get heavenly wisdom and guidance from the visions of God. Each one of us has visions as truly as did these famous men. In sermon and in song, in sickness and in health, in book and in friend, in a score of ways God brings his visions of the Christ and his claims upon us and our duties because of him home to our hearts. If they are to exalt and ennoble us and make our lives glorious for good, it must be because we receive them with open mind and integrity of purpose. As some poet sings, we need to throw open the door to the divine teaching.

> "Open the door of the soul; let in
>   Strong, pure thoughts which shall banish sin.
>   They will grow and bloom with a grace divine
>   And their fruit shall be sweeter than that of the vine.
>   Open the door!

> "Open the door to the heart; let in
>   Sympathy sweet for stranger and kin,
>   It will make the halls of the heart so fair
>   That angels may enter unaware.
>   Open the door!"

I

The supreme purpose for which God gives us visions of heavenly import is first of all the same, whether it be to Paul or to Peter or to you or to me, that we may know the will of God concerning us. God's will is the best thing that can happen to you or to me, and it is his purpose to make known to us his will when we are ready to give allegiance to it. When they led Saul away blind to Damascus, a devout Christian man came, that he might pray with him and instruct him, and that good man said to him, "The God of our fathers hath chosen thee, that thou shouldst know his will, and see that Just One, and shouldst hear the voice of his mouth." From that day Paul sought to know the will of God. His restlessness was conquered. He could afford to be patient, for he was the servant of the King, and was helping to forward the plans of the infinite God. My dear friends, that is the cure for your restlessness and mine. The burdens, the perplexities, and the sorrows of life that would otherwise overwhelm us, if we were fighting our own battle against the world, with all the handicap which we sometimes suffer, become insignificant and of very small account when we really remember that we are the servants of God, chosen to know his will and to do it, and leave the result with him. Life becomes sweet and splendid with such a faith. It is the touch of the Master that calms life's fever and gives us a steady, abiding joy.

I have just been reading a story of a Japanese soldier, who at the siege of Port Arthur, in the

Russo-Japanese War, lost both of his eyes by a cruel bullet. Again and again he begged his comrades to kill him, but they would not. He was brought to one of the military hospitals in Tokyo to be cared for until able to return home. Here also he pleaded with the other soldiers to end his life, and as he began to recover his health he became more and more sad. One day he said: "Well, I will go home and let my family see me just once, then no one can prevent my killing myself. No harm in putting an end to my own misery."

Now every few days a Christian missionary visited this hospital, taking to the sick and wounded soldiers flowers, fragments of the printed Gospel, and Christian tracts, and teaching them about Jesus. Some of the officials of the hospital said to this good woman: "There is a man there who has lost his eyes and seems quite lonely. If you have time, we should like to have you visit him."

They did not tell her how he had wanted to die, and how he had threatened to kill himself. This missionary went to his bedside and talked to him several times. At first he did not take very much interest in anything she said, but gradually he became quite friendly. Finally she asked him if he would not like to learn to read, and he was surprized at such a question, for while he could read before going to battle, how could he ever do so again? But the missionary taught him to read the blind man's Bible just as blind people in America are taught to read, and he became as happy as the blind man whom Jesus healed. Day by day he read the Bible, and became a very happy Christian. The other soldiers would not believe that he could read, and tried to tease him, so he said: "You may pick out any verse you please, and I will show you that I can read." So they kept selecting, and to their astonishment he could read everything and enjoyed doing so, all the more because he wanted to teach the Bible to the other men. When this blind soldier was able to return home, one of his comrades who remembered his earlier despair said to him as he was leaving the hospital, "Are you going to kill yourself after you have seen your family?" And with beaming face he replied, "No, indeed! I am going home to teach my wife and children Christianity; I am glad that I was wounded, for now I am a Christian." Like Saul, through his blindness this man had obtained his sight, and like him he was not disobedient unto the heavenly vision.

And so there is no earthly limitation that can thwart our joy when we come to understand that the will of God is the supreme protection as well as the supreme joy of our lives. Loyalty to God's will is the greatest safeguard of the soul in protecting it from the assaults of evil. Two of the most prominent buildings in London are Buckingham Palace and the Hotel Cecil. Both of these are magnificent specimens of the builder's art. Each is luxuriously furnished and decorated. But there is one great difference between these two buildings. The Hotel Cecil is open to all who are able to pay for accommodations. Rooms in it can be hired for lust, debauchery, or vice of any kind. The one thing necessary is to be able to pay the price. Not so with the Buckingham Palace. No amount of money could hire a single room in it. And why? It is the palace of the King. So it is with a human heart that is completely given over to do the will of God. When the devil taps softly or knocks loudly at the door for admission the reply is, "No entrance here; this is the palace of the King."

II

We have in the study of our theme this further suggestion, that when Christ is revealed to the heart of any man or woman it becomes the duty of the one who has seen the vision of the Savior to be forever after a witness to what he has seen. The good man who brought sight again to Paul said to him, "For thou shalt be his witness unto all men of what thou hast seen and heard." Paul's life bears abundant evidence that he accepted that statement in the most literal way to be true, for wherever he went, to whatever audience he preached, whether it was a great crowd of common people in the street, or before kings or queens, he told the story of his conversion as the greatest thing he had to tell. He held himself above all else to be a witness to Christ and his power to forgive sins. And so every one of us who has had revealed to him the Lord Jesus as his personal Savior is to be a witness for Christ, and our lives and words and characters are to be living testimony for him. God save us from being false witnesses.

In the far East a ship hailing from a German port once drove ashore on the sands of Java. When the master of the ship was called to an account for the disaster, he gave as an excuse that the beacon on shore had settled several feet in the sand, so that it did not register the height from the sea which was ascribed to it in the hydrographic books. Mistaking the elevation of the light, the skipper substituted its indications for those of another light, and went ashore. The beacon, not the skipper, was at fault. Brothers, we are set as beacons in the world. But if our light is shed forth from a lower moral plane than that of Christ, we become false witnesses, and may bring destruction on immortal souls that are influenced by us.

Nothing will take the place of this loyalty to Christ in our lives. First and last, in youth and middle age and old age, we are witnesses to him who has revealed to us his divine purpose and love in the forgiveness of our sins.

One of the most beautiful things that Ian MacLaren ever wrote was the story which he called "His Mother's Sermon," which describes the deathbed of a mother and her plea to her son whom she had dedicated to the ministry.

He was broken that day, and his sobs shook the bed, for he was his mother's only son and fatherless, and his mother, brave and faithful to the last, was bidding him farewell.

"Dinna greet like that, John, nor break yir hert, for it's the will o' God, and that's aye best.

"Here's my watch and chain," placing them beside her son, who could not touch them, nor would lift his head, "and when ye feel the chain about yir neck it will mind ye o' yir mother's arms.

"Ye 'ill no forget me, John, I ken that weel, and I'll never forget you. I've loved ye here and I'll love ye yonder. Th'ill no be an 'oor when I'll no pray for ye, and I'll ken better what to ask than I did here; sae dinna be comfortless."

Then she felt for his head and stroked it once more, but he could not look nor speak.

"Ye 'ill follow Christ, and gin he offers ye his cross ye 'ill no refuse it, for he aye carries the heavy end himsel'. He's guided yir mother a' thae years, and been as gude as a husband since yir father's death, and he 'ill hold me fast tae the end. He 'ill keep ye too, and, John, I'll be watchin' for ye. Ye 'ill no fail me," and her poor cold hand that had tended him all his days tightened on his head.

But he could not speak, and her voice was failing fast.

"I canna see ye noo, John, but I know yir there, an' I've just one other wish. If God calls ye to the ministry, ye 'ill no refuse, an' the first day ye preach in yir ain kirk, speak a gude word for Jesus Christ, an', John, I'll hear ye that day, tho ye 'll no see me, and I'll be satisfied."

A minute after she whispered, "Pray for me," and he cried, "My mother, my mother."

It was a full prayer, and nothing left unasked of Mary's Son.

And when the day came, and the boy came back to preach the first sermon in the old home, he was true to the mother's prayer, and his loyal witness to Christ won all hearts and melted them all into love for their Savior.

My friends, we are all preachers in this highest sense of bearing witness. The supreme need of our time is for this loyal witness to Christ not only in the pulpit, but in the factory and in the shop, in the store and in the great business houses. No man has a greater pulpit to-day than the sincere and honest Christian who stands in tender loyalty to Christ among his employees in business relations. Each one of us in our own place, in our profession, in our business or our social relations, have opportunities peculiar to ourselves of bearing effective witness for our Lord. One of the greatest witnesses for Christ in this country in the splendid influence which went out from it during the past generation, was that borne by Professor Agassiz, our great Christian naturalist. In some scientific circles of his day the loyal avowal of his Christian faith brought upon Agassiz ridicule and scorn. But he never wavered in his teaching on that account. He had beheld the vision of the Christ. He had a great and sacred faith in himself, and his course grew brighter with Christian confidence. He came up out of tribulations of doubt and infidelity into the clear regions of faith, and like Paul he was not disobedient unto the heavenly vision.

A keen sense of what we owe to Christ as our Savior will constrain us to loyalty as witnesses for him. Mr. Spurgeon, a short time before he died, felt such an overwhelming sense of obligation and indebtedness to Christ that he said, "I will sit up in bed during the last hours of my life and cry, 'With His stripes we are healed!'"

Christ has given us wonderful inspiration to loyalty as witnesses. How splendidly he says, "If any man confess me before men, him will I also confess before my Father and his holy angels." If we are loyal witnesses to Christ here, he will be

a loyal witness to us there in the immortal life. We
are now choosing our companions not for time only,
but for eternity. We are making up our friendships not for this world only, but for all worlds. It
is open for us now to enter into brotherhood with
the bravest and holiest spirits of our race, and
share in their glory and triumph throughout eternity. The poet has a vision of that day and exclaims:

"Ah, see the fair chivalry come, the companions of Christ!
    White horsemen, who ride on white horses, the knights
        of God!
  They for their Lord and their Lover who sacrificed
  All, save the sweetness of treading where he first trod!

"These through the darkness of death, the dominion of
    night,
  Swept, and they woke in white places at morning tide;
  They saw with their eyes, and sang for joy of the sight,
  They saw with their eyes the eyes of the Crucified.

"Now, whithersoever he goeth, with him they go;
    White horsemen, who rode on white horses—oh, fair
    to see!
  They ride where the rivers of Paradise flash and flow,
    White horsemen, with Christ their Captain: for ever
    he!"

GOD THE BEST
PAYMASTER

GOD THE BEST PAYMASTER

"The Lord is able to give thee much more than this."—
II Chronicles XXV: 9.

THE words of the text were spoken by a messenger of God to Amaziah, who was at the time king of Judah. He was a war-like man, and desired very much to expand his territory. He seems to have been of soldierly quality, and to have been consumed by ambition for military glory. There is no account in the record of his having been imposed upon in any way, or that his neighbors had given him any reason to make war. He seems to have simply been greedy of conquest and determined to overrun the Edomites, murder the inhabitants, and steal their territory. He was not strong enough to do this alone, and having a good fat treasury at the time, he determined to hire soldiers from Israel. And so he entered into negotiations with the king of Israel, and bargained for one hundred thousand men, for whom he laid down a bounty of one hundred talents of silver, a large sum of money for that day. By the aid of these men he had an army of four hundred thousand

soldiers at his disposal. He gloated at the pros-
pects of victory over Edom, and counted their
lands adjoining him to be as good as his own. Just
then, when he was about to start forth with his in-
vading army, there came a prophet from God with
a message which was a wet blanket on all his plans.
He had left God out of the account, and that is
never wise. The prophet came with the declaration that if he took with him these hundred thousand men whom he had hired of Israel, he marched
to certain defeat. Now it does not appear that
Amaziah doubted for a moment the credentials of
the man of God. But his great dismay was concerning the hundred talents of silver which he had
given as a bounty, and which of course there would
be no chance to get back. Amaziah was a thrifty
soul as well as ambitious, and the thought of losing
all that money grieved him to the heart. But
when he exclaimed, "But what shall we do for the
hundred talents which I have given to the army
of Israel?" the prophet answered without a
moment's hesitation, "The Lord is able to give
thee much more than this."

I

Here, then, is our theme. Amaziah is not the
only man who has come face to face with the prob-

lem of self-denial in the path of duty. But however great the temptation to go contrary to God's
desire, it may be always spoken truthfully to every
man tempted to find his prosperity in sin that God
is able to give him much more than is promised by
evil. Amaziah had been touched in his money-
nerve, and that is a very sensitive nerve. Judas
Iscariot has been held up to condemnation with
peculiar bitterness through all the centuries since
he sold his Lord for thirty pieces of silver. He
has been looked upon as the incarnation of covetous-
ness, and Judas has been thought of as a sort of
inhuman monster. The artists have usually taken
that view. Holbein's face of Judas is one to make
you shudder; a face such as you imagine when you
read Shakespeare's description of Shylock; such a
face as Cruikshank sketched of the vile old Jew
whom Dickens puts in the pillory in "Oliver
Twist;" meanness, cowardice, cunning, malice,
cruelty, all seem to blend together into a face that
is hideous. But I see no reason why we should
think that Judas had a face like that. How can
we believe that Judas lived three years in the inti-
mate association of Jesus Christ, sharing his meals,
conversing with him every day, witnessing his
miracles of healing and of salvation; and yet have
been living a base, vile life of which a revolting

face like that these artists have given him would have been the proper dial-plate. No, I imagine that Judas was very much like men now. The trouble with him was that he was a selfish man, with this rotten spot of money-greed in him, and he did not banish it, but allowed it to live and grow in his soul. I have sympathy with an artist who says, "If I had painted a Judas, I would have selected a smiling, silly-like, nice man." A good many men who are consciously doing wrong for gold, and are closing their bowels of compassion and mercy against the needs of the kingdom of Christ and of their poor brothers among their fellow men, could find out very easily what Judas looked like if they would go and look in the glass the first time they are at home. But oh, the pity and the tragedy of the life of Judas. Over and over again in a hundred ways God said to Judas that he was able to give him much more than was the world, and how much more he did give John and Peter and all the rest of that little band of friends. Judas clutched for the gold and he got the rope of the suicide. Put over against him John on the Isle of Patmos, when he is a man nearly a hundred years old, with heaven in his face and the dreamy far-away look in his eyes, as he beholds those visions of infinite beauty which he has recorded in his great book that closes the Bible.

We are in the midst of a great epoch of physical prosperity in America, when hundreds of thousands of men have gone money-mad. What would have meant a very rich man fifty years ago is not counted much to-day. The old simple life of our fathers has been forgotten, and men scramble to-day, at the cost of their health, of their lives, and often of their very souls, that they may get rich quick. The warning of God's word needs to be rung out again and again. We have been sowing to the wind, and we are beginning to reap the whirlwind. During the last two years in America we have seen more men who were the possessors of great fortunes, and who had great financial influence, who had stood as the synonym of honor and manliness, set in the pillory of public condemnation, and branded as infamous, dishonorable, and contemptible, than we have had in any twenty years before, and it seems quite probable that the end is not yet. Let any man who is tempted to get business success and acquire money at the cost of his religion, at the expense of his peace with God, and his communion with Jesus Christ as his personal Savior, be warned by all these things. I come to you humbly as God's minister to-day, to say to you, as the prophet said to Amaziah, that no matter what is promised you for selling your conscience, "God is able to give you much more than this."

II

This is a time when scholarly men and women, people with bright intellects and cultivated brains, are in danger of being led into an attitude, not of open infidelity and rebellion against God, but of a mocking sneering of wit against religion, against the Bible, against the church, and things that have been esteemed sacred. The sneer is in the atmosphere, in almost every flash of wit at the theatre or the opera; often in the magazines and in the public press; often in the after-dinner speeches at banquets, sometimes made by professedly religious men, the holy name of God, and the church of Christ, and the Bible, furnish barbs for the arrows of witty men and women. The temptation to this sort of thing to-day seems to be very insidious, and I wish to sound the note of warning, that whosoever is deceived into imagining that true joy of mind or heart is to be had in that way is being cruelly deceived. The worst deceived men in the world in our day are those of bright, keen, cultivated brain, who are seeking to get their joy and their happiness at the cost of goodness and of harmony with the purpose of God. Don Marquis, a new poet to me, has published in one of the current magazines a poem, entitled ''The Tavern of Despair,'' which goes to the heart of this very

thing of which I am speaking, and illustrates it
with more force than I can in any other way:

"The wraiths of murdered hopes and loves
    Come whispering at the door,
Come creeping through the weeping mist
    That drapes the barren moor;
But we within have turned the key
    'Gainst Hope and Love and Care,
Where Wit keeps tryst with Folly, at
    The Tavern of Despair.

"And we have come by divers ways
    To keep this merry tryst,
But few of us have kept within
    The Narrow Way, I wist;—
For we are those whose ampler wits
    And hearts have proved our curse—
Foredoomed to ken the better things
    And aye to do the worse!

"Long since we learned to mock ourselves;
    And from self-mockery fell
To heedless laughter in the face
    Of Heaven, Earth, and Hell.
We quiver 'neath, and mock, God's rod;
    We feel, and mock, His wrath;
We mock our own blood on the thorns
    That rim the 'Primrose Path.'

"We mock the eerie glimmering shapes
    That range the outer wold,
We mock our own cold hearts because
    They are so dead and cold;

We flout the things we might have been
    Had self to self proved true,
We mock the roses flung away,
    We mock the garnered rue;

"The fates that gibe have lessoned us:
    There sups to-night on earth
No madder crew of wastrels than
    This fellowship of mirth. . . .
(Of mirth . . . drink, fools!—nor let it flag
    Lest from the outer mist
Creep in that other company
    Unbidden to the tryst.)

"We're grown so fond of paradox
    Perverseness holds us thrall,
So what each jester values most
    He mocks the most of all;
But as the jest and laugh go round,
    Each in his neighbor's eyes
Reads, while he flouts his heart's desire,
    The knowledge that he lies.

"If God called Azrael to him now
    And bade Death bend the bow
Against the saddest heart that beats
    Here on this earth below,
Not any sobbing breast should gain
    The guerdon of that barb—
The saddest ones are those who sport
    The jester's motley garb.

"Whose shout aye loudest rings, and whose
    The maddest cranks and quips—
Who mints his soul to laughter's coin
    And wastes it with his lips—

Has grown too sad for sighs and seeks
　To cheat himself with mirth:
We fools self-doomed to motley are
　The weariest wights on earth!

"But yet, for us whose brains and hearts
　Strove aye in paths perverse,
Doomed still to know the better things
　And still to do the worse,—
What else is there remains for us
　But make a jest of care
And set the rafters ringing, in
　Our Tavern of Despair?"

To any bright young man or young woman
tempted to the gay and giddy path which leads
by many devious ways which shut out its real
direction to "The Tavern of Despair," let me say,
as the man of God said to the old king of Judah,
"God is able to give you much more than this."
The happiest life in the world is the sincere Christian life. The great men who have reveled in
beauty among the artists have been men who communed with Christ. The sensitive souls who have
given us the great music of the centuries have
been those who laid their musical harps at the
feet of Jesus. The great statesmen who have
builded the nations of modern civilization have
been Christians. The poets, the orators, the supreme writers who have known the soul's best,
and whose story we do not need to weep over,

have been those whose imaginations and whose
brilliant gifts were held in obedience to Christ,
and who reverently wrought for their fellow men
in harmony with the law of God. No matter what
is offered you in the path of irreverence and mock-
ery, "God is able to give you much more than
this."

III

Our theme has in it warning and inspiration to
those who are seeking to live the Christian life in
relation to deeds as Christian men and women.
Dr. Dawson, the English evangelist, says that when
he was in Chicago, and was visiting the Armour
Institute, he was very much struck by the way in
which they taught mechanics there. Here was the
room with the scholar's bench, and the scholar's
desk, and all the appliances for quiet instruction,
but opening from this room there was a door that
led direct into the place where were the forge and
the grime and the hard work. When they had
taught a young fellow the theory of how to make
something, they said, "Now, go in there and make
it." It is like that with our Christian lives. Many
of you who are listening to me are saturated with
sermons and with Bible teachings. You have truth
enough. Are you putting that truth to work?
What you need is to take the theory of Christian-

ity, the revelation of Christ in your own heart and
character, and go among your fellow men, and see
what you can do in reproducing a Christian life
in some one besides yourself. The temptation
comes to every Christian sooner or later to live
simply the nominal Christian life, a Christian life
which costs nothing in self-sacrifice, and does bring
a certain respectability and dignity. I want to
awaken from his lethargy every one who is tempted
to be satisfied with that sort of a Christian life and
say to him with all the earnestness of my soul,
"God is able to give you much more than this."
And you must have more than this if you do not
deteriorate from even what you are now. You
cannot hold a thing to be true and yet live as
tho it were not true, without losing the truth
out of your soul. Savonarola, the grand old
Florentine, who gave his life for the truth, used to
say: "We only really believe that which we prac-
tice." And it has been well said that when a man
says a thing is true and lives as tho it were
not true, it becomes a lie to him and poisons his
whole life. Once when an infamous criminal was
executed, the prison chaplain was offering to him
what are often called the consolations of religion,
when the wretched man turned and said: "Do
you believe all that? Do you believe it? Oh, if I

only believed what you say you believe, I would crawl across England on my hands and knees on broken glass to tell men it was true." O my friend, if you are dropping down into a peaceful, self-complacent, half-worldly sort of religious life, let me awaken you to the great truth that "God is able to give you much more than this." No Christian life is worth the living that is not animated by the Christ spirit so that its supreme inspiration is the hope and purpose to bring other men and women to know Christ. A traveler, who had gone over the old St. Bernard Road, past the famous St. Bernard Hospice, tells how he came up over the snow field just as the somber night was gathering. The first thing he saw was the iron cross upon its jutting crag. That was the symbol of redemption. Next he saw the lighted windows of the Hospice, the symbols of succor. But that was not all he saw, for when he entered the Hospice there were the monks, all girded, with lamps lighted, and the great dogs, trained and vigilant, standing ready, waiting for the first sound of distress out in the black night, that they might seek in order to save that which was lost. Brothers, sisters, there is a picture for us. The city is full of lost men and lost women. I do not mean the drunkards, and the gamblers, and the outlaws only,

I do not mean the women who are shamed and dis-
graced only, tho I do mean these also. But multitudes of others who are respectable and proud,
and hold their heads high, are just as truly lost in
the eye of God, lost to all true goodness, as are
these. And these lost men and women will not be
able to see the Cross through the black night, and
they may not be able to find the door of the hospice
of the church; so we must go out and seek. This
is the life to which Christ calls us, and if you are
satisfied with anything less than this you are living
a poor beggarly Christian career, and I shout in
your ears, hoping to make you ashamed of yourself, that, "God is able to give you much more
than this."

Nothing is sadder to my eye than the dormant,
unused power in our churches. Here are hundreds of us who have pledged ourselves to the
Christian life, and we do not mean to be hypocrites,
and we do want to live worthy of our calling, and
yet how poverty-stricken is our expectancy that this
week shall see us bringing lost men and women to
Christ! If all you hundreds into whose eyes I look
felt that you are each of you under obligation to
bring one soul to Christ this week, and were going
to give yourself to it with more fidelity than you
give to your business, with more love than you

give to your family, with more care than you give to your body, then what a power this church would be in the city this week! Brothers, this is not impossible, it is not an idle dream, it is the very common sense of Christian life, and I pray God that the Holy Spirit may inspire in our hearts a deep and vital determination to exhibit in our lives the full measure of the Christ-spirit that God is able to give us!

If we are to do this Christ must be the abiding guest in our hearts. Mary G. Brainard sings:

"O thou, dear Lord, who stayest
    When all the guests are gone,
When in its silent chambers
    The soul sits down alone;
Our garlands all are withered
    Our sweetest songs are sung,
The lamps which lit our feasting
    Have gone out one by one.

"The gladness and the beauty
    Have vanished from our sight.
The footsteps of our dear ones
    Have died away in night.
Yet thanks to thee that ever
    Thou comest at our will,
Thy voice is heard the clearer
    When all the house is still.

"As on the mount of vision,
    Amid the shining three
The overawed disciples

Looked up and saw but thee,
So we, our brightness faded,
  Our sweet companions flown,
Lift up our troubled faces
  To find thou art not gone.

"Thanks to thy name that ever
  In grief thou dost appear,
That by each deepening shadow
  We know that thou art near.
Be Ruler of our feasting
  Thou 'Lord of Love,' *alone,*
O thou, dear Lord, who stayest
  When all the guests are gone."

THE GOLDEN AGE
OF THE SOUL

THE GOLDEN AGE OF THE SOUL

"Now there was long war between the house of Saul
and the house of David: But David waxed stronger and
stronger, and the house of Saul waxed weaker and
weaker."—II Samuel III: 1.

"For the flesh lusteth against the Spirit, and the Spirit
against the flesh."—Galatians V: 17.

"Walk in the Spirit, and ye shall not fulfil the lusts of
the flesh."—Galatians V: 16.

THESE scriptures remind us of the words of
Jesus when he declared that he came not to
bring peace but a sword. In a world with evil in
it, peace can only come through struggle and battle
and conquest. I have associated this Old Testament fragment of story with these New Testament
utterances of Paul, because there are certain pairs
of men contemporary with each other in the Old
Testament which are always used in the New as
illustrating the battle going on between the flesh
and the Spirit, between the good and the evil in
human life. The first pair of these men are Cain
and Abel. Cain stands always for the flesh—the
worldly, sensual, evil man, full of envy, jealousy,
and hate; while Abel stands for reverence, for

humility, for obedience, for goodness. A second
pair are Ishmael and Isaac. Paul refers to this in
this letter to the Galatians when he says, "Now we,
brethren, as Isaac was, are the children of promise." You will note that he is talking to Christians. He goes on to say, "But as then he that was
born after the flesh persecuted him that was born
after the Spirit, even so it is now. Nevertheless
what saith the scripture? Cast out the bondwoman and her son: for the son of the bondwoman
shall not be heir with the son of the freewoman.
So then, brethren, we are not children of the bondwoman, but of the free." Another pair used in
this way are David and Saul. Saul stands for the
flesh, for the worldly, sensual man. Saul stands
for the proud, arrogant man who does not fear God
and will not obey him. David stands for the Spirit.
With all his faults and his sins, and they were
grievous enough, he was a man after God's own
heart. Not because he sinned; but because, sinning, he repented in humility, and gave reverence
and loving service to God. So in this scripture
which I have chosen as the key-note for our study
we have in the battle between the house of Saul
and the house of David the picturesque suggestion
of that great struggle which is going on in the soul
of every man who has his eye upon the golden age

of the soul when Christ shall be Supreme King in the heart and life, and the Spirit shall have completely mastered the flesh.

I do not need to argue with you about the fact of this battle going on in the human soul. It is a battle which each man and woman knows who has seriously undertaken to dispute the domination of the lower, fleshly passions and appetites and to rise up into the Spirit realm of high and holy living. There is not a man or a woman among us who has not inherited enough of the evil tendencies which sin has awakened in our human nature to make the struggle between the flesh and the Spirit a serious thing. Some people simply give up to it, and make the plea of heredity for all their failures. A man excuses his bad temper, which often makes him act like an insane man, to some ancestral taint, and so one sin and another sin is excused because some dead ancestor has bequeathed the bad inheritance. To do that is to give one's self over to eternal defeat. Now the whole theory of Christianity is that our ancestors have no such power over us, but that it is our duty and privilege in the strength and power of the Spirit of God to master our inheritance, and in Christ's name be king over our own lives. Grace Ellery Channing puts it in the strongest and clearest light:

"Lo what am I? A patch of things,
　Mere odds and ends of lives flung by,
Of age-long, rag-bag gatherings
　Pieced up by Fate full thriftily.
Somebody's worn-out will and wit,
　Somebody's habits and his hair,
Discarded conscience, faith once fair
　Ere Time, the moth, had eaten it.
My great-grandfather's chin and nose,
　The eyes my great-grandmother wore,
With hands from some remote—who knows—
　Perchance prehensile ancestor;
Somebody's style, somebody's gait,
　Another body's wrist and waist,
With this one's temper, that one's trait,
　One's taste, another's lack of taste;
Feelings I never chose to feel,
　A voice in which I had no voice,
Revealing, where I would conceal,
　Rude impulses without a choice;
Faults which this ancestor or that
　Unkindly fostered, to my ill;
With others some one else begat
　And made the matter worser still.
They chose, these Masters of my fate,
　To please themselves, bequeathing me
Base pleasure in the things I hate,
　Liking for what misliketh me;
Out of the ashes of their fires,
　After the fashion of their bone,
They fashioned me, my mighty sires,
　And shall I call my soul my own?

"This motley from the Past flung down,
　This work with no artificer,

This prince, this poet, and this clown,
Deific and a driveller;
This bequeathed brain which shall conceive
What things this borrowed frame shall do,—
This will to serve and will to leave
The outworn Old, the untried New,—
This quick made up of all the dead,
And this deep heart inherited,—
I call these mine, and I will be
King, emperor, czar, and Deity.
The tenement may like me ill,
The garment ill-befitting be,
I will inhabit kingly still,
And wear my rags right royally.
These hands shall do my will, not hers
Who fashioned them to other use;
These feet fare not as he prefers
Who shaped them, but as I shall choose;
Mine be the words these lips shall frame.
And through my great-grandmother's eyes
I front my world, not hers, and claim
Under no dead soul's sovereignties,
Aye, borrowed husk, head, heart, and hand,
Slave on and serve me till we die:
I am your Lord and your Command."

I

The victory over the flesh by the Spirit demands
a complete consecration on our part to the Christ
life. We must take Christ to be our Savior and
Leader in so true and real a sense that he will be
able to give the Spirit full control of our lives. It
must be more than mere theoretical Christianity.

Christ must be so completely King that we seek
with perfect devotion to do his will, not our own.

Miss Gordon Cumming tells how, when she was
traveling in Japan, one night as she and some
others stood on the steps of the hotel, they heard
a call that came again and again out of the forest,
and this was what it said. "Me! Me! Me!" "Do
you hear that bird," they said, "calling 'Me!'?"
And they called it the me-bird. There is a me-
bird that is calling in every heart, the me-bird
that is always longing for somebody to be stroking
it down, the me-bird that never likes to see any
one in front of it, the me-bird that is morbidly
introspective. After a while Miss Cumming, on
inquiry, found that what she thought to be a bird
was only a crawling insect which made that curious
sound with useless wings that were unable to carry
it in the air. So there are many people who have
imagined a life of self-cultivation to be a bird with
wings that was going to carry them high above the
earth in the blue vaulted heavens, but have found
to their bitter disappointment, as King Solomon
did, that, at its best, selfishness is only a crawling
insect which can never get above the ground.

The man who is going to win the great victory,
who will rescue his soul from the mire and set it
free upon its high career, must get the control out

of his own hands into the hands of the divine and glorious Christ.

Prof. Henry Drummond, one of the rarest human spirits it has ever been my privilege to come in contact with, was once besought by a lady at whose house he had been entertained, to speak a word to the coachman who was in a few moments to drive Mr. Drummond to the train. She told him that the coachman was giving way to his lower appetites, especially on the side of strong drink, and she begged him if possible to do the man good. And as they drove along Drummond said to the coachman, "Suppose you were on the box and your horses ran away downhill, and you lost all control over them, what would you do?" "Oh," said the man, "I could do nothing." "Yes," said Drummond, "but supposing there were some one sitting by your side stronger than you, who could control them, what would you do?" "Oh," he said, "I would hand him the reins, sir." "Ah," said Drummond, "your life has run away with you, your appetites and passions and lusts are carrying you downhill, and you in your own strength cannot control your life. But, man," he said, "believe me, there is One at your side stronger than you, who offers to take the control of your life and make it what it should be. What will you do?'' And the spirit of conviction seized hold upon the man, and with eyes swimming with tears he exclaimed, "Sir, I will give Him the reins." Are there not some of you here now in just such a plight? You have lost the control of your life, it is running away with you—the passions and appetites and lusts of the flesh are mastering the better impulses and the nobler instincts of your nature. The good you purpose to do you fail to perform. The sense of weakness you have is humiliating, but, my friend, the Christ who says of himself, "I am the good shepherd, and I lay down my life for the sheep," is able to take the reins of your life into his own hand. He can master the flesh and make it your servant instead of your tyrant. He can control your appetites and make them but the steeds that draw you on toward a great and glorious career. Will you not now yield the control of your life to Christ?

II

The golden age of the human soul can only come through the conquest of the soul for goodness under the leadership of Christ. How different this is from any other conquest. It is a conquest that leaves no sorrow in its wake. There has been recently on view in the Paris Salon a picture illus-

trating a very impressive allegory. It is called
"The Pedestal of Conquest." The artist, Mr.
William Laparra, has given a vivid impression of
the sorrows and miseries that lie beneath the pedestal on which the warrior is crowned. At the base
are the widows and the orphans standing on the
edge of the newly open grave in which the hus-
bands and fathers have been cast, their somber
garments and haggard cheeks indicating their desolation. On the opposite extremity of the monument there is a general view of family life, the
bride waiting for the bridegroom who has kept a
tryst with death; other women with the babes in
their arms who have been made fatherless by war.
In the foreground is the wreck of a man whom
death has spared, but who must live on crippled and
maimed. Above are the buttresses of the hideous
temple, in which are the bodies of the slain laid in
ghastly rows, tier on tier, up to the capitals of the
Corinthian pillars which support the roof. In the
front of the temple are the burning ruins of towns
and villages, among which lie other bodies that
are being consumed in the awful holocaust. Above
all is the black horse of war on an abutment of
the temple, with the dome clad in its garment of
smoke behind him, and bestriding him is the warrior brandishing his dripping sword. He has won

fame, but if he would look down he would see the horrors, and the bereavements, and the desolation which have been the price of it. It is a picture of wonderful significance, about which crowds gather, gazing rapt on its sorrowful details. But how different the pedestal of conquest upon which stands the lofty soul that has battled against lusts and passions and evil desires, until under the leadership of Christ he has come to victory—the noble, splendid victory of the Spirit. There are no memories of cruelty and of rapine and murder to haunt his triumph. Instead, there grow beneath his feet the sweetest and most fragrant flowers that grace human life, for what says Paul? "The fruit of the Spirit is love, joy, peace, long-suffering, gentleness, goodness, faith, meekness, temperance: against such there is no law. And they that are Christ's have crucified the flesh with the affections and lusts."

I am sure there are some of you to whom the Spirit of God is speaking with clear voice, and you are drawn by heavenly magnetism to enter upon this struggle with new energy to make conquest of your soul for goodness. I would that I could bring you this morning to that supreme decision. In this story—indeed, in this very chapter, from which I took our first text—it is related that Abner, talk-

ing with the elders of Israel concerning their relations to David, said to them, "Ye sought for
David in times past to be king over you: *now then
do it.*" Do I not speak to some one who in times
past has with more or less earnestness sought to
have Christ king over his heart and life? But
something has interfered and it has never been
accomplished. I come to you and say, "*Now do
it!*" What keeps you back? I was reading the
other day the story of a man who went into one
of the English museums and saw, to his astonishment, in a case at the end of one of the rooms, a
little steel key, apparently hanging upon nothing.
He saw that there was above it a magnet. There
were the two arms of the magnet reaching out to
the key, which was longing, as it were, to come
into that close contact which would let the magnetic
current through it, and keep it close to the magnet.
As the man got a little nearer he saw that there
was a little black thread that had stopt the communication. There had been a downward ten-
dency in the key which had been overcome, or held
in suspension, and there was, so to speak, in that
key an earnest desire for the new magnetic life, but
that black thread held it back; and the gentleman
felt a longing to take off the lid of the case and
cut the thread and let the key go! My dear friends,

I do not know what coarse black thread of earth it is that keeps your soul from yielding itself completely to the heavenly magnetism of Him who said, ''And I, if I be lifted up, will draw all men unto me;'' but I do pray God that that thread may be broken and that you may yield yourself completely to be taken possession of by the life of the Spirit.

Do not for a moment imagine that there is any lack of power in Jesus Christ to give you complete victory over everything that mars or hurts or degrades you. It is the power of love that is required, and the depth of the love of Christ is unsearchable.

When Nansen was looking for the North Pole he once found himself in very deep water. He tried to take his sounding, but his line would not reach bottom. He took his book and wrote the date and the length of his line, and added ''Deeper than that.'' The next day he lengthened his line and dropt it again and again. It failed to touch, and again he wrote down the date and the length of his line and added, ''Deeper than that.'' After a few days he gathered all the line that could be found about his ship, tied it together and dropt it down, but it would not reach the bottom, and once more he took his book and wrote the date and

the length of his longest line, and added the note,
"Deeper than that." But, my friends,

> "Through all the depth of sin and loss,
>   Drops the plummet of the cross;
> Never yet abyss was found
>   Deeper than the cross could sound."

Give your heart to Christ, and the golden age
shall come to your own soul, as it is coming to the
whole world, after a while, under the dominion of
Jesus. No wonder the poet, catching vision of that
glorious day, puts his wreath of tribute on the
brow of our Lord:

> "The world is glad for Thee! the rude,
>   Wild moor, the city's crowded pen;
> Each waste, each peopled solitude
>   Becomes a home for happy men.

> "The heart is glad for Thee! it knows
>   None now shall bid it err or mourn;
> And o'er its desert breaks the rose
>   In triumph o'er the grieving thorn.

> "Thou bringest all again; with Thee
>   Is light, is space, is breadth, and room
> For each thing fair, beloved, and free,
>   To have its hour of life and bloom.

> "Each heart's deep instinct unconfest;
>   Each lowly wish, each daring claim;
> All, all that life hath long repressed,
>   Unfolds, undreading blight or blame.

"Thy reign eternal will not cease;
  Thy years are sure, and glad, and slow;
Within Thy mighty world of peace
  The humblest flower hath leave to blow.

"The world is glad for Thee, the heart
  Is glad for Thee! and all is well,
And fixt and sure, because *Thou art*
  Whose name is called Emmanuel!"

THE UNSHAKEN
PILLARS

THE UNSHAKEN PILLARS

"I know him whom I have believed, and am persuaded
that he is able to keep that which I have committed unto
him against that day."—II Timothy I: 12.

"We know that all things work together for good to
them that love God."—Romans VIII: 28.

"We know that if our earthly house of this tabernacle
were dissolved, we have a building of God, an house not
made with hands, eternal in the heavens."—II Corinthians V: 1.

NOTHING is more apparent in our time than
the lack of restfulness and repose. It is a
nervous, curious, uncertain age. The Bible declares
that "The wicked are like the troubled sea, which
cannot rest," but in our day it is a restless multitude that greets our gaze. Physicians tell us that
there are many new expressions of nervous disease
manifesting themselves in the present time. One
cannot walk along the street in any great city without noting that multitudes of human faces are
marked by anxiety. We live in a rush, apprehensive all the time of danger. Yesterday people
were talking about "the bicycle-face." To-day it
is "the automobile-face," and whether it shall be

"the balloon-face" to-morrow, who can tell. All this indicates an uncertainty and a restlessness in the mind of the people.

The same is true religiously. We are living in a time when a good many very bright people, notably certain novelists, trying to pique public curiosity so as to make a success in fiction, make a business of displaying their doubts. They seem to like to parade their heresies and skepticisms as a sort of evening dress of the soul in order to attract attention. In such a time it is good for us to stop occasionally to take account of stock, and notice some of the great unshaken pillars of our Christian faith which are as solid as ever.

I

First, we have Christian experience: Paul says, "I know him whom I have believed." There is a tonic in that expression. Paul has no doubts, because he knows Christ. When a man speculates and guesses, we may listen or not; but when a great and good man says "I know," we must stop to listen. When we want to know a thing we must go to the man who has had experience. If I want to travel in India, I like to find some man who has lived there, and who knows the people and their methods of transportation, and can tell me all about it. If I find myself in some great sorrow or severe trial, it is not much comfort that any one can give me, unless it is some man who has had the same experience and who comes to me with sympathy in his face, and tells how he was once in that very condition, and how he came out. Then I listen. As one has said, a lecture on a loaf of bread by a man who had never tasted bread might be edifying; but a hungry man who had eaten and been filled could tell a much more interesting story, no matter how much less he might know of the chemical constituencies of bread; so when Paul says "I know," our hearts are lifted up and we turn to him with hope and assurance.

Christian experience is the strong pillar of the soul. Nothing can shake that. As Bishop Charles Gore says: In our everyday-life it is always that which we have experienced concerning which we are most certain. Am I certain that sugar is sweet? that fire is warm? that food allays hunger? that exercise is healthful? that music stills the fears? that love of wife and children and friends is a deep ineffable joy? Certainly! I would stake everything I possess on my certainty of these things, for it is a certainty rooted in experience. When I speak about them I speak what I know. And so we never need be in doubt concerning the great realities of the Christian life; whether God is real; whether prayer is a power; whether the Christian life is worth living. It all depends on your experience of these great spiritual realities. No man who experiences them can possibly doubt them. Uncertainty with regard to them is for him at an end. Out of the experience will come certainty, as a rose opens from the bud. A lady, it is said, once asked James Simpson, the great Edinburgh physician, the discoverer of chloroform, "What is the most important discovery you have ever made?" The great doctor looked at the questioner and replied, "Madam, the greatest discovery I ever made was the discovery that Christ is my Savior." He had no doubt.

Charles Kingsley, in his story of Alton Locke, describing Eleanor's testimony to Jesus, says, "She talked of him as Mary would have talked just risen from his feet. . . . The sense of her own intense belief, shining out in every lineament of her face, carried conviction to my heart more than ten thousand arguments could do. It must be true!" That is what men always say in their inner souls when they hear Christians speaking of Jesus with the certainty born of experience of him! "It must be true!"

The knowledge Paul had of Jesus, which gave

him in his own experience a divine comradeship with the Savior, is possible for every man and woman to-day, and is enjoyed by multitudes.

There is a pathetic little incident in the life of Robert Louis Stevenson which illustrates the sort of comfort that comes from the sense of an unseen comradeship. In his early days Stevenson was a fragile little child, suffering from a hacking cough, which often kept him awake night after night. He had a devoted Scotch nurse, to whom he owed everything—Alison Cunningham—and to whom he dedicated one of his books. Often when the boy could not sleep, this faithful woman would lift him in her arms and croon to him some of the old Scotch songs to pass away the hours of darkness until morning. But sometimes, when the little fellow was more than ordinarily restless, she would carry him to the window in the silent night, and across the square in the front of the house she would point out here and there other lighted windows, "where," says Stevenson in referring to it, "we would tell each other that perhaps there were other little children who were sick, and who, like us, were waiting for the dawn." What a picture it is—the frail little child looking wistfully out into the black night and taking comfort from these lighted windows where, perhaps, there were other

little children who were sick and like him were
waiting for the dawn. It illustrates the wonderful
power of human sympathy! The light of friendship in the dark night of our sorrow that helps us
to wait for the breaking of the dawn. But clearer
and more radiant than any other friendship in the
world are the sympathy and friendship of Jesus
Christ, that come to the reverent loving heart just
as real to-day as when he came walking across the
waves to the frightened disciples long ago, saying
now as he said then: "It is I; be not afraid."
How beautifully Peter puts it: "Whom having not
seen, we love."

A Russian writer tells us of the young count who
went out from the palace on a bitter morning, and
passed a beggar at the gate starved and blue and
well-nigh dead with cold and hunger. And the
count hastily felt in all his pockets, but he had no
coin with him. He felt to see if he had any piece
of jewelry, but he had not even that; and he stood
before the beggar fumbling for the gift that he
fain would give. At last, with a burning face, he
said to the poor starved man, "I have nothing with
me, my brother." An hour afterward he passed
into the palace, and at the gates he found the beggar, not starved and blue, but warm and glowing
and happy. And the young count said, as he heard

the beggar's benediction upon him as he passed, "But I gave you nothing." "Yes," said the beggar; "you called me 'Brother!'" Love and sympathy and brotherhood bridge the great chasm, and the wondrous love of God in Christ Jesus lifts the sinful man out of his sense of hopelessness into a warm, glowing, loving sonship to God, and into a sympathetic brotherhood with Christ Jesus. We may shake some pillars which have been associated with Christianity, but no man can shake the pillar of Christian experience. A man may say he has not known it, but he cannot invalidate the joy, the comfort, and the gladness of multitudes of men and women who do know it. It stands unshaken.

II

The second pillar I wish to call your attention to is *the divine Providence:* "We know that all things work together for good to them that love God." Paul is speaking here also out of experience. With him it was a certainty. He had had his thorn in the flesh, his buffetings and beatings, his shipwrecks; but after them all he declares his absolute assurance, as a matter of knowledge, that all things work together for good to them that love God. It is interesting to match Paul with Napoleon.

Napoleon said cynically that God was always on

the side of the strong battalions, but he lived to see
that it is on the side of right rather than battalions that God always takes his stand.

Lord Rosebery's recent book on Napoleon is
profoundly interesting in its sympathetic and yet
judicial estimate of the most marvelous of modern
conquerors. Napoleon appears to this last biographer so great in his energy, his intellect, his
genius, that he "enlarges the scope of human
achievement." He "fought the Austrians once for
five consecutive days, without taking off his boots
or closing his eyes"; he would work for eighteen
hours at a stretch; "his genius was as unfailing and
supreme in the art of statesmanship as in the art
of war, and he was as much the first ruler as the
first captain in the world." Ordinary measures do
not apply to him; we seem to be trying to span a
mountain with a tape. The conclusion arrived at
is that Napoleon was the largest personal force that
has ever come into the modern European world.

Why, then, did his career end in defeat and
exile? Napoleon's own saying is a revelation on
this point. "I am not a man like other men," he
asserted; "the law of morality could not be intended to apply to me." He believed that religion
was essential to the nation he ruled, but not to himself. He was not antagonistic to it; he patronized

it rather. But for a man as consciously great as he
to obey the Ten Commandments when they ran
counter to his own views, appeared to him absurd.
Humility was in his eyes no virtue, but an entire
mistake. Yet humility alone could have saved him.
The dangerous, the fatal element in Napoleon's
nature was ambition. In youth he was phenome-
nally sane and well balanced. But little by little his
knowledge of his own powers unbalanced him; nothing seemed as important as his own destiny; "the
intellect and energy were still there, but, as in
caricature, they became monstrosities." Then came
the inevitable collapse of insane and impossible ambitions; and at forty-six the man who had dreamed
of governing a world became a captive exile. His
conquests left little mark; the kings he made lost
their thrones; France was beggared and exhausted
by him; and the greatest gifts ever bestowed upon
a human soul since the days of Caesar thus failed
to help forward the world.

If any one was ever great enough to do without
goodness, Napoleon was the man. The result of his
experiment ought to be enough to satisfy anybody.
There is no need for smaller men to repeat the test;
it ought to stand as a finality. Plain, simple goodness is the necessity of great souls as well as lesser
ones; duty is the supreme law, God the Almighty

Ruler. Napoleon failed, not because he was not great enough, but because he was not good enough. "Not by might, nor by power, but by my Spirit, saith the Lord."

Victor Hugo was strongly of this faith about Napoleon. In his "Les Miserables" he paints a graphic picture of the battle of Waterloo, and at the close of it he inquires if it were possible for Napoleon to have won the battle. And he answers "No," and then he inquires why. "Because of Wellington?" "No." "Because of Blücher?" "No. Because of God." And he continues to say that the weight of this monstrous man cast into the scales of human destiny was sufficient to disarrange the balances of the universe, and that overcrowded graveyards and starving children and mothers' prayers were formidable pleaders, and that up from the suffering earth there went cries which God heard. And so in the narrower sphere of human life as well as on the larger canvas filled by the great captains of history there is every assurance and certainty that God's providence and care are over the good and true, and multitudes of Christian men and women are ready to sing with the poet:

"I will not doubt, tho all my ships at sea
   Come drifting home with broken mast and sail,
   I shall believe the Hand which never fails

From seeming evil, worketh good for me,
And tho I weep because those sails are tattered
Still I cry, while my last hopes lie shattered,
   'I trust in Thee.'

"I will not doubt, tho all my prayers return
Unanswered, from the still white realm above;
I shall believe it is an All-wise Love
Which has refused these things for which I yearn;
And tho, at times, I cannot keep from grieving,
Yet the pure ardor of my fixt believing
   Undimmed shall burn.

"I will not doubt, tho sorrows fall like rain,
And troubles swarm like bees about a hive.
I shall believe the heights for which I strive
Are only reached by anguish and by pain;
And tho I groan and writhe beneath my crosses,
I yet shall reap through my severest losses
   The greater gain.

"I will not doubt, well anchored in this faith
Like some staunch ship, my soul braves every gale,
So strong its courage that it will not quail
To breast the mighty unknown sea of death.
Oh! may I cry, while body parts with spirit,
'I will not doubt,' so listening worlds may hear it,
   With my last breath."

III

Then we have this other unshaken pillar of
Christian faith, the assurance of *the immortal life*.
Paul says, "We know that if our earthly house of
this tabernacle were dissolved, we have a building

of God, an house not made with hands, eternal in the heavens.'' Paul had no doubt whatever on this subject. To him it was a certainty. You will look in vain for a single instance in all Paul's teachings where he speculates on the subject and wonders if it is going to be true. Instead, he is always sure of it. He was absolutely sure that the building of God was being made for him. He was certain that it was better for him to depart and be with Christ than it was to remain in the world, and yet cheerfully he waited the call of God. Now this divine assurance of Paul's must have come from a consciousness of the spiritual life within him, from the eternal life which was pulsing in his own veins. He felt that the immortal life was already a part of his inheritance, and he lived it so perfectly every day that to him there was no great gulf between the spiritual and the physical. The executioner who made him a martyr for Christ would only set him free to enter fully upon the spiritual life. We too may be certain of our immortality only by living day by day the resurrection life. If we are risen with Christ in our daily lives, we shall have no doubt of his resurrection or of our immortality with him.

We must not confuse immortality with mere continued existence. To simply go on living is a small matter, and a cheap matter. A jellyfish goes on living, but it is a very poor sort of life. The immortality which Paul calls ''the crown of life'' was a life of noble thoughts, of holy purpose, of divine fellowship, a life of high and holy service to God and to humanity. If we would be as certain as Paul of our immortality, then we must live the same kind of a life. If a man is living a mean, low, vulgar life, a life that is simply animal, it is easy to make him believe that he is only an animal and that he will die as the ox does; but illuminate his soul with great truths, quicken his imagination into lofty flights, bring him into fellowship and communion with God, and great souls; cause him to know the exquisite joy of high service, and there are no arguments that can make him doubt his immortality. To such a soul heaven is not far away and the transition thither is a slight journey. A little child, when her father came to kiss her before she slept, used to say, ''Good-night, father! I shall see you again in the morning.'' And when the little one fell ill, and her father came to kiss her for the last time, that was still her greeting: ''Good-night, father! I will see you again in the morning.'' And if we in the spirit of childhood will live in fellowship with Christ Jesus, we shall be able to speak with that little child's certainty of the morning, and of the better day, and the fairer home, and richer life.

The Bishop of London was visiting a little dying child in the East End of that great city. She was afraid to die. He could not still her terror at once. After pondering for a few minutes, he leaned over the child and said, "Would you be afraid if I were to take you in my arms and carry you into the next room?" "Oh! no;" was the reply. "Well, some one ten thousand times kinder and stronger than I is going to do that with you. Heaven is no further than the next room, and Christ is as near you as I am." After that she was at rest and her heart was full of peace. If we live in close fellowship and friendship with Christ, heaven will never seem far away. When Charles Kingsley lay dying he cried aloud, "How beautiful God is." When Fletcher was too feeble to cry out, he said to his wife, "Wife, help me to cry out, 'God is love.'" Let us not be over-worried at the breaking down of the earthly house. It is God's beautiful gift to us, and we will keep it in good trim while we may; but we are not in despair when it falls to pieces. There is fitting for us a building, a house not made with hands, eternal in the heavens.

"What will be best in heaven?
To see my Savior's face.

To know my sins forgiven
  Through his abounding grace.
To seek no wayside lodging but my preparèd place.

"To find prepared my dwelling
  In beauty none can tell,
Earth's palaces excelling,
  For he doth all things well.
Christ is the Master-Builder, beneath his roof we dwell.

"Beneath his roof are meeting
  The holy and the just.
How tender is their greeting!
How perfect is their trust!
God giveth joy for ashes, and gold instead of dust."

THE MUSIC
OF LIFE

THE MUSIC OF LIFE

"And I saw as it were a sea of glass mingled with fire: and them that had gotten the victory over the beast, and over his image, and over his mark, and over the number of his name, stand on the sea of glass, having the harps of God."—Revelation XV: 2.

MUSIC is nature's high-water mark. It is when the brook is in full tide and goes with strong pulsing current toward the sea that it gurgles and murmurs and sings in delicious music. It is at mating time, when their hearts are swelling with love and their life's fruition is at the full, that the birds burst forth in song. When the writer of the book of Job would give us the noblest idea of beauty and glory, of sound and harmony in the universe, he declares that in creation's dawn "The morning stars sang together." When God would give the most glorious prelude to the birth of Jesus' angels sang to the shepherds on the plains of Bethlehem.

In the wonderful imagery of our text we are told of those who have come to that perfection of human living that the harps of God of right belong to them. That is to say, they have reached life's highest goal. They have come to that station in life, to that stand in character, to that point of triumph, that music is the natural expression of their living. As the best life must of necessity be the ambition of every true man and woman in the world, we surely cannot have a more interesting or helpful task than to study the characteristics of these people who have come to so glorious a triumph.

I

When we enter upon this search we have first *a thought of power*. Our text says that the harps of God are given to those who stand upon "the sea." What a brilliant figure and how suggestive! The figure is not a brook, or even a river or a lake, but it is that of the ocean. It is the wide, deep sea with its almost limitless expanse of wave, with its rising and falling tide, with its marvelous power to toss the giant ships upon its bosom as tho they were playthings, to crush the mightiest works of man with irresistible force. This is the figure used here to suggest the character and personality of the man to whom is given the harp of God. It suggests a strong, resourceful, splendid, glorious personality, and such the Christian character and personality must ever be. It must have a power about it too great to be limited to this

world. The sea has a wide horizon. Its vision is
not hemmed in by any narrow bay or inlet, it
reaches across thousands of miles and touches conti-
nents on all sides of the world. So the Christian
man must have wide horizons, and life must be to
him no mere earth-digging affair. A writer of dis-
tinction was dining some time ago in a palatial
hotel in one of our largest cities with a man of great
wealth, many times a millionaire. This modern
Crœsus said to his neighbor, "It is a good dinner,
isn't it? You know," he continued, "when a man
gets to be my age (he was nearly sixty) this is one
of the very few pleasures of life." Think what a
tragedy that was! Here was a man with such resources as to be able, if he willed, to bless humanity
at many points the wide world round. He could
have reached around the earth to open blind eyes,
unstop deaf ears, and make life sweeter to thousands of his fellow men, and yet one of the few
pleasures of his life was a good dinner. Let no
young man or young woman allow the visions
which always come to youth to narrow into that
of the mere money-grubber. Great-souled men and
women like John Howard, Florence Nightingale,
Carey, and Livingston, and multitudes of others,
had eyes that looked around the earth. They were
men and women like the sea, and they awoke music

in many a darkened land. Such people are too
great for their life force to be spent in this little
world alone. They come to the end of their earthly
experience with their vitality unabated. It was
once said of a Christian master by his servant who
had just come from his death-bed, "He is dying
full of life." Just as a tidal river ceases to be the
river at the spot where the ocean comes in to meet
it, so the great ocean of eternity has been flowing
in to meet the life of the true Christian, and he
dies full of life. Paul died full of life when he
could say: "I am now ready to be offered."
Stephen died full of life when he could cry
triumphantly, "Lord Jesus, receive my spirit."
Death is swallowed up of life in such cases.

II

We have also here in our text *a thought of purity
and sincerity.* This is "a sea of glass." That
indicates the perfection of purity and the absolute
sincerity of life. Dr. Jowett comments on this
scripture, If you were to come to such lives and
take up as it were a tumblerful, it would be as if
from a filtered spring. If you took as it were a
cupful of their imagination, it would be trans-
parent. If you took a sample of their affections,
there would be no mire, no unclean sediment. If

you went into their morality generally, it would be
equally clear and pure, and you would have to
say, "It is a sea of glass." A character like that
may be deep, but you can see to the bottom of it,
you can see clear through it—such characters are
simple, candid, translucent. It is this perfect sincerity of character which is absolutely essential to
music of the highest and noblest sort in human life.
Corrupt imaginations, impure thoughts, unclean
motives, selfish purposes—all these are fatal to the
music of life. It is the open, candid, simple, child-
like men and women, honest and true in their love
to God, in their service for God, unselfish in their
fellowship and service of fellow man, whose souls
are full of music. We may cheat our fellow
men. We may deceive them for a while as to the
sincerity and purity of our natures. But we can
never deceive God so that we shall have the music
of life without sincerity.

Dr. Watkinson tells about a gentleman in London who was a great joker, and on one occasion
he gave a garden party in which he thought he
would surprize his friends with some interesting
little tricks. All the trees in the garden were distinguished by particular associations with which
they were certainly unfamiliar. There was a wil-
low tree with great scarlet blossoms, and an ever-

green bearing roses, an elm tree rich with yellow oranges, and an oak bearing not acorns, but apples. In such a case how would you know a tree by its fruits? You could not, of course. The fruits never unfolded from those trees at all. They were only stuck on, or tied on, to give a certain artificial effect. Now there is a vast deal of that sort of thing in society to-day. There are a multitude of people who are surrounded with Christian environments, and who are so hedged about by the influence of the Christian church that they have a great many virtues in form that they do not possess in essence. They have a great many proprieties tied onto their lives that have no vital root in their consciences or affections. These may be able to deceive their fellow men, but they never deceive God, and such lives never sing. No music will ever burst forth, like the song from the breast of a bird in spring time, from such a heart.

III

We have also *a thought of loving sympathy*. You will notice that it is not only "a sea of glass," which might suggest coldness and ice, as well as purity, but it is "a sea of glass mingled with fire." You cannot fail to get here both purity and heat. It is not only goodness, but it is goodness warmed

with sympathy. It is goodness hot with loving
enthusiasm. The life that gives music to the world
must be permeated by love and sympathy. There
are many people who are as technically good as the
Pharisees and just as dull and unlovable. There
are many people who are good, but good for nothing. They are goody-goody. We may be very
regular and yet very useless. It is not enough to
be good, we must be humanly good. Our goodness
must be electrified by the dynamo of love. We
must have sympathy and self-sacrificing devotion;
then our goodness loses all its stiffness and unat-
tractiveness, and becomes the most charming and
lovely thing in the world. It is love that gives the
value to all human service. Robert Louis Stevenson had a marked power of attracting people to
himself by the very warmth of his personality as
well as by the kindness of his behavior. In one of
his books of reminiscence concerning his life in
Samoa, he tells how one day, when the cook was
away, he told another servant, Sasimo, just to
bring him a little bread and cheese for lunch to
his reading-room. But to his surprize he was served
with an excellent meal—an omelet, a good salad,
and perfect coffee. "Who cooked this?" asked
Stevenson. "I did," said Sasimo. "Well, then,
great is your wisdom." Sasimo bowed and humbly

corrected him! "Great is my love!" It was love that gave skill and deftness to his hands, and added the music of willingness to the repast. Dr. Wayland Hoyt tells of a godly negro whom he knew, who was a cobbler. For years he had been a servant in the house and field, but he began to get too old and crippled for this and so took to mending shoes. One day the doctor said to him, "My friend, after you have done cobbling here have you any hope for the better world?" "Ah! master," he replied, "when I sit here on my stool at work I feel that the Good Master is always looking at me, and when I take a stitch, it *is* a stitch, and when I put on a heel-tap it is not paper but good leather." The old shoemaker had the music of service because he had love in it. It is love that gives the charm to service and is its crown. The poet tells us that—

"One prayed aloud his thanks, and many heard—
But when he passed forth from the house of prayer
He wore upon his face his secrets bare,
While those who met him sighed, and thought with pain
Of all the year had lost them, of the reign
Of grief and sorrow on this earth of ours.

"One wore upon his face the smile of peace,
As if he held communion close with God,
And loved the world and all who on it trod;

And those who met him smiled, and thought how fair
The world must be to him—and straightway there
Rose in their hearts a glad thanksgiving hymn!"

IV

We have here also *a thought of struggle.* The text
holds the vital truth that the music of life comes
only after conflict. It is the reward of victory.
These people who stand upon the sea of glass
mingled with fire and to whom are given the harps
of God are the same people who were but recently
fighting with "the beast" and have gotten the
victory over "the beast." The music springs to
their hearts and fingers because of that victory.
"The beast" stands for all that is selfish and
wicked and mean in human life, and it is against
"the beast" in us and "the beast" in the world
that every one of us must struggle, and there can
be no real music until we have been victorious. We
are not all fighting the same beast. With one it is
as Christ says about Herod, "a fox," sly and
cunning; and again a man is ready to cry out with
David, "My soul is among lions," and another
hears the serpent hiss about his path; and still
another, who is not afraid of any of these, is eaten
with the moths of self-indulgence and idleness. We
cannot pick out each other's beast and know just
which it is, but you know, and God knows, and if

there is to be any music, if the harp of God is to be yours at last, you must get the victory over "the beast." Some scholar has rendered that phrase "gotten the victory over the beast" into "gotten the victory *out of* the beast," which gives another idea, as tho these victors had got hold of the beast and struggled with him until they had taken all his strength and absorbed it into their own natures. And it is surely true that every struggle we make against evil in which we come off victorious adds to our own power and increases the music of life. If we fight "the beast" in Christ's name and for Christ's sake, we may come out wounded from the fight, but they will not be the marks of "the beast," but the wounds of Christ. St. Paul fought with "the beast" and was sorely wounded, yet he never said it was a tiger's claw that had left its mark upon his body, but with a proud note of victory in his voice he cried: "I bear in my body the marks of the Lord Jesus!" This fight with "the beast" is the campaign of the ages. It is the battle of the human race. Every man and woman of us is in this struggle. Some it may be have fought and lost, and have given up to "the beast." If so, God pity you and arouse you to re- new the fight in the strength of Jesus Christ. Some of us have won victories again and again, but none of us are yet free from the struggle, and we shall never come to life's true scepter, nor shall we ever know the soul's perfect music, until our victory is complete.

No doubt many of you have read, in Longfellow's "Tales of a Wayside Inn," "The Legend of King Robert of Sicily." The proud monarch is seated upon his throne awaiting the arrival of his brother, the Emperor, and his second brother, the Pope, and secure in his worldly dominion and in his pomp and pride, listens to the chanting priests as they render the Magnificat—"He hath put down the mighty from their seats, and hath exalted them of low degree"—and he murmurs to himself:

> "'Tis well that such seditious words are sung
>   Only by priests and in Latin tongue;
> For unto priests and people be it known,
>   There is no power can push me from my throne."

Having so said, he falls asleep, and his place is taken by an Angel, his exact counterpart in form and feature. King Robert awakens to find himself condemned to a dark cell, and presently, instead of the king, he is the court jester; and daily as he passes him who has usurped his place the question is put to him by the Angel, "Art thou the king?" Haughty, suffering, unsubdued, King Robert, flinging back his head, hurls forth the sentence, "I am,

I am the king.'' Then comes the day, the dawning Easter day, when a new self is born within him, and as it were the psalmist's prayer is answered, and the heart of flesh has replaced the heart of stone.

"And, kneeling humbly on his chamber floor,
    He heard the rushing garments of the Lord
    Sweep through the silent air, ascending evermore.
        *   *   *   *   *   *

"And when they were alone the angel said,
    'Art thou the king?' Then, bowing down his head
    King Robert crossed both hands upon his breast!
    And meekly answered him: 'Thou knowest best.
    My sins as scarlet are; let me go hence
    And in some cloister'd school of penitence,
    Across those stones that pave the way to heaven,
    Walk barefoot, till my guilty soul is shriven!'

"The angel smiled, and from his radiant face
    A holy light illumined all the place,
    And through the open window, loud and clear
    They heard the monks chant in the chapel near,
    Above the stir and tumult of the street:
    'He has put down the mighty from their seat,
    And hath exalted them of low degree!'
    And through the chant a second melody
    Rose like the throbbing of a single string:
    'I am an Angel, and thou art the King!'

"King Robert, who was standing near the throne,
    Lifted his eyes, and lo! he was alone!
    But all appareled as in days of old,
    With ermined mantle and with cloth of gold;
    And when his courtiers came, they found him there
    Kneeling upon the floor, absorbed in silent prayer."

Let us not lose the lesson. The angel can never surrender the scepter to us until we have conquered our selfishness, until "the beast" is slain and our victory is attained. But victory is within the reach of every one of us, and with our victory the perfect music of human living. The music of life does not depend upon our wealth, or upon our luxuriant surroundings; but it depends upon our victory over "the beast." Blake, the painter-poet, lived in his two rooms in perfect contentment, and said to the great world, "Leave me alone, leave me to my happiness and peace." St. Paul had a very narrow place to live in in Rome—a cell in Nero's dungeon. Some years ago I went down into that old prison, where it is supposed St. Paul spent the last few months of his life, and tho it was a hot August day, I shivered in its gloom and recalled how Paul had asked that his cloak might be brought to him by his friend who was coming to visit him. And yet in that cold dungeon Paul lived in heavenly places in Christ Jesus, and in a spirit so full of joy and song that every soldier who was chained to him to guard him was converted to Paul's Lord. His soul was full of music and has been waking music all round the world ever since. If we would have Paul's victory, and like him, and these whom we have been studying, stand at last with perfect sincerity of soul, with boundless resources of character, and with the flush of victory on our cheeks, on "the sea of glass mingled with fire," we must, like Paul, bravely fight the battles of life which confront us to-day. Let no struggle that threatens to come in the future give us fear or worry. To do our duty to-day, to be sure we are right with God at the present moment, to live this hour with candid sincerity of heart, with strong courage, with loving sympathy, is the open secret of great and harmonious living.

> "Why fear to-morrow, timid heart?
>   Why tread the future's way?
> We only need to do our part
>   To-day, dear child, to-day.
> The past is written! Close the book
>   On pages sad and gay;
> Within the future do not look,
>   But live to-day—to-day.
> 'Tis this one hour that God has given;
>   His *now* we must obey;
> And it will make our earth his heaven
>   To live to-day—to-day."

GOD'S COMMAND THAT WE ANSWER OUR OWN PRAYERS

GOD'S COMMAND THAT WE ANSWER OUR OWN PRAYERS

"Wherefore criest thou unto me? . . . Go forward: . . . Lift thou up thy rod, and stretch out thine hand over the sea, and divide it."—Exodus XIV: 15, 16.

MOSES and his great army of Hebrew slaves, who had but just escaped from their bondage in Egypt and were fleeing toward the promised land of refuge, became entangled in the wilderness. The news of this reached Pharaoh. This proud and wicked king had had severe handling for his sins. The plagues which had come upon Egypt because of his stubborn rebellion against God had broken him down for a time, and he had been anxious in his fright that the children of Israel should depart out of the land. But after they were gone and the loss of these hundreds of thousands of servants began to be keenly felt, Pharaoh and the leading people of Egypt regretted their action, and they wished they had not been so hasty in yielding to God. Now just at this time, when they were well ready for it, came the news that the escaped

Hebrews were confused in the wilderness and would
no doubt fall an easy prey to a pursuing army of
their former masters. Pharaoh decided to follow
them and capture them. So with a large number
of men of war, and mounted soldiers with their
war chariots, he set out, and soon overtook the
crowd of men and women and children who were
traveling on foot.

The knowledge that they were pursued brought
great terror to the Hebrews. They knew they were
no match in battle for the war-like and disciplined
Egyptian soldiers. They pushed forward in their
fear of capture until they came to the banks of the
Red Sea, and there to human eyes ruin seemed inevitable. Behind were the cruel tyrants determined to carry them back to bondage, which would
now, without doubt, be more severe than ever. On
the other side, immediately before them, was the
wide reach of the sea. To be drowned or captured
seemed the only alternative. It was in this emergency that they cried out to God for help, and God
responded to Moses, ''Wherefore criest thou unto
me? Speak unto the children of Israel, that they
go forward: But lift thou up thy rod, and stretch
out thine hand over the sea, and divide it: And
the children of Israel shall go on dry ground
through the midst of the sea.''

We have here a great theme; a subject worthy of our sincere study, not only rich in teaching, but one which should inspire our hearts to the noblest service for God and humanity.

I

The rod was the token of God's presence with Israel. God had promised Moses that he would be with that rod, and when in the course of his duty he used it, it should be accompanied with divine power. So God has promised us that if with reverent and humble hearts we seek to do his will and go forth on the path of duty, his presence shall be with us. The history of the church gives abundant proof that God keeps his promises. One of the old hymn writers voices this faith:

> "Give me thy strength, O God of power;
> Then let winds blow, or thunders roar,
> Thy faithful witness will I be;
> 'Tis fixt; I can do all through thee."

Some one says that it is a kind of stored-up energy that is ours in God: Such as you find in a coiled spring, a sealed fountain, power held in leash; such that, when it is once released, the work is as good as done. A recent article in a scientific magazine declares that "The storage power is the want of the age." In these great Rocky Mountains about us we see illustrations of its importance every day. The great cañons of the mountains are being filled with water, stored up, held back, and made to yield not only irrigation for the wide-stretching, thirsty plains, but power to drive spindles and turn wheels, and heat buildings, and light up towns and villages, and drive trains of cars a hundred miles away. So the Christian, and the church, which is a combination of Christians for Christian service, should be in spiritual things a storehouse of accumulated energy, ready for service—a storehouse filled by God himself. What may not such men accomplish! We are told that Michael Angelo, even after he was seventy years of age, when filled with the sacred fury of genius, would hew away at the marble of a statue and accomplish as much in an hour as would occupy two or three ordinary workmen for a day. A man filled with divine ardor cannot be accounted for by earthly rules. You cannot measure a personality like General Booth, or his wife Catherine Booth, or a man like Chinese Gordon or Bishop William Taylor by ordinary rules. Who could estimate the achievements of a church filled with men and women conscious that the presence of God in them gives them divine power in Christian service?

One of the Scotch professors, speaking of the

threadbare discussion about Shakespeare and
Bacon, says that Shakespeare was a plain man,
therefore they say he could not have produced
Hamlet, or Macbeth, or King Lear. These great
works, they say, must have been written by Lord
Bacon, and Lord Bacon must have been the son of
a queen. Oh, the blindness of it! It is through
inspiration that such works are done, through
laborious embodiment of great ideas, which the
spirit of truth and beauty sent into the soul. So,
in the works to which God calls you and me, we
are, indeed, above the level of our lives. In a real
sense we rise above ourselves, becoming the agents,
the instruments of God. Tho it is impossible
for us to think too humbly of ourselves, it is impossible for us to think too highly of the work
which God gives us to do. It is one of the glorious
rewards of the Christian workman to discover that
his work has a value which he had no title to expect. You undertake some duty with much self-
distrust; blunder in discharging it; persevere with
difficulty; entertain an idea you have misjudged
your vocation; but you learn, as you proceed, that
God is working through you; that what you sow in
weakness is raised in power, and that the works of
which you only saw first that they were good are
also beautiful and noble. It is the old story told

by Jesus: ''Lord, when saw we thee a stranger, or
naked, or sick, or in prison, and came unto thee?
And the king shall answer and say unto them,
Verily, I say unto you, inasmuch as ye have done
it unto one of the least of these my brethren, ye
have done it unto me.''

II

Our theme should teach us that *God requires of
us obedient faith*. ''Faith without works is dead.''
We are not only to believe God, but we are to act
upon our faith. There is nothing in the text to
discourage the man in trouble from praying to
God. We are plainly told to call upon God in the
day of trouble. But the plain teaching is that God
does not do for us what we can do for ourselves.
We are often more ready to cry out for help than
we are to help ourselves. We are more ready to
call for more light, means, and privileges than we
are to use faithfully what we possess. We are often
more apt to complain, as the Hebrews did against
Moses, than to exert ourselves; to wonder at what
God hath done, at what he will do, than we are
to lift our own rod and go forward. The Hebrews
were crying aloud to God for help, yet Moses held
in his hand the rod which God had promised to
attend with the power which controls the universe.

God said to him "Lift thou up thy rod, and stretch out thine hand over the sea, and divide it." When Moses obeyed, the sea divided, and at the command of God the Hebrews marched forward with the wall of waters on either hand. It was not prayer alone, but obedience, and doing of duty faithfully, that they needed to achieve their triumph. The same is true to-day in all our Christian work. I was reading the other day Campbell Morgan's story of Moody's meetings, held in Oxford University, England. Morgan, then a very young man, was present. Moody was a man with but the barest rudiments of an education, and Oxford was the center of the world's learning. Moody had only one thing in his favor. That was, he believed God, knew God was with him, and faithfully held up his own rod over human hearts, trusting that God would furnish the divine influence. A more unlikely man than Moody, to human eyes, for reaching university men it would be impossible to imagine, and during the first days he had to stand the insolence and the derision of hundreds of young students. Morgan says it was a sight never to be forgotten. His perfect self-composure, never losing his temper, keeping up the steady, loving appeal to them without a sign of discouragement. One evening Morgan went into the room of the

hotel where Moody was speaking, and just as
the after-meeting began there came into the room
four or five men, well known to the University, because they were on the University Cricket Eleven.
They had all been dining, and were considerably
excited, and they came into the room and began
to make loud and rude comments, and to interrupt
the meeting. Young Morgan put his hand upon
their shoulders, and urged them to be quiet. They
turned around and abused him, and continued
their interruption; but Moody, who was watching
the thing from the platform, in a moment came
down the aisle, stept to the one who happened to
be the captain of the University Eleven, and the
best-known man at the time at Oxford, took him
by the buttonhole, and said: "I want to speak to
you a moment." The man got up and Moody led
him into a corner of the room. Morgan saw no
more of what happened that night; but on the following evening he went up onto the platform of the
meeting. The room was crowded with undergrad-
uates. He noticed that there were four empty
chairs at the front, and just before the meeting
began he saw walking up the aisle those four members of the University Cricket Eleven. They came
on quietly, and took their places in the seats that
were vacant. Moody said nothing at the time, but

spoke to those college men exactly as he would to a crowd of workingmen. Indeed, it was the only way he knew how to speak. The Holy Spirit fell on the audience, as it did when Peter was preaching in the house of Cornelius. A spell fell upon that crowd of students which no one could resist. He told those young men of the sins which were killing them, he told them of the Savior who could save them, and there were very few of them unmoved, and those few who were unmoved at the beginning could not resist at the end, for as he came to the end he turned to the four men in the front, and said, "Now, you men, I am very much obliged to you. You promised me you would come and would listen, and you have done it, and I am very much obliged to you, and may God bless you and save you." And that captain of the University Cricket Eleven became a devout and earnest Christian, and the influence spread through his family and through the University. Obedient faith such as Moody exercised never fails of the blessing of God in the manifestation of his presence.

III

God puts the burden of the world's salvation upon us. He does not send us out alone, but he proposes to work through us to save our brothers.

And wherever men and women have done great
service for humanity they have felt this keen sense
of responsibility for what they saw needed to be
done to help the world. They have heard God
saying to them, "Lift thou up thy rod and go forward," and they have obeyed. In the days of the
Crimean War there was an unknown young woman
in England by the name of Florence Nightingale.
God laid the condition of the sick and wounded
soldiers on her heart, and she obeyed the heavenly
vision. Some of you have read of those dark, dis-
mal sheds which passed under the name of hospitals, and you remember the vision that night
after night was seen in those dreary sheds, a vision
that will not fade for centuries from the memory
of the world.

Lo, in that house of misery, a lady with a lamp I saw
Flit through the glimmering gloom
And pass from room to room;
And slow, as in a dream of bliss,
The speechless sufferer turns to kiss
Her shadow as it falls
Upon the darkened walls,
As if a door in heaven should be
Opened, and then closed suddenly,
The vision came and went;
The light shone and was spent.
In Britain's story, in the long hereafter of her speech and
    song,

That light its ray shall cast
There proudly of the past,
A lady with a lamp shall stand
In the bright history of the land
A type of noble, good, heroic womanhood.

Florence Nightingale worked miracles in behalf of the suffering soldiers because she lifted the rod in her hand and in the strength of God did her best.

Some seven centuries ago there was a young Italian keeping the feast with his friends one night; and he wearied of the feast and of the jests. There was nothing wrong, only a friendly feast. He quietly withdrew and went out and stood thoughtfully beneath the blue Italian sky. By and by his friends came out, and they walked home together, and they said to him, "You are in love." He said nothing, but he had a far-away look upon his face, like a man who is looking into another world. "You are in love. Who is it?" the friends said. "I am," he replied, "and my bride is called Poverty. No one has been anxious to woo her since Jesus lived, and I am going to serve her all my days." That young Italian became immortal as one of the greatest Christians who ever lived, under the name of St. Francis. He felt the burden of responsibility to serve the world. He lifted up his rod in God's strength and went forward.

My friends, it seems to me that one of the greatest needs of the church to-day is a keen sense of personal responsibility felt by the individual Christian for the salvation of the community. An English preacher quotes an old Scotch divine who once said, "What troubles me is not the non-church going, but the non-going church." A very wise and keen criticism. You know the old oft-repeated story of the boy who was asked if his father was a religious man. "Yes," he said, "but he has not been doing much at it lately." And I think that there is much in that story applicable to our churches. Somehow, for some reason or other, many Christian men and women do not keep the passion of their souls for Christ, and for the salvation of humanity, fresh. We have all heard Cowper's hymn criticized, but I think he knew human nature very well when he wrote:

> "Where is the blessedness I knew
> When first I saw the Lord?
> Where is the soul-refreshing view
> Of Jesus and his word?"

I doubt not there are many who hear me who do not feel the same glow, who are conscious that they do not have the same responsive spirit, the same whole-hearted passion of enthusiasm for Christ and for the conversion of their neighbors, as they had five, ten, or twenty years ago. Let us ask the reason why? And if we were to pursue that question from one pew to another, and from one heart to another, we would no doubt find that under various forms it is worldliness that has crept in and smothered the divine flame. Schiller says it is a scientific fact that the animal nature of man, if let have its way, becomes dominant over the spiritual toward middle life; and John Henry Newman says that unless they are subdued by high religious and moral principle, material interests inevitably submerge man's whole nature into selfish indifference toward all with which self is not concerned. And Dante places in his immortal poem man's encounter with the three animals—the fierce lion of wrath and pride; luxury, the spotted panther; and the gaunt, hungry wolf of avarice—in the middle period of man's life. There can be no doubt about it that men and women nearing middle age need to be aroused to the necessity of keeping close to God as the only source of fresh impulse to righteous and holy service.

All that I have been saying should have quick and powerful application in our own hearts and lives. The Red Sea of difficulty and trouble, the sea of human need, confronts every one of us. With some of you it is your unconverted children.

You are ready to pray to God for help to bring about their salvation; but is it not true that so far as you personally are concerned you have dropt into lethargy on the subject? God is saying to you, "Why criest thou to me? Go forward! Lift thou up thy rod!" How many times I have seen an awakened mother, or an aroused father, pour out life and soul in such a stream of gracious and loving influence that the children were immediately won to Christ!

IV

I must not close without a word to those of you who are not Christians, but who stand confronting the Red Sea of your condemnation. Your sins follow you as the cruel and angry Egyptians followed on the heels of those Hebrew refugees. God is commanding you also to lift up your rod and go forward. Do you ask me what rod a sinner has that shall divide the sea before him, the sea of his guilt and condemnation? I answer, it is the cross of Jesus Christ. Your prayers alone can never save you. Look to the cross with confidence and love, and go forward in obedience to God. When Butler, the author of that famous book known as "Butler's Analogy," lay dying, he called for his chaplain, and said, "Tho I have endeavored to avoid sin, and to please God to the utmost of my power, yet from the consciousness of perpetual infirmities, I am still afraid to die." "My lord," said the chaplain, "you have forgotten that Jesus Christ is a Savior." "True," was the answer, "but how shall I know that he is a Savior for me?" "My lord, it is written, 'Him that cometh to me, I will in no wise cast out.'" "True," said the dying man, "and I am surprised that tho I have read that scripture a thousand times over, I never felt its virtue until this moment; but now I die happy." So, my friend, it is Christ, the Christ on the cross, the Christ who gave himself for you, who is your rod of salvation. There is a beautiful passage in Browning's "Saul," where David has been playing before his melancholy master, and trying to lift from him the veil of madness, and at last has begun to feel the passion of love for the fallen king, and he conceives the Redeemer coming into human form in order to save Saul, and he sings:

"'Tis the weakness in strength that I cry for! My flesh that I seek
 In the Godhead! I seek it, and I find it. O Saul, it shall be
 A Face like my face that receives thee; a Man like to me
 Thou shalt love and be loved by for ever; a Hand like this hand.
 Shall throw open the gates of new life to thee! See the Christ stand!"

THE FAG-ENDS OF
THE TREE OF LIFE

THE FAG-ENDS OF THE
TREE OF LIFE

"And the residue thereof, he maketh a god."—Isaiah
XLIV: 17.

THIS is one of the most graphic pictures in the
Bible. It portrays a man who feels within him
some instinctive necessity of being religious, so he
goes out among the trees in his woods and selects
an ash tree, and he cuts it down and takes it home.
By this time he is hungry, and so he uses the tree
partly for fuel with which to bake his bread and
to roast his meat. Then the cold weather comes on,
and he uses still more of the tree to build a fire
to warm himself. At last there is nothing left but
the chips and the twigs, and he seems to be con-
science-stricken a little that he should have forgotten entirely the main purpose for which he cut
the tree down, and so he gathers up these fag-ends
and makes him a god. The word picture as painted
by the writer of this book is very striking: "He
planteth an ash and the rain doth nourish it. Then
shall it be for a man to burn; for he will take thereof, and warm himself; yea, he kindleth it and

baketh bread; . . . He burneth part thereof in
the fire; with part thereof he eateth flesh; he
roasteth roast, and is satisfied; yea, he warmeth
himself, and saith, Aha, I am warm, I have seen the
fire: And the residue thereof he maketh a god.''
Was there ever anything more graphic, more real-
istic in its outlines, more keenly ironical in its
heart-searching description?

Now it seems to me that this incident is of important suggestive interest to us, and that we
should find in it lessons of the greatest possible
value. All the forces of life may be compared to
a great tree with its wide-spreading branches. A
man has about so much force of every sort which is
his heritage as a man. If he uses it in one way, he
cannot use it in another. If a man gives all his
force and power to worldliness, it is certain he cannot give anything but the fag-ends of his life to
God. That is the serious theme I bring to you for
consideration, that *many people are giving the fag-
ends of their lives to him who has a right to the
first and the best.* When we recall what God has
done for us not only in our creation and in the
marvelous adaptations of the beautiful world of
sights and sounds and harmonies in which we live,
but in his revelation to us in Jesus Christ our Lord
and Savior, it is evident to us that any keen appre-

ciation of relative values must put our love and our duty to God in the place first of all.

Some of you remember the story of Karshish, the Arab physician who at the time of Christ's earthly ministry was sent by his royal master Abib to travel throughout the then known world that he might gather up everything of interest and value known in medicine. In his travels he made regular reports to his master. In the course of these journeys he came to Bethany, and met Lazarus, the brother of Martha and Mary, who declares that

> "He was dead and then restored to life
> By a Nazarene physician of his tribe."

Naturally this was in Karshish's line as a physician. Nothing could be more interesting and nothing more improbable to a doctor than this story. So he follows Lazarus around and gives him the closest attention. He finds him as he says to be a man "with the spiritual life around the earthly life."

"His heart and brain move there, his feet stay here."

Karshish hears the remarkable story that—

> "This man so cured regards the curer, then,
> As—God forgive me! Who but God himself,
> Creator and sustainer of the world
> That came and dwelt in flesh on it awhile!"

This Oriental doctor had never heard of such
a God, who not only cared for but loved his children.   The idea was very strange to him.   He
even thought it necessary to apologize to his master
for inserting such an improbable story.   Nevertheless, it fascinated him, and little by little it drew
his interest away from everything else.   All the
new diseases he had discovered, all his curious
spiders, his snake stone, and the wonderful recipes
he had found on his long journeys, all were nothing to him now as his imagination took fire at the
thought of a God who really loves men enough to
seek to help them.   In the awakened passion of his
soul he writes to his master:

> "The very God!   Think, Abib; dost thou think?
> So the all-great were the all-loving too—
> So through the thunder comes a human voice
> Saying, 'O heart I made; a heart beats here!
> Face, my hands fashioned; see in it myself!
> Thou hast no power nor may'st conceive of mine;
> But love I gave thee, with myself to love,
> And thou must love me who have died for thee!'"

It is impossible to fully appreciate the wondrous
revelation of God in Jesus Christ without feeling
as Karshish did that it is of supreme importance
and demands the best there is in us.   Charles
Kingsley once wrote, "You may not believe it
now, but there will come a time when all these

voices will be hushed, and then you will know that
better than riches, better than fame, better than
power, is goodness." And does not Jesus say,
"Seek ye first the kingdom of God and his righteousness"?

One of the few unconditional commendations
which Jesus uttered during his life and ministry
was upon the woman who brought the costly oint-
ment and poured it on his head. He declared that
that should be remembered of her to the end of
time, and to the end of the world, wherever his
Gospel was preached. Why? Because she had
done her best. "She hath done what she could,"
said Jesus. The wise men who came from the East
to worship Jesus at his birth brought the best
things, the most precious treasures that the world
held. Ian Maclaren has written very beautifully of
the guest-chamber for which Jesus asked, where he
might come with his disciples. He asks for the
"upper room," the best room, the lightest, sunniest
room, the room nearest heaven, the love-chamber
of the soul. Ah, how we blunder when we give
Christ the little out-of-the-way room somewhere in
the attic or in the cellar. Some room that can be
spared without sacrifice. You think you have not
time to be hospitable to Jesus. Your own ambitions and selfish desires fill all the beautiful upper

rooms. You would not turn Jesus out, that would shock you to think of, and yet you never dream of bringing him to the front, making him the chief guest, and giving him the best place. Your soul's upper room is alive with all the gayeties of your selfish pleasure, but the world never sees the face and the form of Jesus in that crowded room. How unworthy to thus give Christ the fag-ends of your fellowship.

I

Many Christians give Christ only *the fag-ends of their money.* To support this statement it is not necessary to bring forward exaggerated types, such as the man who spends a dollar a week for some single personal luxury and counts himself generous if he gives half as much to the support of public worship in his church and the upbuilding of the kingdom of God in his community, or the other type of man who is like the colored brother in his giving to the Lord.

"Yes, sir," he said, "I gives the truck off one acre ebbery year to de Lord."

"What acre is it?" was asked.

"Well, dat is a different question. Truf is, de acre changes most ebbery season."

"How's that?"

"In wet seasons I gives de Lord de low land, and

in dry seasons I gives him de top acre of de whole plantation.''

''In that case the Lord's acre is the worst in the whole farm: for in wet seasons it would be quite flooded, and in dry times parched.''

''Jus' so. You don't allow I'se going to rob my family of de best acre I'se got, did ye?''

Of course, in both these cases, and they are typical of great numbers, it is simply the fag-ends of the tree of life so far as money is concerned which is given to God.

Nothing is excluding Christ from the hearts of profest Christian men and women to-day so much as the love of money. Christ says ''Ye cannot serve God and mammon.'' Paul says, ''They that desire to be rich fall into a temptation and a snare and many foolish and hurtful lusts, such as drown men in destruction and perdition. For the love of money is a root of all kinds of evil; which some reaching after have been led astray from the faith, and have pierced themselves through with many sorrows.'' Notice that a man may not be rich, but it is the man with the fierce thirst for it, the man that ''reaches after'' money, who is in danger. It is the reaching out of the racer, every muscle on the stretch until the soul burns with a passion for money. Some one says, it is a com-

mon thing to say of such a man, whose whole soul is
on fire for money, ''He has got all his wits about
him.'' But that is just what he has not, for half
his wits are dead. What are wits? Wits are
powers of alertness, powers of discernment,
powers of perception; and a man who has all his
wits about him has his wits alert toward God. The
magazines are full just now with long discussions,
philosophizing over the extravagance, and the sins,
and disgraceful follies into which the bright crowd
of the younger rich men farther east have fallen
within a few years. These men are bright men so
far as money-getting goes, but they are blind on
the side of God, on the side of a pure, wholesome,
noble personal and family life. And the tremendous peril to the Christian church to-day is
that many people in the church are unwilling that
their religion should interfere either with how they
get their money or with how they spend it. Some
one has written a poem about those people at
Gadara who besought Christ to leave their country
because the devils had entered into their swine and
their herds had been destroyed:

> '' 'Rabbi, begone! Thy powers
>   Bring loss to us and ours.
>   Our ways are not as thine,
>   Thou lovest men, we—swine.
>   Oh, get you hence, Omnipotence!

And take this fool of thine!
His soul? What care we for his soul?
What good to us that thou hast made him whole?
Since we have lost our swine.'

"And Christ went sadly,
 He had wrought for them a sign
Of Love, and Hope, and Tenderness divine,
 They wanted—swine.
Christ stands without *your* door and gently knocks;
But if your gold or swine the entrance blocks,
He forces no man's hold—he will depart,
And leave you to the treasures of your heart.

"No cumbered chamber will the Master share,
 But one swept bare
By cleansing fires, then plenished fresh and fair
 With meekness and humility and prayer.
There he will come, yet, coming even there,
He stands and waits, and will no entrance win
Until the latch be lifted from within."

Christ departed from the Gadarenes and never
came back, and you may depend upon it, my fellow
Christians, that if we are to save our souls, and
enjoy the blessings of God, it must be because we
hold our lives open to God's inspection, and recognize Christ as supreme ruler both in the making
and the distributing of our money. I have for
some time been ever more and more interested on
the subject of tithing. For a long while I felt,
like a great many others, that while tithing, the
giving of one-tenth of one's earnings or income

definitely to God, had the divine sanction under the Mosaic dispensation, it had been done away with in the new Christian dispensation under which we live. But more recently I have been led to look into the matter, and I am now thoroughly convinced that that position is untenable. In the first place, the tithing system was in existence many centuries before Moses was born. Abraham was a tither. When he came back from the rescue of his nephew Lot he gave tithes to Melchizedec, the priest of the Most High God. And Jacob, when he had the wonderful vision of the heavenly stairway with its angels coming and going, at Bethel, vowed to God that he would throughout his whole life give a tenth of everything that was bestowed upon him to the Lord. Christ did not do away with the tithes. The only place that could be regarded as a criticism upon it is where he is rebuking the Pharisees, not for giving the tithe, but for failing in the spirit of love and brotherhood in which the tithes should be given. Surely we modern Christians, with all the light, and beauty, and glory which have come to us through riches of salvation in Christ Jesus, should, at the very least, give as large a percentage of our substance to God as the old Jew who looked through a glass darkly. I do not think that one-tenth is as much as many of us should give.

Many of us ought to give three times that much to the service of God. But I do honestly believe that that ought to be the minimum, the very least which any servant of God gives, or, perhaps the better word would be, pays. We ought not to give what we bestow upon the church in support of God's kingdom with any thought whatever of charity. There is no charity about it. We are in partnership with God. If we use nine-tenths of what we earn for ourselves and our friends, the other tenth belongs to God, and it is not a question of charity, it is paying our honest dues to the Most High.

And God has promised that if we are loyal to him, and faithful in this partnership, he will bless us in basket and in store, and multiply our resources in physical as well as in spiritual matters. If you are satisfied with the security, you can pay your tenth with all gladness of soul. Harvey Reeves Calkins tells the story of a young German, Gustav Schwan. He was converted one February, and, in March, he began to pay his tithe unto the Lord. He had a little shop down town. Trade was very dull for a while. Nobody came to buy. To make matters worse, his stock was running very low. He could not collect certain large bills that were due. He had no credit at the wholesalers, and only a very small balance in the house with which to conduct the business and buy food for his wife and the children. He looked into the "Lord's box," where they kept their tithe, and found that he had a considerable sum which had been accumulating a little at a time. At first he thought he would borrow the Lord's money, but on praying about it concluded it would not be honest, and so took it, hard prest as he was, and gave his pastor two-thirds of the amount to send to China to support a little orphan boy in one of the church schools, and the rest he sent to the church treasurer for current expenses. Telling about it, the young German said, "It seemed to me just like this: God will look down and see his box empty; he must have money to supply his work, so he will begin to fill his box again; and while God is filling his box, I will be getting the business." Well, the very morning that the young German sent the sacred money on its way to do God's service, a gentleman called and paid a large bill, saying something had reminded him as he was passing that way. Two more remittances came that day by post, and a large number of cash orders followed, some large and others small. In three days he was able to replenish his stock, paying cash for all he bought, his business was greatly increased, and the family had turkey for dinner. But the best of all was, the Lord's box was almost full again. And the young German ends his testimony, for this story was told at the prayer-meeting by the man himself, "I have proved that tithing is good business for a young man just starting for himself."

Dear brethren, more and more I feel sure that there is a growing desire in our church for a great outpouring of the Spirit of God upon the people, resulting in our own spiritual culture and in the salvation of those who are without. Surely we should not overlook the direct and definite promise of God that if we will enter into partnership with him, and give at least one-tenth directly to his service, he will give us spiritual blessings, greater even than we dare to ask or think. Is not our case perfectly typified in that described in Malachi? God said then: "Even from the days of your fathers ye are gone away from mine ordinances, and have not kept them. Return unto me, and I will return unto you, saith the Lord of hosts. But ye said, Wherein shall we return? Will a man rob God? Yet ye have robbed me. But ye say, Wherein have we robbed thee? In tithes and offerings. . . . Bring ye all the tithes into the store-house, that there may be meat in mine house, and prove me now herewith, saith the Lord of hosts, if

I will not open you the windows of heaven, and pour you out a blessing, that there shall not be room enough to receive it.''

II

There are many others who give to Christ only *the fag-ends of their physical and intellectual strength.* A man uses up his physical strength in his ambition to get on in business or professional life, or to succeed in some honorable position for which he struggles, and he makes that an excuse for giving the fag-ends of his powers to the spiritual work of the church of God. A man works so hard through the week that he thinks it a legitimate excuse to make to his pastor for staying away from prayer-meeting, or remaining at home from the Sunday-evening service. My brother, as God's messenger let me ask you, in all frankness, what right you have to take God's time for your business so that you are too tired for more than one service on Sunday, and feel compelled to stay away from the prayer-meeting at the middle of the week. Why should you give God the leavings, the twigs, the chips, the fag-ends of all that tree of physical strength and power which he has bestowed upon you? The more you think of it the worse it will look. The more you study it out and investigate it the more ashamed you will be that you ever used such an excuse or ever allowed it to be necessary to use such an one. Where do you get your strength? Who gives it to you? Your breath is in God's hand. He alone has power to guarantee you strength and life. He breathes upon you, and you sicken and die, or at his smile you may be filled with vigor and power. Why, then, will ye rob God? Why will you give all your force and the flower of your strength and vigor to your business or social or political life, and bring only the worn-out fag-ends to the development of your soul, to the spiritual exaltation of your own life, and the uplifting of humanity in your city? My friends, the way to great triumph, the way to true success lies along the line of humble, reverent, loving service of God and blest fellowship with God. Let us never forget that supreme law written on all human life, given by the Master, "Whoso loseth his life for my sake shall find it."

THE LIMITATIONS
OF THE DWARF

THE LIMITATIONS OF
THE DWARF

"A dwarf . . . shall not come nigh to offer the bread of his God."—Leviticus: 20-21.

UNDER the old Hebrew priesthood the dwarf, while permitted to partake of the holy bread, was restrained from offering it to others. He was not to blame for being a dwarf, but only men without blemish, and who had the full measure of manly power, were permitted to exercise the functions of that holy office. There is in this significant fact the suggestion of a great theme. Every department of human life is full of illustration. The saddest limitation of poverty to any true man is that he cannot bestow charity on the poor. It is the bitterest sorrow of weakness that a man cannot render aid to the helpless. And in the higher realm the sorest pang that a man can know is that he is so dwarfed in his spiritual nature that he cannot offer the bread of his God to his fellows. The physical dwarf is very often, and indeed usually, without personal blame. It is his misfortune, which may have come to him by inheritance, or by accident.

But the spiritual dwarf, while the conduct of others may have contributed to his lamentable condition, is in the last analysis personally responsible, for the power to emerge from such a condition is always within his reach.

Our theme ought to have a helpful message for all men and women who desire to live a good life, a life not only harmless before God, but one full of benediction and blessing to their time, but who yet find themselves continually handicapped in efforts to be helpful to those about them by a sense of spiritual poverty and weakness. I wish to speak with all my heart, and I crave divine aid to speak, to those of you who in your better hours have dreams of righteousness which you never realize, and visions of service which you never perform, and which it may be you are never roused to sufficient courage to seriously attempt to perform. I wish to speak to you who have high appreciation of people who seem to you to be spiritual geniuses because there goes forth constantly from their rare souls the bread of God to others, yet when you attempt to offer it your hands seem empty, and hungry souls starve in your very presence. Now where can we find the secret of this failure on the part of many people who have good desires, and who are often conscious of a longing to be a bless-

ing to the world? The secret must be in a lack of
the presence of God known and felt in the heart
and life. When we study the great men who have
lived in the different epochs of the world, who have
been almoners of God's bread to their fellows, men
like David, and Wesley, and Bunyan, and John
Knox, we are convinced that this is true.

Take up the Psalms anywhere and read a hundred words and you will learn the secret of David's
power over the men of his time. God was with
David. Whether he wandered in the wilderness,
or hid in a cave on the mountain side, or went forth
to battle, or led the song in the temple service, God
was present with him. To David the world was
full of God. The eagle soaring in the sky made
him think of the wings of God flying to his help.
The mountain cavern was but a type of his hiding-
place in God's heart. No wonder that this man, to
whom every tree, and flower, and bird, and cloud,
and mountain crag spoke of God, was fitted to offer
the bread of God to the world of his time.

John Bunyan could write "Pilgrim's Progress"
because he had lived the life himself. He could
write of angels, for they had ministered to him. He
could make the Hill Difficulty seem possible to
human feet because God had led him step by step
to the summit. He could paint pictures of deliver-

ance from Doubting Castle, and from the lions by
the way, because God had delivered him.   The
dungeon might be small and gloomy, but the presence of God who had redeemed him, and who
abode in his heart, made that jail more splendid
than the palace of the king who had imprisoned
him.   Bunyan is still feeding the bread of God to
the world in nearly all languages, because God was
so continually present in his own heart and life.

John Wesley was able to quicken the religious
life of every church in the world, and to start into
being a new army of Christians which to-day has
millions of adherents, and is preaching the gospel
to the ends of the earth, because God was with
him more evidently than with any other man on
the earth in his day.   Other men were more eloquent, other men were as scholarly, other men had
more splendid physical presence, but no man of
his age so made men feel that the Almighty God
dwelt in frail human flesh to offer the bread of
life to hungry souls.   Once two boys filled their
pockets full of stones, and climbed up into the
loft of a house where Wesley was to preach, intend-
ing to stone him when he had got going well.   But
when the good man began to pray a wonderful awe
fell over all who heard him, and the larger of the
two boys said to the other, ''He is not a man!   I

tell you, he is not a man!" And so those boys lay
there in astonishment with a feeling that they were
in the presence of God. And so absorbed were
they with this impression that when the meeting
was over they slipt down to the gate where
his horse was tied, and as Wesley came along talking with some of the people, the smaller of the boys
crept up beside him and pinched his leg through
his trousers, and cried out loud, "He is a man!
I tell you, he is a man!" Wesley looked down at
the boy with a face lighted up with holy kindness,
and putting his hand on the boy's head said, "God
bless you, my lad, and make you a preacher of his
word." The boy never got out from under the
spell of that hand, that spirit, and that blessing,
and became one of the most powerful of Wesley's
preachers.

But I fear these great names often largely fail
in their influence with us. They fail not only because of oft reference, but because in the grandeur
of the distance they seem lifted so high above us
that we somehow feel that they are not real examples for men and women of common quality like
our own. But, my friends, our own day, the age
in which we live, is full of illustrations among the
common people which prove to us the same great
truth, that the soul may be enlarged, that the per-

sonality of men and women bred in the commonest walks of life may be so transformed and exalted by the presence of God that they may become the bread-givers of God to their fellows. The Hebrew priest that was born a dwarf, or who had been dwarfed by accident or by cruel treatment in childhood, could never become anything else. No penitence, no care, no culture could ever give him the broad shoulders, the splendid presence, and the noble personality of the full-grown and mature manhood necessary for his office. But God is more gracious in spiritual things, or rather the spirit is not subject to the limitations of the flesh, and the man who has been dwarfed by poverty, or affliction, or harsh treatment, into narrowness of vision and experience, may through devotion and self-surrender to God emerge out of the dwarfed manhood he now knows into the large and splendid personality which shall give him the privilege of offering the bread of God to humanity. In illustrating this fact one is only embarrassed by the wealth of resources.

Forty years ago a young medical student without money or friends was pursuing his course of studies in a London hospital, trying to fit himself to go as a medical missionary to China. There was nothing uncommon about him in any way. His father was a German, his mother was an English woman, and he himself had been born in Ireland. As he was emerging into manhood the Spirit of God got hold of him, and he was happily converted. He became so intensely Christian that he longed to be of service in making Christ known to the most neglected, and so he came to London to fit himself for that work. His heart was burning with love to God. He was fired with a desire to help everybody, and so he soon came to know of the frightful conditions of multitudes of homeless children in London. He began by helping one boy who had no home, and soon his hands were full of them. He first used a donkey stable for a refuge. But his heart was on fire, and God was with him and found him friends. His own heavenly magnetism inspired everybody who came in contact with him, and before long Thomas John Barnardo, ''The Father of Nobody's Children,'' became known throughout the whole world. Great institutions, which not only served as a refuge but as schools of preparation, accommodating thousands of boys and girls, grew up under his hand. Tens of thousands of hopeless, outcast youths, rescued by this man, educated and reclaimed, were sent out into all lands where English power has gone, and ninety-eight per cent. of them turned out well. Now

the wonderful thing about Barnardo, that which
everybody noted who came into touch with him,
was that he was a man of God. The spirit of love
and faith, the habit of prayer, an element of intensity and quiet self-sacrifice, of joy and radiance
and hope, pervaded his work and revealed the contact and communion he ever had with the perpetual source of supply and strength. Prayer to
God was his secret. An atmosphere of heavenly
warmth and light shone forth from the man and
his work.

Let us turn now to a very different illustration.
The first year after I went to Boston I found that
center of culture wonderfully stirred by the death
of a woman named Jennie Collins. Naturally I
looked into the matter. I found that Jennie Collins was born in poverty and struggled with it for
more than half of her life to win in the shops of
Boston her daily bread. Finally she succeeded in
getting a little money ahead and determined to
try to fulfil her long-cherished dream of assist-
ing her less fortunate fellow workers. So it was
that "Boffin's Bower" came into existence, and
over this swarming hive of needy girls and women
Jennie Collins was undisputed queen for years.
If ever there was a Christlike soul it was that of
Jennie Collins. All a woman needed in order to win

Jennie Collins for a friend was to be in need and to be friendless. God was present in every hour of her life. As the years went on, hundreds and thousands of women who afterward became true wives and mothers were saved on the ragged edge of the precipice by Jennie Collins. They called her the "Queen of Boffin's Bower." Sometimes her scepter was a bowl of gruel, sometimes a temporary loan, sometimes needed clothing; again it was only a kind word, the clasp of a warm, womanly hand, or a cheery smile that rebuked all despairing circumstances. Whatever was needed —gruel, smiles, tearful sympathy, or money—with rare insight into woman's nature Jennie Collins found out and set herself to provide.

Especially in the winter the amount of work performed by her was marvelous. Her rooms at that season were crowded with women of all nationalities, out of work, sick, in disgrace, in despair, none were turned away. She had the heart of Boston. That was her great power. Many people could not speak of her without tears. They felt God was with her.

During all her experience with the poor, the helpless and ofttimes the vicious, she retained the same faith in humanity, and the same long-suffering patience for it that God shows. If any one had seen this shop girl at thirty years of age and estimated her power to bless the women of Boston, he would have said, "She is a dwarf." But ten or twenty years later if he had watched her ministrations and known the streams of blessings that issued from her Christlike heart and gracious life he would have said, "She is a queenly woman." What was it? It was a woman surrendered to God. It was heaven in a woman's heart. It was the presence of God in a woman's soul and life.

On July 9, 1884, with great civic honor that stirred the city from end to end, a statue was unveiled in the city of New Orleans. It represents Margaret Haughery. It is not idealized, but shows a broad plain woman with the common dress she wore, an arm encircling an orphan. Who was this woman, that a square in a great city should be named after her, and a statue of her set up among the great of earth? She was a plain Irish Catholic girl, who became a nurse. Later she was married, and during the first year of her wedded life her husband died and left her a widow. As she must support herself, she managed a dairy in an orphan asylum for awhile, and then she opened a little eating-house of her own. Now this young Irish woman, in some way, I know not how, had

come into wonderful nearness to God. Something
of the pain and agony of Jesus Christ for the poor
and the suffering had come to bear upon this
woman's heart. She came to know the fellowship
of Christ's sufferings and her heart longed to succor the neglected children about her. She did not
wait until she got rich, but she opened a little eating-house, and began to help as much as she could
the needy within her reach. Looking about for
opportunities she saw that the deck-hands along
the river front were being swindled out of their
money, and were stupefying themselves with drink,
and then lay about boozing-dens till they were
pushed out. So she opened a little shop where they
could have wholesome food and drink cheaper than
at the saloon. And so she went on. She never
started into any enterprise to make money without
a benevolent motive at the back. In everything
she went into partnership with God. She was
trying to do the Lord's work. It is wonderful
how a thing goes when God is your partner. Margaret prospered. Her wagons covered the city.
She might easily have died a millionaire. But
she had no such poor purpose as that. Her heart
went out to the orphans. She had been one herself. She knew what it was to be left without
father or mother, and to get no education, not

even enough to read. In the course of her life this Irish girl either founded or largely aided eleven orphan asylums—Catholic and Protestant, black and white, alike.

In February, 1882, this good woman died. Never was there such a funeral in Louisiana. As far as I know she is the only woman in America who was ever buried with public honors. The Governor and ex-Governors of the State were among the pall-bearers. Delegations from her eleven orphan asylums attended the burial. The New Orleans Fire Department was in the procession. The bells all over the city tolled as the cortege moved along the streets. When it reached the Chamber of Commerce an unheard-of thing happened. The members marched down to the sidewalk and stood reverently with uncovered heads, and many of those strong business men with faces wet with tears, while the body of Margaret was carried past them to its rest. They built her a monument from contributions which poured forth from all classes, from newsboys to bankers.

"And she died; and so the people set
  Amid their heroes, with a proud consent,
   This simple woman-crownèd monument,
    And carved thereon the one word,—'Margaret.'"

What was the secret of Margaret's life? It was the presence of God with her.

A little while ago a man died in Indianapolis who was known popularly as "Uncle Billy Jackson." He had lived in Indianapolis since 1840. When Henry Ward Beecher, in his young manhood, was pastor there and conducted a great revival of religion, young William Jackson was converted to God. It was a conversion which carried his whole heart and nature with it. He consecrated himself completely to the service of God. He became a railroad man, and from 1853 on to the time of his death in 1900 he was continuously in the service of the Union Railway Company. He had great opportunities to make money, but he saw the evil effects of money-making upon so many people that he early decided not to take the risk for himself, but instead he gave his life constantly, every day for seventy years, for he lived to be ninety-one, to doing Christlike deeds in the service of men and women and children around him. He never married, but lavished his holy love and devotion on every hand. All men were his brethren; and all little folks were his children. For a number of years he lived among the very poor in the simplest and plainest way, that he might get closer to them. His heart and mind were so in harmony with God that a singular magnetism of kindness shone from his eyes and reflected from his countenance. He was no doubt unconscious that his love had broadened to that rare and beautiful degree exemplified by the description of the Master, that he had "compassion on the multitude." The rich and the poor of Indianapolis loved him alike. He had a great Sunday-school class of poor boys, and after he was eighty-three years of age took them at his own expense in detachments to the World's Fair, spending nights of travel and days of hard walking that they might have the privilege of seeing the great exhibition. And that is only a suggestion of what this man was doing for nearly three-quarters of a century. His whole life went out to others. When he died, all Indianapolis mourned. The city stood still at his funeral. The daily newspapers had columns of editorials of eulogy about him, and these secular editors, every one of them, confest that the secret of his life was that he was God's man, that the presence of God was in him. I saw a friend a little while ago, who told me that a year or so before William Jackson's death he spent several days with him, and traveled about with him in the cars, and said he: "I did not feel as when I am with other men. It seemed to me I could feel his holiness. There was something so saintly, something so convincing of the presence of God in his very countenance, and

in his conversation, that I felt it all the while.''
There was the secret. His soul and his life were
enlarged by the presence of God until he could
feed the bread of life alike to the rich and to the
poor of his city.

My friends, I have piled these illustrations, one
upon another, that they might stir our hearts to
this great truth. We do not need to be weak and
powerless. We need not go along the way of life
spiritual dwarfs. God is no respecter of persons.
He is seeking for men and women to offer the
bread of life to hungry souls. All that is needed
is that we should surrender ourselves to him for
the highest and holiest service. What folly that
for a few paltry dollars, or for a few years of
sensual pleasure, or a few shouts of applause from
unthinking crowds, we should miss the building up
of soul and character into those splendid propor-
tions that shall fit us for divine usefulness. Oh,
that we may see with clear eyes the relative values
of spiritual and temporal things! How clearly
James Russell Lowell characterizes these values in
his picture of ''St. Michael the Weigher.'' There,
says Lowell:

> "Stood the tall Archangel weighing
> All man's dreaming, doing, saying,
> All the failure and the pain,
> All the triumph and the gain,

In the unimagined years,
Full of hopes, more full of tears
Since old Adam's hopeless eyes
Backward searched for Paradise,
And, instead, the flame-blade saw
Of inexorable Law.

"Waking, I beheld him there,
With his fire-gold, flickering hair,
In his blinding armor stand,
And the scales were in his hand:
Mighty were they, and full well
They could poise both heaven and hell.
'Angel,' asked I, humbly, then,
'Weighest thou the souls of men?
That thine office is, I know.'
'Nay,' he answered me, 'not so:
But I weigh the hope of Man
Since the power of choice began,
In the world, of good or ill.'
Then I waited and was still.

"In one scale I saw him place
All the glories of our race,
Cups that lit Belshazzar's feast,
Gems, the lightning of the East,
Kublai's scepter, Cæsar's sword,
Many a poet's golden word,
Many a skill of science, vain
To make men as gods again.

"In the other scale he threw
Things regardless, outcast, few,
Martyr-ash, arena sand,
Beechen cups of men whose need
Fasted that the poor might feed,

Disillusions and despairs
Of young saints with grief-grayed hairs,
Broken hearts that broke for Man.

"Marvel through my pulses ran
Seeing then the beam divine
Swiftly on this hand decline,
While Earth's splendor and renown
Mounted light as thistle-down."

THE CHRISTIAN'S HIDDEN
SOURCES OF DELIGHT

THE CHRISTIAN'S HIDDEN
SOURCES OF DELIGHT

"In the multitude of my thoughts within me thy comforts delight my soul."—Psalm XCIV: 19.

I WAS once in company with a friend fishing in a large stream in the Northwest, when as we were working down the river we came unexpectedly on a tributary so deep and strong of current that we could not cross it. We were amazed, because as we gazed up its course we looked less than a mile away to a solid wall of hills with no cañon through which it might have come, and yet judging from its size one would suppose it needed forty or fifty miles to have gathered so much water into its bosom. Our curiosity awakened, we decided to follow up the stream and find from whence it came. We followed it for perhaps three-quarters of a mile, till we came to the hills and saw where it sprang full-born from the earth. Twenty feet from the source it was too deep for a man to wade, and plunged away across the valley to the river. I never shall forget the impression that it made upon me. Back in the subterranean caverns of the mountains somewhere there was a mighty reservoir, which, seeking an outlet for the water from the melting snow above on the higher mountains, was ever forcing its way out through this stream to the sea. From the multitude of the waters hidden away in the crevices of the great rocks this joyous stream had its continual supply. No drought affected it. Its sources were drawn from the great secret reservoirs of the hills.

This utterance of David reminds me of that stream. This chapter is full of suggestion of the trials and hardships which beset the life of the Psalmist. Indeed, the whole Psalm is a cry for help against the wicked and cruel treatment of the oppressor; but in the midst of it David gives us the secret of his greatness and the immortal work which he accomplished when he declares that notwithstanding all the machinations of powerful and wicked foes, ''In the multitude of my thoughts within me thy comforts delight my soul.''

Our thoughts form the hidden sources of our lives, whether for good or for evil. Caroline Butterfield, in a beautiful poem entitled ''Thought Wings,'' pictures this very clearly when she sings:

> "Strange things are thought-wings,
>   Fleet as a ray of light,
> Nay, fleeter far—
> For they reach the star

That is far beyond the sight,
And are back again
To the dusty plain,
     Swift as a keen delight.

*   *   *   *   *   *   *

"Sad things are thought-wings,
     Drooping with taint of sin,
Heavy with pain
From scar and stain,
     Where wrong has entered in
And marred with crime
The soul sublime,
     The spring of life within.

"Fierce things are thought-wings,
     Fierce as a vulture's beak
To rend and tear
With wild despair
     Who gaping vices seek.
Shame's nameless stain
And gnawing pain
     Defile their victim's cheek.

"Free things are thought-wings,
     Free as the eagle's breast.
On strong brave will
There waiting still
     The fleet thoughts seek rest;
The good and true
The lofty too
     Bear men to the Isles of the Blest."

I am sure it cannot but be profitable for us to
search out these thoughts that gave David peren-

nial joy. I remember once reading of two simple men who were standing by one of Stephenson's locomotives in the early days of the steam engine. And as these men stood by the engine, full of curiosity and wonder, one of the men said to the other, "Mate, she'll never stir." When the engine moved, the man said, "Mate, she'll never stop." Finally he said, "Mate, I am going to get the secret of what makes her go." Of course, for the locomotive, in order that she may go, there must first be fire, but there must also be the two rails lying parallel along the track. I am sure it will be good for us if we can find the track along which ran David's thoughts which gave him such great power and such sources of delight that his wonderful career was possible.

I

The first of these thoughts of David he makes very clear to us in this Psalm. It was the thought of an immanent God in the world, one who hears and sees and cares. "He that planted the ear, shall he not hear? He that formed the eye, shall he not see?" Here is the starting point of David's hidden source of joy. God is in his world. He made it and he rules it. Here is the source of courage that will never grow weary.

The recent death of one of the first of the missionaries who went to the Sandwich Islands has recalled the work of civilization which has been wrought there. One of the most picturesque incidents connected with the overthrow of idolatry in Hawaii was the defiance of the volcano Pele by the Princess Kapiolani. Pele was the most dreaded deity of the Sandwich Islands, a goddess supposed to be of great and terrible power who resided in the crater of the volcano of Kilauea. Superstition in regard to this revengeful spirit who dwelt in the fiery seething pit was hard to dislodge from the savage mind.

When Princess Kapiolani became a Christian, and had enshrined in her heart this wonderful thought of God which filled the soul of David with delight, she set out on a journey one hundred miles, most of the way on foot, to the crater of Kilauea. The missionaries at Hilo, twenty-five miles from the volcano, heard of her pilgrimage, and one of them who had no shoes walked barefoot over the stony hills to meet her at the mountain.

The Princess was much affected by this meeting with the missionary. The two, watched by a company of about eighty natives, descended from the rim of the crater to what was known as the "Black Rock." There, in full view of the terrific panorama, Kapiolani gave her great testimony. She cried aloud, "Jehovah is my God. He kindled these fires. I fear not Pele. If I perish from the anger of Pele, you may fear the power of Pele. If I do not perish, all the gods of Hawaii are vain." She then sang a hymn of Christian praise, and returned to the wondering, fearful company unscathed. In those few moments she had given the death-blow to the remaining idolatry in the Sandwich Islands. In the multitude of her thoughts of God she had found a great source of delight, a source which is open to every one of us.

II

Another thought that was a constant source of delight to David was the conviction that God was the defender of those who trusted him. He cries out in this Psalm, "The Lord will not cast off his people, neither will he forsake his inheritance. But judgment shall return unto righteousness: And all the upright in heart shall follow it." And in another one of his great Psalms, having this same thought in mind, David says, "The Lord shall keep thee from all evil; he shall keep thy soul." The Rev. Percy Ainsworth, commenting on this Psalm, says that this is a promise that can fold us in divine comfort and peace, and can help us to

interpret every coil of difficulty and every hour
of pain. But if we are going to get the comfort we
ought to get from these great words we must think
about the soul as God thinks of it. We live in a
world where souls are cheap. They are bought and
sold in the market every day. Is it not very
strange that the only thing many people are not
afraid of losing is the one thing that is really
worth anything to them—their souls? Sometimes
the lusts of the world drag down our heart's desire,
and we have to confess with shame to epochs in our
experience when we have not been concerned with
what became of our souls so long as the desire of
the hour was satisfied. God will keep the soul of
the man who will do his bidding and set his heart
upon the noblest and highest living. The man who
gets "the best of the bargain" is always the man
who is most honest, for the most precious thing
that a man stands to win or lose in any deal is the
cleanness of his soul. The man who gets the best
of the argument is always the man who is most
truthful, for a quiet conscience is better than a
silenced opponent. The man who gets the best
of life is the man who keeps the honor of his soul,
for has not Jesus said, "What shall it profit a
man if he gain the whole world and lose his
own soul?"

III

Another thought that gave David great delight was his discovery that much of the sorrow and trial which he experienced was not punishment, but chastening and discipline. In his joy of this faith he exclaims, "Blest is the man whom thou chastenest, O Lord, and teachest him out of thy law." This reminds us of what Paul says in his letter to the Hebrews, "Whom the Lord loveth he chasteneth, and scourgeth every son whom he receiveth. If ye endure chastening, God dealeth with you as with sons; for what son is he whom the father chasteneth not? . . . Now no chastening for the present seemeth to be joyous, but grievous: nevertheless afterward it yieldeth the peaceable fruit of righteousness unto them which are exercised thereby." David had got hold of this great thought of God's chastening love, and it was a source of delight to him; and it cannot help but be a source of perpetual delight to us if we will treasure this thought in our hearts and keep it to live by day by day. Mr. Beecher once used this illustration. He said when a great organ was built the lead and the zinc did not know what the men were about when they were melting them, and making them into pipes, and when the work was distributed through the different shops, among different hands.

And when the various stops were but partly com-
pleted if you had tried them in the factory you
would have run out with your fingers in your
ears, and cried, "Lord, deliver me from that sort
of music!" With all the different parts of the
organ separately made, unconnected, nobody can
tell what is coming except an experienced workman; but by and by, little by little, the frame is
erected, the stops are all arranged and in connection with the wind-chest, and now that it is an
organic whole every part plays into every other
part. As a whole it is magnificent; but the separate stops were poor and weak and unsatisfactory.
God makes stops on earth, but he builds the organ
in heaven; and many a man will never know until
he comes there what was the reason of that providence by which he was trained and fitted to be a
part of that great band of music in the heavenly
home. It takes all the bitterness out of life and
fills all our sorrows with pathos and tenderness if
we can keep this thought of God's fatherly care
and love uppermost in our minds. A woman who
was very troubled, hurrying through the town to
a railway station with an aching heart, overtook
two little mites of children, happy and cheerful
looking, who were talking over their school-lessons.
As she came up to them she heard one child say to

the other with the ring of a child's loving pride,
"Father teaches me." And then came the answer
from the other child, "How nice to have a father to
teach you," with a certain emphasis which showed
that she knew something, small tho she was, of
what a father's love and teaching should mean.
The woman's face brightened as she heard it, and
she turned with a grateful smile to the two little
ones, pausing to look at them for a minute before
she went hurrying on again. And as she went her
face kept its brighter look, her heart lost its bitterness, because this thought was singing in her soul,
"Surely, many beside that little child can say,
'My Father teaches me.' "

IV

Another thought that gave David delight in his
hour of darkness, so far as his outward circumstances were concerned, was the thought which he
cherished that in the time of great emergency he
could depend upon God's mercy. In connection
with our text he says, "Unless the Lord had been
my help, my soul had almost dwelt in silence.
When I said, My foot slippeth; thy mercy, O Lord,
held me up. In the multitude of my thoughts
within me thy comforts delight my soul." So we
may be sure that this was one of the thoughts that
was forever a hidden source of delight to David.

His heart rejoiced in the mercy of the God who comes to the rescue of the man in peril, whose feet have slipt and will go to disaster without help. It is the glory of our Christianity that it has a word about mercy to the man whose feet have slipt.

Samuel Chadwick, the English preacher, tells how he was once holding a series of meetings in Leeds, England, and a number of atheists and agnostics, who were also socialists and reformers in their way, sent up to him a note before he began to preach. "Don't preach us a sermon," they said; "we would like you to tell us frankly and simply and in a straightforward, unconventional way, why you believe in Jesus Christ." He did so, and afterward met with these men in another room to discuss the matter. Quite a number of them came, and they sat there and talked until two o'clock in the morning. When they rose to go he turned to the leader of the group and said, "Let me ask you one question. You have propounded a philosophy for a cult. In the things you are hoping for you assume the existence of a certain quality of humanity. You have said nothing about those who do not reach that standard. You know that in this city, by the thousands, there are men who have lost their manhood, whose tastes are de-

praved, whose wills are destroyed, the victims of
passion, the slaves of lusts, the despair of civilization. What will you do with these?'' A cynical
smile lighted up the agnostic's face. ''Oh,'' he
said, '.'I would make you a present of that lot.''
Then more seriously he added: ''I am free to confess that if there is any hope for such men anywhere it is in the Christ you preach.'' Every religion must be judged by its power to heal the
crippled and save the lost. A religion that has
no Savior in it is useless for this world. David
found in the mercy of God a religion that took him
out of the mire and the clay and set his feet upon
a rock, and established his goings, and inspired a
new song in his heart and on his lips, even a
song of praise unto God. This thought of God's
infinite mercy and love to the sinning soul is a
source of continual comfort and delight. The
mercy and the love of God melt the hard
heart, take the bitterness out of the soul, and
inspire our faith and our courage. David in
another place has borne testimony that it was the
gentleness of God that made him great, and George
Herbert, in his beautiful little poem entitled ''Discipline,'' strikes the same note. He sings—

> "Throw away thy rod,
>   Throw away thy wrath;

      O my God,
  Take the gentle path.

"For my heart's desire
  Unto thine is bent;
     I aspire
  To a full consent.

"Not a word or look
  I affect to own,
     But by Book,
  And thy Book alone.

"Tho I fail, I weep,
  Tho I halt in pace,
     Yet I creep
  To the Throne of Grace.

"Then let wrath remove;
  Love will do the deed:
     For with love
  Stony hearts will bleed.

"Love is swift of foot;
  Love's a man of war,
     And can shoot,
  And can hit from far.

"Who can 'scape his bow?
  That which wrought on thee,
     Brought thee low,
  Needs must work on me.

"Throw away thy rod;
  Tho man frailties hath,
     Thou are God:
  Throw away thy wrath."

THE SOUNDING
LINE OF PRAYER

THE SOUNDING LINE OF PRAYER

"Make thy petition deep."—Isaiah VII: 11 (Marginal rendering).

AS this scripture stands in our authorized version the entire verse reads, "Ask thee a sign of the Lord thy God; ask it either in the depth, or in the height above." But the marginal rendering, designing to give a short cut to the direct message, is as I first read it, "Make thy petition deep." And as that expresses perfectly the theme which I wish to study with you, we will let it stand as our text. This rendering exactly fits the circumstances surrounding the utterance of the text. Ahaz, the king of Judah, was a timid and helpless man. He lacked promptitude and courage. His religion was of the most formal kind. He looked upon God not in a definite loving sense as his own personal Heavenly Father, but as the God of Judah. He did not even believe that God was as efficient and powerful as the god of Assyria, for he had about made up his mind to apply to the king of Assyria, and was already mixed up in intrigues with that heathen king, thinking him a more trustworthy helper than Jehovah in the difficulties with which he was surrounded. Hence, when God told him through his prophet Isaiah to ask a token from the God of heaven and earth, and to make his petition deep, Ahaz responded "I will not ask," and then he adds in a hypocritical canting strain, as tho he could deceive God, "Neither will I tempt the Lord." The fact was that Ahaz was irreligious and worldly and had given himself over to intrigue with these people who were the enemies of God. He did not want to earnestly and truly pray for a token from heaven. He did not want a token from heaven. He was not willing to pay the price for it. He wanted to go his own way and he feared that if he sought an answer from God it would only bring to light his own sins, and make it impossible for him to carry on his intrigue with the king of Assyria. In short, Ahaz was a coward, and, as Emerson says, "God never gives visions to cowards." He does not because he cannot. Cowards close the door, they pull down the shades on the windows of vision and shut God out of their lives. The light of heaven cannot enter the soul when a man is timid and cowardly, and all the entrances to his higher life are blocked.

Perhaps it has never occurred to you that it

takes great courage to pray. If it has not it is because you have not studied the matter very deeply.
Oh, I know, any coward can say his prayers, and
many cowards do say them with the regularity of
a parrot; but to really pray, with that depth of
petition that longs for the coming of God into the
heart and soul, and into the mastery of the life,
such a prayer takes courage. Look back over the
roll of the men who have been famous for their
prayers and you will notice that they were all as
famous for their bravery. It was no mere accident that Havelock's prayer-meetings among his
soldiers during the Indian mutiny produced the
men that were always called upon to lead the for-
lorn hope. It was not a happy accident only that
Chinese Gordon's white handkerchief outside his
tent, which meant that he was at prayer with God,
was a sign of the hero that the whole world knew
him to be. Here, then, let us find our theme. Let
us study our own duty and privilege in regard to
prayer to God.

I

We should surely find suggested in our theme
that it is our duty as well as our privilege to make
our prayers as deep as our needs. And when we
come to that point we cannot deal with it in whole-

sale, for each one of us has our own peculiar and personal relation to God, and our own personal needs, which we should bring to God in earnest and sincere prayer.

1.   There are some of you who have never known Christ as your personal Savior. That you have sinned against God, and that sin unforgiven rests upon your conscience, and lurks as poison in the depths of your heart, you are conscious of whenever you permit yourself to have a thoughtful moment. Your need is as deep as that sin, and your cry to God should have the depth of your great necessity for deliverance. It is a terrible thing to live day after day knowing that you are a sinner against God in whose hand your breath is, and yet doing nothing to bring forgiveness. Some poet sings:

> "Weep not for broad lands lost;
> Weep not for fair hopes crossed;
> Weep not when limbs wax old;
> Weep not when friends grow cold;
> Weep not that death must part
> Thine and the best-loved heart;
> Yet weep, weep all thou can—
> Weep, weep, because thou art
> A sin-defilèd man."

Conscious of your sin, why do you not pray with a petition so deep and strong that it would revolutionize your life? Is it not that, like Ahaz, there is some timidity or cowardice which holds you back from such a prayer? That as yet you are not willing to have that prayer answered? The spell of Christ, I am sure, has been over your spirit again and again. You have heard his knock at the door of your heart, and your hand has been almost raised to turn the key and open the door, and then you have thought of the demands of Christ, of how he will claim that your business, political, and social life shall be carried on purely, and honestly, and righteously. You have thought of certain things which if Christ were a guest at your table you could not practise, and you have turned away with a sinking heart, and a blush of shame, and with a new sense of failure and personal deterioration you have said, "I cannot let him in! God knows I would like to be a good man, I would like to be free from sin, but I cannot pay the price." And so it was your cowardice that turned back heaven from the door of your soul. My friend, I call you again to your duty and your privilege, and beg of you to make your petition as deep as your sins and your need of salvation.

2. Those of us who are Christians, but are conscious that we are not as fruitful Christians as we ought to be, that we are not winning souls to the

banner of Christ, and shrink from the attempt, or dare not make the attempt, or when we do attempt it find ourselves helpless, ought to be inspired by our theme to make our prayers as deep as our need of spiritual vitality and power for service. The great need of the church to-day is for fruitful Christians. Not only for men and women who can keep from swearing and lying and stealing, but for Christian men and women who live close to God, whose lives are fragrant with the spirit of Christ, and in whom spiritual vitality is so manifest that they charm and conquer sinning men and women about them and bring them penitently to the Savior. I most heartily agree with Campbell Morgan when he says that he is getting a little tired of the men who want to win heaven—Oh, for the men and women that want to win the earth for God! Oh, for men and women with deep and holy passion to have fellowship with Jesus Christ in winning souls!

Now as I speak I am sure that I look into the faces of scores and hundreds of Christian men and women who are conscious, and sadly conscious, that compared with the vital, courageous, and whole-hearted Christian life which it is your privilege to live, the life you really do live is flabby and helpless. But when I come with this theme, and drop the sounding line down into the depths of your soul, is it not true that you hold back from making your petition deep as your needs, because you are not willing to pay the price of having your prayer answered? Dr. Alexander MacKenzie said not long ago to his congregation that if God should answer the prayer which some brother had made that morning, in which he had asked, "God take care of the poor," the answer to that prayer would come out of that brother's bank account, and would probably cost him five hundred dollars. If we are to be God's men and women we must make our prayers as deep as our needs and be willing to take the risk. We must commit ourselves to God's commandments, and invoke God to work his will with us and shine in our obedient hearts. Then both the light and the power will come. Believe me, spiritual peace and spiritual power can never come to us except when we keep close to God, so that our prayer is the deep outgoing of the heart as of friend to friend. Dante spoke of the duties of men being ranged like a pyramid. When you are at the top your purpose is single and your conduct is simple, for there is not much room to range about. But, as you come down, the sides of the pyramid spread, and then you have a broader plane. Now if you stand on the top of the pyramid, just room enough for God and you, whatever labor or pleasure you have, you have there, right in God's presence. Whatever work you have there, you are close to the law of God. But you get restless and uneasy. You think you want a little more liberty, and you gradually descend. Now your plane widens. You have more things. You are not so much held to the duties of a Christian life as you used to be. You are more like the world around you. You have not those differences that separate. Now you are on a broader plane, and the widening of the plane has been a separating of yourself from God. But as you have gotten away from God you have gotten away from peace, you have gotten away from spiritual power, and you are no longer a fruitful, useful Christian as you once were. There is only one way to live a great life, vital with the power of God, and that is to climb upward. Turn to the other wing of our text, which would be, "make thy petitions high," as well as deep. Let the sides of your life, let the things you do, lessen. Up and up and up, fewer things to do, and more strength to do them. Climb upward toward the top of the pyramid, where all the pleasure you have, and all the duty you have, and all the work you have, and all the life you have are in fellowship with God. Will life lose because it becomes narrower? No, indeed. It will become rich and strong and mighty with the vigor of the power of God. Call the roll of the men and the women who have added supreme glory to the race, the men and women whose lives have had about them the breath of unselfish service, the spirit of holiness, the glory of a joy and a gladness that neither sorrow, nor persecution, nor failure, nor death could dampen, and they have all, no matter in what age they lived, or of what race they were born, been men and women who lived close to God, and whose petitions were as deep as God's willingness to give beauty, and power, and glory to his children.

3. We should make our prayers as deep as the needs of the multitudes about us who are unsaved. How little we appreciate the need of Christian fidelity. We recognize the needs of the drunkard, and the gambler, and the lost woman whose shame is apparent to the world; but, alas! in the midst of our cultivated, and well-to-do, and socially moral communities many men and women are living and dying in their sins without Christ, who need, beyond words to describe, that their Christian neighbors should have spiritual vitality and power enough to bring to them the message of the gospel.

A beautiful woman lay on her death-bed in a

well-to-do home in one of our cities. A company of friends, respectable, intelligent, and well drest, stood by her. "Read me something new," she said, impatiently, to her friends who were trying to divert her with interesting books. While her sister went out to search for "something new," the nurse, a sincere Christian, took out her pocket Bible and began to read the Sermon on the Mount. The sick woman paid close attention to the end. "Beautiful!" she said. "That will create a sensation. Who wrote it?"

"Why," replied the astonished nurse, "that is the Sermon on the Mount—in the Bible, you know."

"The Bible! anything so good and beautiful as that in the Bible?"

"Surely; what else but good did you think could be in it?"

"Oh, I don't know. I have never looked into a Bible in my life. My father wouldn't have one in the house."

"But you have certainly heard the Bible read in the church?"

"I have never been to church much. Sunday was always our holiday. We sometimes went to places of amusement, but seldom to church. I never thought much about the Bible. I never supposed it contained such beautiful things. I wish I had known it before!''

She begged the nurse to read again the prayer in the Sermon on the Mount that was so new to her—''Our Father, which art in heaven.'' And she died, saying with her last breath: ''I wish I had known it before! I wish I had known it before!''

Friends, these people are all about you. God says that he who winneth these souls is wise, and that those who turn many to righteousness shall shine as the stars forever and ever. Shall we not make our petitions as deep as the needs of these starving souls? Ah, do we understand the value of a soul?

> "The value of a soul!
> 'Neath sin's encrust
> Look with Faith's visioned gaze, then pay thy toll—
> In patient trust—
> Of work and prayer; the slumb'ring seed that lies
> Hopeless to all, save Christ-anointed eyes,
> The sunbeam's thrust
> May quicken into life, beneath the sod,
> As lilies bloom, in the fair fields of God,
> From out the dust.
>
> "Measure it by Christ's love,
> His life, his cross;
> Take angel's reed, and scales of courts above,
> Weigh gold, weigh dross!
> If from the firmament fell one bright star,

If but one shining planet wandered far,
     How great the loss;
Yet is the profit of a whole world won
Not to be measured with one soul undone.
     Gone from its course."

II

We should make our prayers as deep as the promises of God and his power to perform. Time will not permit me to make a catalog of the promises of God which reach to all our needs, and cover every longing, and every possible condition of the human heart and life. Let me rather call your attention for our comfort and inspiration to Paul's great conclusion. After thinking the whole matter over he bursts forth with this triumphant exclamation: "What shall we then say to these things! If God be for us, who can be against us? He that spared not his own Son, but delivered him up for us all, how shall he not with him also freely give us all things?" He who gave his Son for our salvation will not fail in anything else we need. There is a legend which they tell you at Niagara Falls. It is said that in olden times among the Indians it was the custom to offer every year a sacrifice to the great spirit of the mighty falls. Those children of the forest thought they caught glimpses of the Great Spirit in the mist that rises

and in the marvelous lunar rainbow that is seen,
when the moon shines, to hover over the edge of
the falls. The sacrifice sought was the most gentle
and beautiful girl of the tribe. She was chosen by
lot. One year the lot fell on the only daughter of
a chief, whose wife was dead. He showed no sign
of surprize or sorrow. But behind this mask of
stoicism, inwardly, his grief was intense. Life
without his only child was empty. Moreover, he
knew that she would be alarmed and horrified at
the fate that awaited her. The yells and shouts of
the men might drown her cries and tears. The
flowers that decked her canoe-coffin were bright,
but the dizzying depth of the terrible cascade was
appalling. She gazed about her—her father, where
is he? What, not one last look, ere she is pushed
out into the foaming rapids! She has not even a
paddle to help steer her canoe, and to clear her of
the projecting rocks. But her father soon comes
near. Just from beneath some branches of a huge
tree a canoe shoots out. Her father is in it. He
smiles, and with terms of endearment cheers the
affrighted little soul. He gets quite close to her,
and, holding her hand, sweeps onward himself to
death with her. Love triumphs, love upheld, love
joined hands. So God the Father was with Christ
in our redemption. In this tender legend we have

a faint suggestion of how, if in every time of need we make our petitions deep and earnest, God will draw near to us, and reveal himself to us in the full and perfect satisfaction of all our needs.

Dr. R. J. Campbell of the City Temple in London tells how a woman once came to him in great anxiety about her boy. She was a proud and not over-wise woman. The preacher suspected that the boy had learned much of his folly through her weakness; but she loved him with all the intensity of a mother's heart. He was an exile from home, had been away a long time, and his father's heart was hard concerning him. If he were to come back, she had said to herself many a time, she must be there, otherwise his welcome would be harsh. One pathetic sentence she uttered which Dr. Campbell noted: "I always knew he must come back, but I did not wish him to find things changed when he came." What she really meant was that she had hoped God would spare her life that she and not a sterner soul might meet her son; for if she were gone the probabilities that the boy would be saved would have been very small. Is not this illustrative of the teachings of God's word concerning his willingness to answer to our needs? While that boy was away from home, and while he was picturing to himself the all but impossibility that he should be received at home again with kindness or mercy or pity, much less with love, the unchanging love of a mother-heart was going out to him. It is no mere sentiment, that figure: before his penitence called to her, love had answered; before his desire for home had formed itself into a purpose in his heart, his mother's desire for him was reaching him, was ever toward him, and it conquered in the end. The prayer, even of a weak woman, brought her boy to her side again. She had not changed her solicitude for him; when he turned toward her he was but responding to that desire. How like that is that wonderful promise of God in this same book of Isaiah: "And it shall come to pass, that before they call I will answer; and while they are yet speaking, I will hear."

CHRIST THE SUPREME OBJECT OF HUMAN CONSIDERATION

CHRIST THE SUPREME OBJECT OF HUMAN CONSIDERATION

"Consider Him."—Hebrews XII: 3.

PAUL gives us these words as a key to the solution of the problem of a Christian life in the midst of the allurements and distractions of this present world. Keep your eye on Christ and nothing shall disturb you. There is a story of a young man in the East who was sent one day by his teacher through a crowded bazaar with the instructions to carry a vessel full of water—full to the very brim—through the bazaar, and to bring it back without having spilled a drop. He returned, pleased and triumphant, because he had succeeded in obeying the command. Not a single drop had been lost. The wise old teacher praised him, and then asked him what he saw as he was passing through the bazaar. "Saw!" cried the young man, "Why, I saw nothing." "How can that be?" replied the teacher. "For I know that the very time when you were in the bazaar the Sultan with some of his chief attendants went by." "Well, that

may be," said the young man; "but how could I
see anything, or anybody, when I had my eyes
fixt upon the water the whole time, and could
think of nothing but how to carry it without spill-
ing, as you told me to do?" "Ah!" said the
teacher, "now you can understand how we may
be so entirely occupied with some work that God
has given us to do as to be quite unconscious of the
sinful allurements of the world, which strive to
attract our attention as we are passing through
them."

Our text is in the midst of a triumphant paragraph sounding the note of encouragement. Paul
has been calling the roll of the heroes of faith, and
inspired by the memory of them he exclaims:
"Wherefore seeing we also are compassed about
with so great a cloud of witnesses, let us lay aside
every weight, and the sin which doth so easily beset us, and let us run with patience the race that
is set before us, looking unto Jesus, the author and
finisher of our faith; who for the joy that was set
before him, endured the cross, despising the shame,
and is set down at the right hand of the throne
of God. For consider him that endured such con-
tradiction of sinners against himself, lest ye be
wearied and faint in your minds. Ye have not yet
resisted unto blood, striving against sin. And ye

have forgotten the exhortation which speaketh unto
you as unto children, My son, despise not thou the
chastening of the Lord, nor faint when thou art rebuked of him. For whom the Lord loveth he
chasteneth.''

I

Consideration of Christ will comfort and *reconcile us to the difficulties of our lives, and give us
fortitude in bearing the burdens necessary to helpful service for humanity.* When we are wading
against the current in our daily experience, we
sometimes feel that we are getting more than our
share of opposition, and are carrying more than
our shoulders are able to bear of the burdens of
life. At such a time it cannot help doing us good
to look at Christ and consider what he voluntarily
endured for us. One of the quaint old students of
the Bible once said, ''Our troubles are but as the
slivers and chips of his cross.'' If we consider
Christ even when he was most abused, when he
was spit upon and railed at, and crowned with
thorns, and beaten with many stripes, we see that
he was silent and patient under it all. Christ
was willing to let his life, his deeds, stand as testimony against all the world could say. And how
well the history of the world has vindicated Jesus
in that silence, for in the end a man's faithful work

is his only defense in the court of time. Ole Bull, the great violinist, was once offered space in the *New York Herald* to answer his detractors. He declined with these words: "I think it is best that they write against me and I play against them." The finest argument against any one's enemies is a faithful doing of the very best one can do. And if we keep our mind and heart in steady consideration of Jesus it will not only be easy for us to do that, but we will get the blessing which is always wrapt up in such patient endurance. We will come to understand the poet who sings:

"If all my years were summer, could I know
  What my Lord means by his 'Made white as snow'?
 If all my days were sunny, could I say
  'In his fair land he wipes all tears away'?
 If I were never weary could I keep
  Close to my heart, 'He gives his lovèd sleep'?
 Were no graves mine, might I not come to deem
  The life eternal but a baseless dream?
 My winter, yea, my tears, my weariness,
 Even my graves may be his way to bless,
 I call them ills, yet that can surely be
 Nothing but good that shows my Lord to me."

Consideration of Christ is sure to comfort us in the many discouragements which always come to any one sincerely trying to benefit and bless their fellow men. In no service can we get so close to Christ as in that, and in none are we so sure to experience the secrets of Christ's career and come into the fellowship of Christ's sufferings. John Ruskin once said: "You cannot save men from death, but by suffering it for them; you cannot save men from sin, but by resisting it for them."

> "All through life I see a cross,
>   Where sons of God yield up their breath,
>   There is no gain except by loss,
>   There is no life except by death.
>   There is no vision except by faith,
>   Nor glory but in bearing shame,
>   Nor justice but in taking blame.
>   And that eternal passion saith,
>   Be emptied of glory and right and name."

And in harmony with that Jesus says, "If any man will come after me, let him deny himself, and take up his cross daily, and follow me."

II

Consideration of Christ alone can give us *a just estimate of the value of humanity.* The world is always judging men by what they have, by the amount of their goods and possessions, rather than by what they are. When Robert Browning went wooing at the home of Elizabeth Barrett, the father of the lady asked her one day with a sneer, "Has that man been here?" To the elder Barrett's notion a man whose income was only five hundred

dollars a year was, decidedly, "that man." Yet
Robert Browning managed to save his soul, build a
character in the world like a white pillar, and earn
for himself an immortality which only goodness
and genius combined can give.

The Christ attitude toward man is very different.
The other day I saw a story about Cecil Rhodes,
which warmed my heart. After he had become one
of the richest men in the world and was living in
his great house in South Africa, a man called to
see him on business. Mr. Rhodes had four footmen,
very proper footmen, uniformed and powdered.
The man who called was plainly drest and looked
poor. Of course, he was received in footman
fashion, kept waiting a long time, and finally
ushered, with scant respect, into the great man's
presence. After the little business matter had been
transacted the visitor said, "Mr. Rhodes, I think
you will thank me for telling you that your footmen are not altogether courteous to men that look
poor!" Those footmen were out of the house in
ten minutes, hunting a new job. That, I take it,
is the spirit of Christ in his attitude toward men.
Does he not say, "Him that cometh to me I will in
no wise cast out"? He gave the same welcome to
Zacchæus, the grafting politician, as to Nicodemus,
the respectable ruler. He was as good to Peter,

the swearing, blundering fisherman, as he was to
Paul, the cultured aristocrat. He was as kind to
a sick, beggared woman as to the man who lived
in the best house in the town. To Christ, manhood
and womanhood were the precious things worth
living and dying to redeem, no matter what their
surroundings, and the more we consider Christ the
truer will be our attitude toward mankind.

Joseph Parker on one occasion, in his pulpit in
City Temple, London, told how some minister had
complained to him that he had only added one
member to his church for a good while, and that
was a poor washerwoman, and Parker replied, "Oh,
indeed! any family?"

"A large family—six boys."

"And you added the mother of six boys to your
church! Who can tell how many you added when
you added that laundress? These may be six
kings, six leaders of men, six apostles." That is
the true Christian spirit. May we all learn it from
Jesus Christ through earnest and faithful consideration of him until humanity everywhere is
sacred to us.

III

Consideration of Christ will give us *a clear vision
of the proper spirit in which the noblest work of
life must be done.* In him we find the perfect *un-*

selfishness which is always necessary as a condition of the noblest work. No man who does his work simply that he may get money from it, without the true spirit of service, will ever do his best work. See Balaam, brilliant, imaginative, noble-visioned, a strong man in many ways, but his vision is distracted by the lust for gold, and his tragedy is one of the most terrible in the Old Testament day. David Watson says that whenever a poet begins to write verse to order, to sing for gold, and not merely because he must, as the lark at heaven's gate, he sells his inspiration, he sins against the Holy Ghost, and no true poem was ever written under these conditions. Verse may be written, but not a poem. Not a line that Burns wrote for money is worth reading, and none knew that better than Burns himself. Ask any poet or any artist, and he will tell you that the verses he wrote or pictures he painted merely for money are the most unsatisfactory things he ever did. They lack genuine inspiration, they lack soul; they were pot-boilers, as they call themselves. They were hack-work. Of course, such work must be done, for men must live; but be very sure of this, that no work of art which is a thing of beauty and a joy forever, like the Venus de Milo, no grand poem, like the "Divina Commedia," the "In Memoriam,"

and the "Ancient Mariner," uplifting the souls of
men, was ever produced for gold; and the same is
true of the world's work generally as done by the
blacksmith, or the carpenter, or the cook, or the
dressmaker, or the lawyer, or the doctor, or the
preacher. It is not for filthy lucre that any one
of us will ever do our best work. We must have
our wage that we may live, but in the spirit of
Jesus Christ there must always be in our minds
and hearts the pleasure of doing our work well for
the joy of knowing it is well done, for the pure
satisfaction of using our gifts as God would have
us use them to produce from them the highest results possible.

As we consider Christ we will catch his *courage,*
that will hold us brave and true when other men
are ready to fly from the struggle. Lord Rosebery, in his recent life of Napoleon, recalls a saying of that great man of war. Napoleon says:
"There is a moment in every great war when the
bravest troops feel inclined to run; it is the want
of confidence in their own courage." And then
Napoleon adds: "The supreme art of generalship
is to know just when that moment will come and
to provide for it. At Arcola I won the battle with
twenty-five horsemen. I anticipated the moment
of fright and flight, and I had twenty-five men

ready, of cool nerve and decision, and just at the appropriate moment I turned the twenty-five into the host and the battle was won.'' Twenty-five men who had not lost their nerve brought back confidence to a host who were inclined for fright and flight. The man who was cool for fight brought back the hordes who were ready for flight, and that has its analogy in every department of life. Again and again we see one brave and true member of a family save a whole household from a cowardly yielding to sin. And often one young man in a group, with the courage of honest principles, saves all of them from the hell of dissipation. Now, my friends, there come times to every one of us when we are tempted to run. No matter what we do, the battle seems to be going against us, and we are ready to fly. When we feel like that there is one sure refuge, and that is to consider Jesus. He never loses his nerve, never runs, is always brave and true, and if we study him we shall breathe into our souls his courage.

If we consider Christ we shall catch his *spirit of obedience to God* and shall become practised in that *discipline of faith* which is so essential to make any man or woman an efficient soldier of Jesus Christ. I shall never forget how thrilled I was in my young boyhood in reading the story of how

Wolfe took Quebec. With almost breathless interest I followed the boats as they dropt down the St. Lawrence River, the one order to the men being, "Perfect silence," no shout, no whisper, but wait. And then, in the dead silence, the awfully perilous ascent of the heights of Quebec that led up to the Plains of Abraham. A company of men, through the night, winding their way up that narrow trail. If the enemy once hear them, if the enemy once suspect their presence, nothing can save them, for half a dozen men can hold the defile at the other end. Everything depends upon discipline, obedience, silence, the mounting the heights until the last man is ready for the captain's word to strike the blow. And we know how those men ascended. No sound was heard. Up and up, through the hours of the night, until the last man was upon the heights, when the word was given, and Quebec was taken. The church of Jesus Christ needs to learn that great lesson to-day. Guerrillas and bushwhackers and stragglers have never yet fought a great battle or carried a great cause to success. We need to so consider Christ that we shall catch his spirit of supreme obedience to God and supreme loyalty to united and federated effort for the salvation of men.

IV

It is only as we consider Christ that we are fanned with the breath of the eternal world, and are able to breast all difficulties and sorrows with *an undying hope*. Dr. J. H. Jowett tells us that he had a friend who, in his matured life, published a book on which he had bestowed the hard labors of many years. Some time before its publication his wife died, and he was left alone. The book received an enthusiastic welcome, and now enjoys high eminence in its own department of learning. Jowett spoke to his friend of his well-deserved reward and of the triumph of his labors. His face immediately clouded and he quietly said, "Ah, if only she were here to share it." His loneliness culminated there, and his sharpest pang was experienced in his sunniest hour. It is not otherwise with the moral triumphs of the soul. When we fall into sin and falter in the fight, we feel that we need a companion to whom we can tell the story of our defeat; and with equal need when we have some secret triumph we want a companion to share the glow and the glory of the conquest, or the glow and the glory will fade. Even when we conquer secret sin the heart calls for a companion in the joy! And here He is! Does not God say, "My presence shall go with thee"? And if we will admit

Christ into our hearts and consider him day by day we shall not be without a Companion, a precious friend, who will not only be with us in this life, but who will lead us into the immortal life beyond. Aristotle said that "Death is the most terrible of all things, for it is an end." But the man who lives in fellowship with and under the leadership of Jesus Christ knows that death is not an end, but an entrance upon fuller, nobler existence and blest reunion with those loved ones who have preceded us through its silent door. Browning's triumphant words of cheer and hope ought to warm our hearts and ring in our ears:

> "One fight more,
> The best and the last!
> I would hate that Death bandaged my eyes, and forebore,
> And bade me creep past.
> No! let me taste the whole of it, fare like my peers,
> The heroes of old.
> Bear the brunt, in a minute pay glad life's arrears
> Of pain, darkness, and cold.
> For sudden the worst turns the best to the brave,
> The black minute's at end,
> And the elements' rage, the fiend-voices that rave,
> Shall dwindle, shall blend,
> Shall change, shall become first a peace out of pain,
> Then a light, then thy breast,
> O thou soul of my soul! I shall clasp thee again,
> And with God be the rest!"

THE LORDSHIP
OF CHRIST

THE LORDSHIP OF CHRIST

"For we preach not ourselves, but Christ Jesus as Lord."
—II. Corinthians IV: 5. Am. Rev.

DURING the last few months there has been
awakened in England a great deal of
discussion concerning what has been called "The
New Theology." Innumerable sermons have
been preached, the religious papers have been
filled with articles, editorial and otherwise, in
regard to the vagaries of a popular young
minister concerning the nature and character
of sin and the personality and mission of Jesus
Christ. The discussion naturally has drifted
over the ocean, and aroused more or less attention in our own pulpits and religious press. At
such times it is always profitable to comfort our
hearts with the great fundamental certainties of
our religion. The Rev. J. H. Jowett, preaching recently in Christ Church, Westminster, speaking of
the great need humanity has for Christ, exclaimed:
"But it must be the real Christ, the risen, glorified, personal Christ; not a fine man, not the finest
of men, but the Lord of Glory, Christ unique and
alone, above all men, governing all men, holding all

men. Jesus Christ my Lord shall not be to me a mere historic personage whom I revere, whom I admire, whom in some degree I love; he shall be to me a living, bright reality, in touch with me now; not a mere statue in the Abbey, but a presence filling the Abbey. When I speak to Jesus, does he hear me? Is he a living, immediate Presence, with his hand on me? Is he a great superlative man in history, or does he know me now? He is my Lord. He knows his sheep by name. If he does not hear my voice now, I have got no Savior, and I have got no redemption. I must have a Lord who can lay his hand on me now, who knows my infirmity, who is not on the summit of some great mount calling to me with a voice like a great Excelsior to climb to him, but who will come down to the base of the mount and deal with me there. When I speak to him, he hears. I can say that of none other. I cannot speak of Luther, I cannot speak of Augustine, I cannot speak of saintly men of all ages like that. I know not that they can hear, or can help. But I speak of Jesus, and

> " 'Thou, O Christ, art all I want.
> Freely let me take of thee.' "

It is this Christ, who is King and Lord over all, into whose presence I wish to lead our thoughts reverently at this time. For, after all, the center

of our religion is Jesus Christ. It is a personal
religion, and it must stand or fall by the person of
Jesus Christ. I will not take up my time worrying
over criticisms concerning the shell of religion so
long as it is all right between my soul and Jesus
Christ.

I

Some thirty years ago, at a time when questions
regarding evolution and inspiration were stagger-
ing the faith of some people, an Oxford professor
wrote in a private note-book these lines:

> "I have a life with Christ to live,
>   But ere I live it must I wait
> Till learning can clear answer give
>   Of this and that book's date?

> "I have a life in Christ to live,
>   I have a death in Christ to die,
> And must I wait till science give
>   All doubts a full reply?

> "Nay, rather, while the sea of doubt
> Is raging wildly round about,
> Questioning of life and death and sin,
> Let me but creep within
> Thy fold, O Christ, and at thy feet
> Take but the lowest seat
> And hear thine awful voice repeat
> In gentle accents, heavenly, sweet,
>   'Come unto me and rest,
>   Believe me and be blest.'"

Christ has proved his Lordship in the atonement which he made for sin and in the revelation of his power to forgive sins. Nothing was kept more completely at the front throughout the whole public ministry of Jesus than the claim made by himself that he came to make atonement for the sins of men. He says, "The Son of man came to give his life a ransom for many." He calls himself "The Good Shepherd," who "giveth his life for the sheep." He distinctly says, "I am the good shepherd . . . and I lay down my life for the sheep." To emphasize these sacrifices he speaks as no mere man could speak when he says: "Therefore doth my Father love me, because I lay down my life, that I might take it again. No man taketh it from me, but I lay it down of myself. I have power to lay it down, and I have power to take it again." Again and again, by parables, by allegory, in public sermons and in private conversations, by illustration and in the plainest possible speech, Christ announced the fact of his coming death as a sacrifice for the sins of men. Christ stood in our place, and took on his shoulders the blow that was meant for us. Our race had fallen behind, crippled and ruined by sin, and Christ came in infinite love to search after humanity when it was lost.

Some of you have heard the story of the little

drummer-boy who was left behind to perish. When Napoleon was going with the troops across the Alps, and they were making their way to the plains of Italy, a little drummer-boy slipt down many hundreds of yards with an avalanche of snow. He was partly covered and wedged into the snow-drift, and it was utterly impossible for him to get out without help. The soldiers who witnessed the accident looked back, but they dared not stop and go to his rescue without orders. The little boy commenced to play on his drum the relief call, and the soldiers heard him, and they longed for orders to relieve him; and Napoleon himself was told of the accident, but in some moods the life of a little drummer-boy was of no value to him; so on they went and still he played the relief call. He watched the army fast disappearing, and no help or relief coming; and when the brave little fellow saw there was to be no rescue, he began to beat his own funeral march, and many of the veteran soldiers wept as they heard it, and after they reached home they told the story to their wives and children, and they also wept. That is not the way God treated us in our fallen and lost condition. He heard our relief call and came to our rescue. He did not leave us behind to perish and to beat our own funeral march and die; but he came in Jesus Christ, our

Savior and our Lord, to our rescue and deliverance.

Nothing shows the lordship of Jesus Christ more clearly than his power to forgive sin. You remember what trouble the friends of that poor paralytic man took to bring him to Christ. They were seeking simply the healing of his body. They hoped to see him walk again. But when they let him down before Christ, the Master, looking on him, went to the root of the matter when he said: ''Thy sins be forgiven thee.'' And to the poor sinful woman who came to him in the house of the Pharisee, Christ said, ''Thy sins are forgiven thee. Thy faith hath saved thee; go in peace.'' Tennyson has painted this scene in matchless words:

> "Her eyes are homes of silent prayer,
>   Nor other thought her mind admits
>   But, he was dead, and there he sits,
> And He that brought him back is there.

> "Then one deep love doth supersede
>   All other, when her ardent gaze
>   Roves from the living brother's face
> And rests upon the Life indeed.

> "All subtle thought, all curious fears,
>   Borne down by gladness so complete,
>   She bows, she bathes the Savior's feet
> With costly spikenard and with tears."

So completely is Christ Lord over sin that he has power to take away the sting and sense of bitter remorse and shame out of the heart of the forgiven sinner. A man who had lived for many years the Christian life told Dr. Charles MacFarland that there was a place in a street in a certain city which was associated with a sin. Every time in his early life when he passed that place, it brought back again the keen remorse and shame. It seemed to stain his life afresh whenever he saw the very place. But when he came to God and gave his heart and life to Christ, the first time he passed that place afterward his soul was filled by a great transport of joy that all that was done, that it was no longer a part of his life, that God had forgiven and forgotten, and cast it behind his back. And he entered for a moment at least into the perfect joy of soul, he forgot the shame of his youth and remembered the reproach no more. Thank God for the ever-increasing multitudes of redeemed men and women who are able to say with Paul, "This is a faithful saying, and worthy of all acceptation, that Christ Jesus came into this world to save sinners, of whom I am chief."

II

Christ has proved his lordship not only by revealing to us the perfect pattern of a human life, but by giving us power to live that life in fellow-

ship with him. Campbell Morgan says: Jesus
Christ becomes the Lord because he communicates
to man the new energy, the dynamic of life. By his
Holy Spirit he writes the law of God no longer upon
the tables of stone at which men are to look, but
upon the heart; by that same Spirit he constrains
the rebellious will of man until, instead of lifting
itself against God, it sings the song of his law, and,
catching the music of Christ's own life, repeats it:
"I delight to do thy will, O my God;" and by the
self-same Spirit he not only writes the law of God
upon the heart and constrains the spirit of man to
obedience, but energizes man so that, standing erect
in the presence of a past impossibility, he says,
"Now I can do all things through Christ who
strengtheneth me."

Christ shows his lordship in giving to common
men victory over their selfishness, and the grace to
imitate himself. Tennyson describes it in those
melodious lines: "Love
>   Smote the chords of self, which, trembling,
>   Passed in music out of sight."

It is told of Leonardo da Vinci that when he was
painting his wonderful picture of the Last Supper,
he had a bitter quarrel with another artist, and he
thought that he would strike a lasting blow at him,
and show what he thought of him, by painting his

face in that picture for the face of Judas Iscariot.
And so he did. The enemy whom he hated he set
in the picture as Judas Iscariot, that men might
know what he thought of him. And then he worked
on at his picture until he came to paint the central
figure—the face of our Lord; and he tried and
tried again, but he never could satisfy himself with
it. Always it was at fault. Always it was clearly
behind what he wanted to get. Meanwhile there
had been growing in his heart some sense of sin
and shame at what he had done toward his enemy.
This feeling grew in him as he worked on, until at
last he got quite ashamed and repentant, and made
up his mind that he had done a wrong; and so at
last he sponged out the face of Judas Iscariot. And
that night he saw in a dream the face of our Lord
which he afterward sketched and painted in the
picture. There were the lineaments and the look
that he had been longing to sketch, but which he
could not portray until he had put away selfishness
and bitterness out of his heart.

Our Lord, who was made perfect through sufferings, is ever able to lead his disciples over the path
of pain and struggle to the saintliest and holiest
life. We are told in Mark's gospel that "He was
with the wild beasts; and the angels ministered
unto him." The same ministration still comes to

tempted and tried men and women who live in fellowship with their Lord. J. M. Barrie has a beautiful chapter in "Margaret Ogilvy," entitled "How My Mother Got Her Soft Face." It is a beautiful description of a sweetness of life that came through suffering and bereavement. The "wild beasts" may snarl and sometimes wound and tear our lives, but if Christ is Lord there shall be the ministry of angels, and there shall be the peace of God. The highest life can only come through struggling and climbing in fellowship with the Master. Some one says that saintliness is like the Alpine edelweiss, which, as Dora Greenwell so beautifully sings, lives "in the mist and the cloud," and must be sought and found only by brave hearts and strong souls:

> "I bloom for the eagle's eye,
>   I bloom for the daring hand;
> I live but for God, and I die
>   Unto him, and at his command."

III

Christ is Lord of immortality. He brought life and immortality to light. He made it the common heritage of mankind. The supreme hope of the world centers in immortality revealed in Jesus Christ. Professor Fairbairn, in a recent discourse on "The Keys of Hell and of Death," recalls the

vision of one of the early seers of literature, who
dreamed that once God called up into heaven the
soul of a man, and he said to the angels that stood
by, "Strip that child of earth from his robes of
flesh. Put on him sail-broad wings for flight. Show
him over all my house, only touch not the human
heart, the heart in him that weeps and trembles."
So they left that human heart to the child of earth.
They put sail-broad wings for flight upon him;
they stript him of his robes of flesh; then, under
the guidance of a mighty angel, they shot sheer
from the battlements of heaven out into space.
There they went through a wilderness of dead
worlds; whatever world they saw looked like a
burned-out cinder. That wilderness of extinct
worlds frowned upon the heart and prest heavily
upon the soul of the child of earth. Out from there
they swept, and they came into a universe where
every world was new, where star sang to star in
the mystic excellence of voice that speaketh only
of him who had newly made them, the great Creator
of all. From this they swept into a universe where
no world was, where only from far immensity there
floated dim and distant the dust of worlds that
were to be, star-dust, it might be, yet dust still of
worlds in the making. The child of earth felt the
heart within him grow sad, and the soul within him

grow sorrowful. He fain would see a face; only atoms, atoms of extinguished, atoms of new made, atoms that were still the germs of worlds that were to be. On he went, until he said, ''Oh, angel, angel, pause; is there no grave where I can lie down and hide from the persecution of the infinite, for to this universe there is no end.'' ''No end,'' said the angel, ''to the universe of God; know also there is no beginning.'' And as they thus looked, and the child of earth would fain have lain down in a silent grave, he gazed into the far horizon, and he saw a cloud no bigger than a man's hand come toward them. It grew into the face of a child; it drew nearer, the face of the child broadened into the face of a man; as it came nearer still, lo! the child of earth saw Jesus of Nazareth passing him by in the great universe, and he cried out, ''O Lord, receive me.'' And the Lord received him, opened wide his arms and embraced the child of earth. He had now no use for a grave and did not want to die, if the universe had, as its very heart, and its very essence, and as its very home, the great Rest of man, the Heart of love.

It is Christ that makes immortality tender and loving and attractive to us. It is the Christ who stood among the graves of earth and said, ''In my Father's house are many mansions. . . . I go to prepare a place for you. And if I go and prepare a place for you, I will come again, and receive you unto myself; that where I am, there ye may be also.'' We are making no pilgrimage into the dark. We are traveling toward our ''Father's House.''

"The stars shine over the earth,
The stars shine over the sea,
The stars look up to the mighty God,
The stars look down on me.
The stars shall live for a million years,
A million years and a day,
But Christ and I will live and love
When the stars have passed away."

THE BREATHING
PLACES OF THE SOUL

THE BREATHING PLACES
OF THE SOUL

"They that wait upon the Lord shall renew their strength; they shall mount up with wings as eagles; they shall run, and not be weary; and they shall walk, and not faint."—Isaiah XL: 31.

IN more than one of the great cities of the world I have found it refreshing and full of interest to go out into some of the parks, especially on a hot afternoon, when the crowded streets were filled with dust and heat and noise and turmoil, and I have rejoiced again and again at the quiet and restfulness to be found but a few minutes' walk away from the busy marts of the city. There tired men and women had a chance to breathe; and the refreshing green which met the eyes, the singing birds, and playful squirrels, and the innocent and unannoyed prattle of the children, and the restful liberty which was everywhere renewed my strength. Such parks are very aptly called "the breathing places" of the great cities.

Now the soul needs to breathe as well as the body, and our text suggests not only the necessity but the

possibility of these breathing places for the soul.
It assures us that God has not forgotten this need,
and that with sleepless and unwearying vigilance
he is ever ready to supply it. The whole paragraph
of which our text is the final clause is marvelously
beautiful and sublime: "Hast thou not known?
hast thou not heard, that the everlasting God, the
Lord, the Creator of the ends of the earth, fainteth
not, neither is weary? there is no searching of his
understanding. He giveth power to the faint; and
to them that have no might he increaseth strength.
Even the youths shall faint and be weary, and the
young men shall utterly fall: But they that wait
upon the Lord shall renew their strength; they
shall mount up with wings as eagles; they shall
run, and not be weary; and they shall walk, and
not faint."

It is our pleasant and, I trust, helpful study this
morning to consider some of these breathing places
of the soul, where we may wait upon the Lord and
find our strength renewed and our souls refreshed
for the journey of life. Bunyan understood the necessity of such breathing places, and in his "Pilgrim's Progress," in which he traces Christian's
pilgrimage through shadow and sunshine to the
Celestial City, he grants him every now and then
a breathing place for visions by the way. On the

way up the Hill Difficulty, he takes him aside to the
Interpreter's House, with his happy talk and his
frescoes and parabolic pictures of the hidden forces
and the ideal incentives of the Christian life. On
the top of the hill he gave him a pause in the House
Beautiful, where he was comforted and cheered by
the Three Graces. After the fight with Apollyon, he
sees the vision of the Hand holding forth some of
the leaves of the Tree of Life, "the which Christian
took and applied to the wounds he had received in
battle, and was healed immediately." After Doubting Castle he came to the Delectable Mountains,
where were gardens and orchards, vineyards and
fountains of water; where the pilgrims drank, and
washed themselves, and did eat freely of the vineyards. And then, at last, before the crossing of the
river, they stopt a while in Beulah land, where
they were in sight of the city they were going to,
and saw that it was built of pearls and precious
stones, and also the street thereof was paved with
gold, so that by reason of the natural glory of the
city, and the reflection of the sunbeams upon it,
Christian with desire fell sick to be there. Always
after some great struggle and victory, or before
some dark and trying experience, Bunyan gives his
pilgrim these heavenly visions to reward him, and
to sustain him in the narrow path to the end. And

in all this Bunyan is only true to the Christian life
and its divine possibilities.   God has provided
breathing places for our souls where we may find all
the refreshment we need on our way to heaven.
Let us prayerfully consider some of them.

I

The first breathing place of the soul is *Bible
reading.* The Bible is preeminently the Christian's
book.   It is the book of the spirit; the book of the
soul.   The rich farmer in the Gospel found he could
not feed his soul on "much goods" stored in his
barns, and God called him a fool for trying it.
Souls can only be fed and refreshed through fellowship, and the Bible beyond all other books in the
world is a book of high and holy fellowship. Lyman
Abbott comments very beautifully on this truth.
He says that a book is a friend; a good book is a
good friend. It will talk to you when you want it
to talk, and it will keep still when you want it to
keep still—and there are not a great many friends
who know enough for that. A library is a collection
of friends. You go into your library of an evening,
and you look over its shelves and pick out the
friend you want to talk to you. It may be you are
weary and worried with turmoil of the present and
you want to get into the past, and you ask Homer

to talk to you, or you may want to forget this world
and think of the other, and you ask Dante to talk
to you, or your mind is too weary to dwell with such
themes, and you ask Thackeray to chat with you.
Or you want to know what the Twentieth Century
itself is in its essential spirit, and you ask Rudyard
Kipling to interpret it to you. A book is a friend;
a library is a collection of friends. The Bible is a
library. We go to it, not as we go to a school-book
to get information, accurate or inaccurate, about
something outside of the men who wrote it. It is a
library, a collection of friends; and we go to it that
we may see what they saw, feel what they felt, walk
as they walked, share their struggles with them,
ask them to share our struggles with us—that, in a
word, we may live their lives. There is not a doubt,
not a skepticism, not a perplexity, not a temptation,
that assails any honest, earnest, sincere man in this
morning of this twentieth century, that does not
find some hint or suggestion in this splendid collection of friends—all the more friends because they
have been through the dark places I must go
through, have wrestled with the temptations I have
wrestled with, have climbed the heights step by step
as I must climb—aye, and have wandered to the
right hand and to the left from the beaten track,
as I too am tempted to wander.

I said the Bible was a book of souls. It is more than that—it is the book of souls in their relation to God. Open your Bible to these first five books of law. Much that is in these books so far as immediate application is concerned has long since been laid aside, but they have not lost their value because of that, for illuminating them all is the great fundamental declaration that God spoke these words. Behind all to the Jewish law-giver was God. Law was to him the interpretation of God. No man can breathe in that atmosphere without refreshing his soul. Turn to these next books of history. They deal largely with little petty events. They are not by any means all the great deeds of great men. They are very frequently the mean deeds of mean men; but they were written by men who saw God in history. We sometimes look on life as one might look upon a chess-board in which the pieces play the game themselves. Now it is a knight, now it is a castle, now it is a pawn, now it is a bishop, now it is a king, that moves; and why they move back and forth, and what the end of it all will be, we are puzzled to determine. But these great historians of the past who wrote the Bible saw God's hand on the chess-men, saw him move them, and knew that at the end white would checkmate black, and sweep the black off from the conquered board. No man can look at the game of life through the eyes of the Bible and not refresh his soul.

Then there is the poetry of the Bible. Purely as poetry we may not like it so well as more modern poetry and yet not be irreverent. But for the sublime purpose for which it was written it surpasses all poetry. Over the holy of holies of the Egyptian Temple was written: "Who shall draw aside my veil?" The poetry of the Bible draws aside the veil and shows us that behind nature and behind human life is God. When the clouds gather in the western sky, and the lightning illumines the clouds back and forth, and presently the thunder crashes along the hills, take down the eighteenth Psalm and read the poet's picture of a thunder-storm as he saw it forty centuries ago on the slopes of Lebanon:

"Then the earth shook and trembled,
The foundations also of the mountains moved
And were shaken, because he was wroth.
There went up a smoke out of his nostrils,
And fire out of his mouth devoured:
Coals were kindled by it.
He bowed the heavens also, and came down;
And thick darkness was under his feet.
And he rode upon a cherub, and did fly:
Yea, he flew swiftly upon the wings of the wind.
He made darkness his hiding-place, his pavilion round
    about him;

Darkness of waters, thick clouds of the skies.
At the brightness before him his thick clouds passed,
Hailstones and coals of fire.
The Lord also thundered in the heavens,
And the Most High uttered his voice;
Hailstones and coals of fire,
And he sent out his arrows, and scattered them;
Yea, lightnings manifold, and discomfited them."

The poet saw God behind the thunder-storm. And so you can go to the Bible in law, or history, or poetry and have a new revelation of God given you. And still more truly in the New Testament, where you are brought into close, breathing fellowship with Jesus Christ, the friend of sinners; the comforter of the sorrowing; the brother of the tempted, the immortal conqueror over death, your soul is enlarged and exalted and comes to its throne.

II

Secret prayer and meditation is another breathing place of the soul. The great saints have been noted for their prayerfulness. When Thomas à Kempis had guests he used to say to them, when the time came for his private devotion, "Brethren, I must go. There is some one waiting for me in my cell." No wonder he wrote a book about "The Imitation of Christ" which all ages, and all nations, and all schools of Christians find the next book to the Bible. His soul had daily breathing room. The saintly Bengel went into his closet at stated times, and remained there perfectly silent with the open Bible before him. There he would sit thinking most deeply, not unfrequently until the midnight hour; then he would fold his arms over the open book and say, "Lord Jesus, thou knowest me," and immediately fall sound asleep. True Christian advancement will never be made except through prayerfulness. The soldier who talks of deeds he is going to perform in the battle, while he allows his sword to rust in its scabbard or forgets his ammunition; the sentinel who lets his enemy creep on him unawares while dreaming of the blows he will strike him when he comes within reach—we know what becomes of them. How can we hope to survive in the spiritual warfare if we sleep away our hour of preparation? What spiritual blow can be struck by the men or women who neglect the exercise of prayer? "Advance on your knees"; the great missionary Morrison said in speaking of the spiritual conquest of China. "Advance on your knees!" is the motto of all who would conquer the world, the flesh, and the devil. The failure of many people to stand in the face of temptation is simply the failure to hold secret communion with God in prayer. Many a Christian pilgrim has found strength to go on with soul refreshed and encouraged simply by pouring

out the story of his trial and sorrow when none but
God heard.

Some of you have read that remarkable story of
"Kim" which Kipling gave us a few years ago. In
it we have the incident where the little lad, "the
little friend of all the world," overborne by strain,
fatigue, and the weight upon his years, broke down
and sobbed at the feet of the aged man for whom
he begged in the dawn, held the weary head on his
lap during the noonday heats, fanned away the flies
on the hot afternoons until his wrist ached, begged
again in the evening, and rubbed the tired, aged
feet at night.   The wise old man said gently:
"Thou hast never stept a hair's breadth from the
way of obedience, child. I have lived on thy
strength as an old tree lives on the lime of a new
wall. Therefore, not through any sin of thine art
thou weakened. Be comforted." And "Kim" was
comforted. That is only a story told by a master
hand, but it is true of the deepest life. Pour out
your soul to God in prayer, and tho you have
been weary and broken through heavy burdens, he
will wipe away your tears. You shall have precious
communion with heaven and you will go forth from
your devotion comforted and refreshed, as "Kim"
went forth from his old friend's benediction.

Prayer is not asking only, it is as much listening

as it is asking. The Psalmist says, "Cause me to hear . . . for I lift up my soul unto thee." When alone, if we open our hearts to God, and meditate upon him, and commune with him, and listen to him, that is true prayer. Some poet says:

> "In the quietness of life,
> When the flowers have shut their eye,
> And a stainless breadth of sky
> Bends above the hill of strife
> Then, my God, my chiefest Good,
> Breathe upon my lonelihood!
> Let the shining silence be
> Filled with thee, my God, with thee."

III

Sorrow—Affliction—Trouble. These also are breathing places for the soul. Some one has wisely said that God has two great instruments for the deepening of the soul—love and sorrow. If you will not learn by the one, you must learn by the other. Sorrow strips off the layers of our self-complacency, materialism, and worldliness, and throws us back upon reason. The old environment is shattered that the soul may have room to grow. The awakening may be painful, but it is salutary and effective. If I speak to any who are in the midst of sorrow and trial, do not, I beg of you, take your sorrow bitterly. The saddest hours of grief, the most trying business troubles, have great possibilities for you in your higher nature. A fire once raged over a long reach of the Pyrenees Mountains, destroying many of the vineyards. The villagers were greatly distrest at the loss of their vines, but to their delight and astonishment they found that the terrible heat caused by their destruction had made great cracks in the rocks, and in the fissures could be seen molten silver, of whose existence they had hitherto been utterly unaware. The fire was a friend and not a foe; it left them much richer than it found them. So Paul says, "Our light affliction, which is but for a moment, worketh for us a far more exceeding and eternal weight of glory."

Mr. Mallock, in his book on Cyprus, says that it is an enchanted isle, that it is almost always sunshine there. He says there are cloudy days, but the charm of Cyprus is that in the clouds there is no gloom; they are warm, soft, like the breast of a dove, and when they pass they have sown a thousand garlands to give up the smell of flowers. That is like the clouds of sorrow in this world when a man lives in the love of God and walks in the path of the true Christian; there are clouds, but no gloom in them; the horror, the ghastliness, the despair of sorrow are no more. Watkinson says: "If you want to suffer nobly, suffer high up, and if you do that, sorrow and sighing may come to you, but sighing will say to sorrow, 'I cannot get my breath,' and sorrow will say to sighing, 'the tears are dried up in my eyes,' and sorrow and sighing shall flee away.''

Migratory birds never fly close to the earth; the atmosphere is too dense. They have to get up thousands of feet, where there is no mist, and no resistance, and then in a single day they will often sweep from a northern to a summer climate. Let us learn the lesson of the birds. Fly high, live with a wide vision, see in sorrow and trouble and difficulty some providence of God in which you should learn a lesson. Wait upon the Lord in the midst of sorrow and it shall be an atmosphere in which you shall mount up with wings as eagles.

IV

Old age is a breathing place of the soul. This is such a breathing place as those of us who are young cannot presume upon, for as the average of human life is under forty years, it must be evident that a large proportion of us will never see old age. We will fall in the midst of the battle with the harness on. But for those who have been permitted to pass through youth and middle age, and come into that realm of relaxation which comes with continued years, there are great opportunities and privileges.

Old age is free from many of the cares and many of the burdens that belong to the early years of life. It is also free from many of the ambitions that chafe and spur a man while he is young. It is a glorious thing when the crown of age is upon a man's brow to see him giving his soul a breathing place. Old age is a fruitful garden for the spiritual graces. Many of the most beautiful flowers of the Christian life thrive better then, and seem to grow more luxuriantly than at any other period.

Age should be accepted when it comes as an honor and a promotion. There is no greater folly than to try to seem young by ignoring age. Charles Dickens once had a handsome center-piece given him by one of the admirers of his writings, the design of which was figures representing the seasons. Winter, however, was omitted, as the donor shrank from including that gloomy season in his gift to one with whom he connected so much that was bright. Pointing to it afterward, Dickens remarked to a friend, ''I never look at it that I do not think most of winter. The very absence of it in the design made the thought of it more conspicuous. Winter is one of the seasons of life if you live long enough to enjoy it.'' If we are honored by the opportunity, let us accept old age gratefully with the glory of the sunset upon our faces.

"The tallest lilies droop at eventide,
  The sweetest roses fall from off the stem;
The rarest things on earth cannot abide,
  And we are passing, too, away like them;
    We're growing old!

"We had our dreams, those rosy dreams of youth!
  They faded, and 'twas well. This afterprime
Hath brought us fuller hopes: and yet, forsooth,
  We drop a tear now in this later time
    To think we're old.

"We smile at those poor fancies of the past—
  A saddened smile, almost akin to pain;
Those high desires, those purposes so vast,
  Ah, our poor hearts! They cannot come again!
    We're growing old!

"Old? Well, the heavens are old; this earth is, too;
  Old wine is best, maturest fruit most sweet;
Much have we lost, more gained, altho 'tis true
  We tread life's way with most uncertain feet.
    We're growing old!

"We move along, and scatter as we pace
  Soft graces, tender hopes on every hand;
At last, with gray-streaked hair and hollow face,
  We step across the boundary of the land
    Where none are old."

THE SENTINELS
OF THE SOUL

THE SENTINELS OF THE SOUL

"Every man hath his sword upon his thigh, because of fear in the night."—Solomon's Song III: 8.

THIS is a picture taken from that wonderful love poem of the Bible known as "Solomon's Song." The king is represented as traveling under guard. "Who is this that cometh out of the wilderness like pillars of smoke, perfumed with myrrh and frankincense, with all powders of the merchant? Behold his bed, which is Solomon's; threescore valiant men are about it, of the valiant of Israel. They all hold swords, being expert in war; every man hath his sword upon his thigh because of fear in the night." There is the picture. It does not need much imagination to bring it back before the eyes. The king is being carried through the wilderness in Oriental luxury. This chariot or palanquin, the pillars of which are silver, and the bottom of gold, covered with the royal purple, carried by his devoted servants, with sixty tried veteran soldiers guarding him from danger, make a procession worth looking at. But as the darkness falls and night comes on, fears are no strangers to that com-

pany. The night may bring attacks of wild beasts,
or still more vicious men. "Uneasy lies the head
that wears the crown." That old proverb has done
service for a long time and bids fair to do service
a good while yet. It is our sorrow and shame that
three of our own Presidents have died at the hand
of the assassin, and no man in great place of power
feels entirely free from "the fear in the night."
This explains the guard about the king, the tried
soldiers, expert in war, who guard Solomon and
give him safety and peace.

Perhaps you are saying, What message can this
have for us? We are neither kings nor queens,
and no one is seeking our lives. And yet is it not
true that every one of us has known the terror of
the "fear in the night"? Have you never known
what it meant to be in the night of trouble, and to
have a multitude of the ghosts of possible sorrows
and miseries throng about you and threaten you
with their keen weapons? Have you never known
the night of sickness, the night of doubt, when "the
fear in the night" brought agony that was hard to
still? There are terrors of this sort from which no
money can buy respite, and no learning and no
strength can give assurance of safety. What are
the sentinels, then, that the soul may summon to
stand guard in all the emergencies of life—senti-

nels with such skill and courage and power that the soul shall be free from the terror born of "the fear in the night?" I think it will do us good to look at some of these sentinels that are within the reach of every human soul and who may be summoned to guard us and give us peace.

I

The first sentinel of the soul, that which it seems to me must always be of most value in bringing us true peace and safety, is a clear conviction of the dignity of the human soul, a conviction that we are dear to God and that he cares for us more than he cares for the mountains or the plains or the rivers. Make a man believe that and you have gone a long way to guard him from the panic that comes from "fear in the night."

There is a picture called by the painter "The Return of the Flock." The sky is marvelously depicted, gorgeous in its coloring, and the splendor of the setting sun is thrown back upon the screen with wonderful skill. There is a little village in the valley, the smoke rolling loosely but gracefully above the chimneys, the brook with the willows upon the banks, the outstretching meadows, the country road going down the hill toward the village, the flock of sheep moving on to the comfort of the sheepfold—all this beautifully indicates the remarkable power of the artist. But all this is designed only to lead us to the central point in the picture—behind the flock the shepherd lad, with his slouched hat drawn down over the mystery that is the vital art of the pictured life, and in which the whole picture has its reason for existence. Looking at it you cannot but recall what Jesus said, "How much then is a man of more value than a sheep!"

Man's greatest guard against folly must be this high conception of himself as a being worth while and capable of great things. If man is insignificant and little, a beast only, then he can afford to waste himself on any trifle. Robert Browning in one of his lines speaks of "all hell let loose on a butterfly." And we see people let loose all the passions of the heart about something that is of no more importance than a butterfly. If we are to be saved from such things we must have a nobler conviction concerning ourselves.

Tennyson, in his picture of the magic Hall of Camelot, shows us four great zones or belts of sculpture. On the lowest belt he represents beasts slaying men. On the next higher, men are slaying beasts. On the third are warriors, perfect men; while on the highest are men with growing wings; and over all, the ideal men, beckoning upward to those beneath. This is a powerful parable of the worth of man and his ability to grow toward higher things. David, in the eighth Psalm, deals with this same thought when he says: "When I consider thy heavens, the work of thy fingers, the moon and the stars, which thou hast ordained; what is man, that thou art mindful of him? And the son of man, that thou visitest him? For thou hast made him a little lower than the angels, and hast crowned him with glory and honor. Thou makest him to have dominion over the works of thy hands; thou hast put all things under his feet: all sheep and oxen, yea, and the beasts of the fields; the fowl of the air, and the fish of the sea, and whatsoever passeth through the paths of the sea. O Lord, our Lord, how excellent is thy name in all the earth!" Now to David's view when he wrote this Psalm man had already tamed the wild beasts. He had made the ox his slave. He had almost saddled the winds to his chariot. He had harnessed the fury of the fire, and found a way for his commerce in the seas. But nothing of this exhibition of dominion stirred the heart of David so much as the consciousness that God thought upon him and visited him. And it is true that that which testifies to man's greatness most is not that he can conquer the wild beasts of the forests, or even the wild beasts in his own heart, great as that is; but the greatest thing that you can say of him is that he can hold communion with God, and walk the path of life serene in the consciousness that the eternal God is his Father and his Friend. It is the supreme glory of our Christianity that it brings man to a knowledge of himself and of the divine worth that is in him.

A traveler in South Africa stopt one day at the door of a settler's dwelling, at which a boy was amusing himself throwing stones. One of the stones fell at the traveler's feet; he picked it up and was in the act of laughingly throwing it back to the boy, when something in the stone flashed and set his heart beating fast with excitement. The child was playing with a diamond as a common stone; the settler's foot had kicked it aside; the wheel of the ox-cart had crusht it; but this man with eyes skilled for precious stones saw in it the priceless jewel. So men were dealing with one another as tho they were common stones of the earth, when Jesus came and saw in the poorest and humblest of humanity the image of God that might be restored. Some one says we are glib to repeat Carlyle's morbid nonsense of contempt for a man "saving," as he puts it, "his own miserable soul." But only the unsaved soul is miserable. The un-

saved soul is only a partial, a diseased, soul. The
saved soul is the healthy child, capable of growth
into the image of God. The saved soul is the jewel
taken from the mine, in the hand of the craftsman,
to be cut and polished, that it may be set in the
crown of the King. The saved soul is the paint on
the palette, being swiftly blended into some glorious picture on the artist's canvas. My friend, sit at
the feet of Jesus and learn the value of your soul,
and that conviction will stand as a guard to keep
you from the haunting "fears in the night."

II

A second sentinel which God himself has set at
the door of every human heart on the threshold of
life, to keep watch over man's safety and peace,
is what has been called *the instinct of moral
danger*. Dr. Robertson Nicoll declares that the
sense of the soul's value makes the soul protect itself against peril. How this should be is one of the
mysteries in our nature, but, strange as are its
workings, the instinct is both constant and characteristic. This seems to be true not only of man,
but of all God's creatures. Most living things
shrink from contact with plants or animals that
would injure them. Even the insects share it.
Hereditary associations keep them from visiting

certain flowers which would poison them. Instinct warns them, as in a higher form it warns ourselves, against that which is evil and corrupting. Cardinal Newman once said, "It is one great security against sin, to be shocked at it." We are born with an innocence that instinctively recoils at the touch of sin. Conscience forewarns us against certain associations and makes us feel uncomfortable in the company of people whose spirit is evil. These dislikes may be vague, we are not always able to explain them or to put them into words, but they are nevertheless instincts planted in our very nature to protect us. We need to cherish with the greatest possible fidelity this sentinel which God has placed for our protection, for it is easy to break it down and destroy it. There is an old fable which tells of a blacksmith who curst because the hot iron burned his hand, and wished that some power would harden his skin so that it would be incapable of pain. And the fable tells us that the evil spirit that waits upon such wishes came from the neighboring wood, and rendered his flesh insensible to heat or cold, and the blacksmith foolishly rejoiced. He grasped the metal boldly, but ere he was aware of it his hand was now seared and charred to the bone. The loss of sensitiveness had become a curse to him. So we are tempted sometimes to wish that our spirits were not so responsive to pain, sorrow, and temptation; but this sensitiveness is our one hope of soul-enriching and ultimate victory over these things. A petrified conscience is the sure precursor of a destroyed soul. To tremble and shrink from evil is the prophecy of its power yet being broken.

If we allow this natural instinct of moral danger to become dulled or hardened through indifference to its recoil against what is evil, we throw ourselves open to the enemy of our souls. Isaiah tells us that while some people are bound by sins that are like cart ropes that anybody can see, others are first bound with iniquity as with cords of vanity, light, gossamer, tender threads. When the Lilliputians wanted to bind down Gulliver in servitude they began with gossamer threads, and went on and on until the giant was captured. Tennyson, in his "Palace of Sin," describes a young man when he first goes into the dominion of sin. The tempter comes and leads him by the curl on his forehead. He leads him by his vanity, by his pride. If he does not recoil from this delicate seduction to evil, the day will come when he will be led by cart ropes that can be seen a block away by every passerby. But if that sentinel is kept on guard, what peace to the soul within! There is no "fear in the night'' that can ruffle the soul at whose gate stands Innocence with the sword upon his thigh.

III

Another sturdy sentinel equipped with invincible armor to defend the soul from ''the fear in the night'' is a consciousness that we are doing right, that our lives are pleasing to God. A vast deal of the restlessness, and uneasiness, and the kind of fears that crowd out peace, comes from a consciousness that our lives are out of harmony with God, that we are not doing our duty. No amount of gayety and surface pleasures can take the place of conscious rectitude. A great many people are very gay at times, and very miserable afterward, simply because their lives are not mastered by any high purpose and they have a conviction that they are wasting themselves. Balzac, the great French writer, puts this truth very clearly when he says, ''After all, what is less pleasing than a house of pleasure?'' And no one ever yet has tried making life simply a round of enjoyment, no matter how refined or cultivated, but he has come to Solomon's final decision, that ''All is vanity and vexation of spirit.'' If the soul is to have a conviction of safety and of peace, it must come from a consciousness that it pleases God. That assurance banishes "the fear in the night." Christ's teaching is very plain on this point. He says, "Every one that doeth evil hateth the light, neither cometh to the light, lest his deeds should be reproved." And again, "He that doeth truth cometh to the light, that his deeds may be made manifest." You will notice the positive word there, "Doeth." Many people are haunted by fears who are not active sinners, but who do not "do" the right which appeals to them. As Dr. O. P. Gifford says, that word "doeth" means practising. "Many people spend their time practising trifles, wasting opportunities, living an unreal, aimless life, wandering, not walking; drifting, not rowing; rotting, not growing."

You know what it is to practise law, medicine, to give life to the professions; some men practise idleness, dawdle, trifle; do not waste substance in riotous living, but in a moral way they do nothing. God has so made the world that such people cannot be happy permanently. Jesus says, "My father worketh hitherto, and I work." The world is saved by work. "Work out your own salvation with fear and trembling," says the Holy Book, "for it is God which worketh in you both to will and to do of his good pleasure." The man that does the will of God day by day is not without an armed

sentinel standing at the door of his soul to guard
his peace. Two of the most beautiful expressions to
be found in the Psalms are these: ''I will both lay
me down in peace and sleep,'' that is, when you are
going to bed and going to sleep; and ''When I
awake, I am still with thee.'' What a picture it
brings to the mind. A mother is putting her child
to bed at night. What is the last thing that the
child sees? He looks up into his mother's face.
Her face grows less and less distinct. The child's
eyelids fall, there is nothing more. Then, in the
morning, the light comes in, and the child lifts up
his eyes, and he sees the same mother's face.
''When I awake, I am still with thee.'' That is the
way God is always waiting for the man who is
conscious that he is doing the will of his Heavenly
Father. He is waiting for us to wake; more than
that, he is coming with the sunbeams to waken us.
And there can come no night of trouble, no night
of perplexity, no night of old age, that shall have
haunting fears strong enough to break through the
sentinels that guard such a soul. Some of you look
forward, it may be, with a certain shrinking and
sense of fear to the time when ''the pale horse and
his rider'' shall stand before your gate, and you
shall be called into the shadows of the dying. But
tho you fear it now, you will not fear it then,

if you live now in the sweet consciousness that you are doing God's will and to the best of your ability the work that he gives you to do. The old Shepherd Psalm will be realized in us, and we shall be able to make our own its precious utterance, ''Tho I walk through the valley of the shadow of death, I will fear no evil; for thou art with me: thy rod and thy staff, they comfort me.''

I am sure I speak to many who need this great message. Your souls are restless and uneasy. No success in business, no associations with thoughtless friends, no exhilaration of spirit can save you from forebodings and fears that often drive peace from your pillow.

I am glad to bring you the message of God, your Heavenly Father, who loves you; the message of Jesus Christ who redeemed you, that only in goodness, in complete surrender to righteousness, in doing with all your heart the will of God is there assurance of a guard for your soul that will give you the peace that ''passeth all understanding.'' In such a life only can you be secure in all the emergencies that can come to you. With such confidence no storm that can beat upon your head will rob your heart of its sense of security. The poet's song of the bird singing in the rain may then become your song:

"He began his song in the sunshine,
    For the world was fair to see,
And his little heart o'erflowing
    With love and melody.

"The starry flowers of the meadow
    Looked up at him and smiled,
And the sky was blue above him
    As the guileless eyes of a child.

"But soon across the heavens
    Was drawn a cloudy pall,
The sunlight fled affrighted,
    And the rain began to fall.

"The flowers were bent and broken
    Beneath the stress and strain,
But the bird sang on undaunted
    Amid the driving rain.

*   *   *   *   *   *   *

"It is easy to sing in the sunshine,
    When the soul can gaze above
Thro a veil of cloudless azure
    Right into the face of Love.

"When tender hearts surround us
    And eyes that smile in ours,
In the morn of life's brief summer,
    In the dewy time of flowers.

"But when the storm is raging,
    And hearts once gay are bowed,
Give me the faith that seeth
    The light beyond the cloud.

"The love that never faileth
    Thro doubt, or grief, or pain:
The dauntless hope that dareth
    To sing amid the rain."

THE DIVINE ROMANCE IN
CHRISTIAN CHARACTER

THE DIVINE ROMANCE IN
CHRISTIAN CHARACTER

"Now unto him that is able to do exceeding abundantly above all that we ask or think, according to the power that worketh in us, unto him be glory in the church by Christ Jesus throughout all ages, world without end."— Ephesians III: 20-21.

I HAVE heard the story of a great Welsh preacher, celebrated for his eloquence, who was preaching in English to a large congregation in London. His soul was in his message. It flashed in his eye, it fired his tongue, and he was so exalted by the nobility of his theme, and the thoughts within him burned and breathed at such a rate, that the English language would not do, and he paused a moment and said, "Oh, if you only understood Welsh!" He felt that he would have been able, in his more familiar tongue, to climb somewhat higher toward the point he aimed at. When you read Paul's wonderful sentences you cannot but feel that he had a similar thought. He exhausts the resources of language, and then he says, in substance: "It is not enough." It reminds us of that other wonderful utterance of his in which he compares the light afflictions of the present with the glory of the future, exclaiming: "For our light affliction, which is but for a moment, worketh for us a far more exceeding and eternal weight of glory." And if we analyze this scripture which we are to study we shall find that it will take a long time to read it. Let us look into it for a moment. "God is able." That is a most significant sentence, but there is more yet. "God is able to do." Plenty of people can boast. "God is able to do." Then Paul goes farther and says: "God is able to do abundantly." Then his vision expands, the horizon widens, and he rejoices: "God is able to do exceeding abundantly." Then he goes a step farther. "God is able to do exceeding abundantly all." Then his courage grows, and he takes another step: "God is able to do exceeding abundantly above all." Surely, you think, he is at the end of his tether now. But he is not. "God is able to do exceeding abundantly above all that we ask." Then he takes one last flight on the wings of thought, but still he cannot reach the bounds of God's power to bless his children, and exclaims: "God is able to do exceeding abundantly above all that we ask or think." Here he flung down his pen, like the Welsh preacher who ceased to try in a foreign tongue, with a feeling that it was impossible to describe the ability of God to work wonders in a human heart and life.

One writer commenting on these wonderful utterances says that Paul climbed up the ladder to the very highest rung that words could take him; and then he got on a higher ladder, and climbed up as far as thoughts could take him; and then he wanted Jacob's ladder to reach to the throne of God in order to tell us what God will do for any man who says in his heart, "Be my God."

I

The romance of Christian character lies in the fact that God is working in men and women to produce a personality more saintly and more heroic than any man in cool blood without the assurance of spiritual aid believes possible. Many men looking on the life of Jesus, while they are full of admiration and reverence, look upon that wonderful life as they look upon a snow mountain, as something standing apart, too good for human nature's daily food. But the hope of humanity rests in the great truth that the life of Christ, the character of Jesus, is only a sample personality, a sample career, and every man and woman is called upon by the Spirit of God to seek to reproduce that character

and that career under the circumstances of their
own lives. If Christianity were a mere creed, it
would amount to nothing. Thank God, it is more
than that. It is a life, and the value of Christianity to you and to me will be measured only by
the extent to which we live it. The glory of our
religion is in the transformed life which it shows
to the world. The doctrines of Christ are only
explained in full comprehension to men who live
like Jesus. Christ says: "If any man will do his
will, he shall know of the doctrine." God is ready
to do exceeding abundantly above all we can ask
or think when we undertake to live the life of
Jesus. Practise makes perfect in Christianity as
in everything else. Prof. Henry Drummond once
said: "What makes a man a good cricketer?
Practise. What makes a man a good sculptor, a
good artist, a good musician? Practise. What
makes a man a good man? Practise." There is no
magic or trick about the Christian religion. When
we turn our faces toward Christ and seek to reproduce his life in our own, all the powers of the
universe work together to bring about our triumph,
and every man that gives himself with whole-
hearted surrender to that work always succeeds
beyond his dreams.

Do you remember that morning when the time

had come for Elijah's translation? Elisha started
forth with his master, and the young prophets
called to him in a mocking mood: "Knowest thou
not that thy master is to be taken away from thee
to-day? Surely it were better for thee to stay with
us than to accompany a man who will vanish out of
sight." "Oh! I know," Elisha replied, "but I
shall go with him as far as I can." And so with
trembling heart, but with deep, abiding, loving
purpose to keep close to Elijah until the end of his
journey, he crossed the river with him. That day
Elijah mounted to heaven in a chariot of fire. The
next day Elijah's mantle was worn by another
man, but by whom? By one of those overwise,
careful, prudent fellows? No, indeed! It was worn
by Elisha. And if you want to wear the mantle
of Jesus Christ, you must surrender yourself to a
complete following after him. The power of God
will work in you as you work the will of God.

Some of you will recall how Longfellow brings
out this thought in his "Legend Beautiful." The
monk was kneeling on the stone floor of his cell,
bowed in deep contrition, when

> "Suddenly, as if it lightened,
> An unwonted splendor brightened
> All within him and without him
> In that narrow cell of stone;

And he saw the Blest Vision
Of our Lord, with light Elysian
Like a vesture wrapt about him,
Like a garment round him thrown.

"Not as crucified and slain,
Not in agonies of pain,
Not with bleeding hands and feet,
Did the monk his Master see;
But as in the village street,
In the house or harvest-field,
Halt and lame and blind he healed,
When he walked in Galilee.

"In an attitude imploring,
Hands upon his bosom crossed,
Wondering, worshiping, adoring,
Knelt the monk, in rapture lost.
Lord, he thought, in heaven that reignest,
Who am I, that thus thou deignest
To reveal thyself to me?
Who am I, that from the center
Of thy glory thou shouldst enter
This poor cell, my guest to be?

"Then amid his exaltation,
Loud the convent bell appalling,
From its belfry calling, calling,
Rang through court and corridor
With persistent iteration
He had never heard before.

"It was now the appointed hour
When, alike in shine or shower,
Winter's cold or summer's heat,
To the convent portals came
All the blind and halt and lame,

All the beggars of the street,
For their daily dole of food
Dealt them by the brotherhood;
And their almoner was he
Who upon his bended knee,
Rapt in silent ecstasy
Of divinest self-surrender,
Saw the Vision and the Splendor.

"Deep distress and hesitation
Mingled with his adoration;
Should he go or should he stay?
Should he leave the poor to wait
Hungry at the convent gate,
Till the Vision passed away?
Should he slight his radiant guest,
Slight this visitant celestial,
For a crowd of ragged, bestial
Beggars at the convent gate?
Would the Vision there remain?
Would the Vision come again?
Then a voice within his breast
Whispered, audible and clear,
As if to the outward ear:
'Do thy duty; that is best;
Leave unto the Lord the rest!'"

Straightway he started to his feet and with lingering gaze upon the Vision he went to the convent gate and ministered to the necessities of the poor and the suffering. Then, still wondering as to whether he had done right, he turned his face anew toward his cell; and, behold! the convent was bright with a supernatural light.

"But he paused with awestruck feeling
At the threshold of his door,
For the Vision still was standing
As he left it there before,
When the convent bell appalling,
From its belfry calling, calling,
Summoned him to feed the poor.
Through the long hour intervening
It had waited his return,
And he felt his bosom burn,
Comprehending all the meaning,
When the Blessed Vision said,
'Hadst thou stayed, I must have fled!'"

Let us get the great lesson deeply rooted in our hearts, that if we would have God present in our hearts and lives, working in us, to will and to do of his own good pleasure, building up holy and attractive character, we must make it the habit of our lives to fashion our living after the Christ who went about doing good.

II

The Divine Power that worketh in us in the building of Christian character is not interested so much in our temporary circumstances as in final results. Here is where many people make mistake. Many an arrogant man who is making money fondly imagines that God is pleased with him because he is prosperous in business, and many a sincere poor man, whose business has gone all awry,

is cast down and discouraged because he has experienced adversity, thinking God is displeased
with him. Both these men are mistaken. Many
another Dives, whose heart is as hard as the man
whom Jesus pictures, fares sumptuously every day,
while many another man as good as Lazarus goes
bankrupt. But that is only a small fragment of
the picture. Christ draws aside the veil and shows
that in the great immortality Lazarus associates
with the noblest and highest in heaven, while Dives
is gnawed and haunted by remorse. God is building men and women to live forever, and many a
man whom the world calls a failure is in the eyes
of God a stupendous success, and many another
whom the world envies as a successful man will
come after a while to know himself as a tragic failure. Ruskin says: ''The only failure a man needs
to fear is failure in cleaving to the purpose he
knows to be the best.'' This is one of the great
truths we need always to keep in mind, for human
life is honeycombed with illustrations of it.

I have seen a story of a woman, a mother, who
when she was dying called her eldest daughter to
her side and said, ''You will stop with the children
until they are wed, and you will care for your
father.'' She said, ''Yes, mother; I will.'' She
did not know what she was promising. Shortly

after, love looked in at the window of her life, and said, "Will you follow me; will you wed me?" And she loved, and her heart leapt out to the love of her life. Love said: "Will you come now?" "I cannot." "Make haste!" "I cannot; I must stay here." "Then I cannot wait." And the love faded away and her heart died. And she pursued her path, a lonely woman. The boys married, the girls went into homes of their own, and the father died, blessing her for her care. And in late middle life she looked around upon other girls whom she had known, in their happy homes; and often her heart felt sadness as it cried, "Never for me." But as she went to and fro among those children, and the babes were called by her name, and the little boys and the young fellows grew up almost to worship the ground on which she walked, she came to be the queen of the whole family, and came to know that no self-sacrifice, no honest effort to serve in God's name, ever fails in the building of our lives.

Perhaps nowhere in modern literature is the ultimate object of life drawn more clearly than in that wonderful poem on old age, by Robert Browning, which he calls "Rabbi Ben Ezra." It opens with the bold challenge:

> "Grow old along with me!
> The best is yet to be,

The last of life, for which the first was made:
>   Our times are in His hand,
>   Who saith, 'A whole I planned,
Youth shows but half; trust God; see all, nor be afraid.'"

Then the poet faces this very thought which we are
studying—the fact that adversity, hard struggle,
and inequalities of worldly fortune are to be taken
only as accidents and temporary experiences, and
used as helps to bring about the great result which
God is seeking to produce in making us noble and
holy personalities. The poet bravely says:

>   "Then, welcome each rebuff
>   That turns earth's smoothness rough,
> Each sting that bids nor sit, nor stand, but go!
>   Be our joys three parts pain!
>   Strive, and hold cheap the strain;
> Learn, nor account the pang; dare, never grudge the
>   throe!"

Then the poet takes up the scriptural metaphor of
the potter's wheel drawn by Jeremiah, and which
so many people have thought heartless, and in-
terprets it, showing how the potter is seeking
always the final usefulness of the cup which he
fashions. He begins with tracing the lines in love
about the base of the cup which he is molding,
"And as he nears the rim he fashions skulls in
order grim." But all the time he is working toward
the use to which the cup shall be put; to be held
by the Master's hand and used as he will.

"What tho the earlier grooves,
Where ran the laughing loves,
Around thy base no longer pause and press.
What tho about thy rim,
Skull things in order grim
Grow out, in graver mood, obey the sterner stress?
Look not thou down but up
To uses of a cup,
The festal board, lamp's flash, and trumpet's peal.
The new wine's roaming flow,
The Master's lips aglow,
Thou heaven's consummate cup, what needst thou with
earth's wheel!"

It is impossible to live the noblest life without keeping ever in mind that this present life is only the vestibule of our career, and that goodness, and the building up of character, must hold our complete loyalty.

There is an ancient myth which says that upon the confines of the earth there is a huge gateway which separates this world from the next. All the souls of the departed must pass this portal before they enter the other world. The gateway has two large pillars, one on either side. On the summit of these pillars are carved the heads of two massive dogs. Each of these dogs has two faces, the one looking before, the other looking behind. One faces the new world into which the soul enters, the other faces the old world from which the soul has come. There is in this a vein of eternal truth and a serious warning for the Christian who has failed to give whole-hearted devotion to the Christian life. One face regards the glories of the spiritual world. The other is set upon the things of this world. But when men play the double part they are doomed to certain tragedy in the spiritual life. The Christ who died to redeem you deserves and must have all your love. If he would work his purpose in you, he must reign supreme in your soul and in your life.

I have gone before now into a great factory, full of noisy, clanging, roaring looms, and the conductor has taken me from room to room, showing me many interesting things. In the midst of the factory I have sometimes found a room with entrances leading to it from all the great halls in which was the machinery and the hundreds of busy workers. And I have found that that room, in the heart of the factory, was where the manager sat at his desk. There he was in instant communication with every department. He had power to control every one and could call any one to him in a moment. The will of this one man dominated everything. Every worker, every loom, every spindle, was silent, or awhirl with life, at his beck or nod. My friend, as God looks down into your heart today what does he see? Who sits in the manager's room of your soul! If Christ is there, controlling your thoughts, your words, your actions, then every good thing that is possible to man, that is good enough to be true, can be realized in you, since he that worketh in you is able to do exceeding abundantly above all you can ask or think. Let us consecrate ourselves anew to-day to the full and complete building of Christian character, to the supreme purpose which God has for us in all worlds. And if we do that, we cannot do better than to make our own the prayer of dedication with which Browning causes old Rabbi Ben Ezra to conclude his philosophy of life:

> "So take and use Thy work,
> Amend what flaws may lurk,
> What strain o' the stuff, what warpings past the aim!
> My times be in Thy hand!
> Perfect the cup as planned!
> Let age approve of youth, and death complete the same!"

CONTACT WITH GOD
THE SOUL'S
SUPREME NECESSITY

CONTACT WITH GOD THE SOUL'S SUPREME NECESSITY

"And it came to pass, when Joshua was by Jericho, that he lifted up his eyes and looked, and, behold! there stood a man over against him with his sword drawn in his hand: and Joshua went unto him, and said unto him, Art thou for us, or for our adversaries? And he said, Nay; but as captain of the host of the Lord am I now come. And Joshua fell on his face to the earth, and did worship, and said unto him, What saith my lord unto his servant? And the captain of the Lord's host said unto Joshua, Loose thy shoe from off thy foot; for the place whereon thou standest is holy. And Joshua did so."—Joshua V: 13-15.

THE supreme hour of Joshua's life was fast approaching. He was in a singularly lonely position. Of all the men and women who had marched out of Egypt forty years before under Moses, he was, save Caleb, the only one left. All the rest had fallen by the wayside in the wilderness. It was a new army of young men and young women which he led. During all the years of their pilgrimage Moses had been leader. Now he was gone. Aaron and Miriam were dead, and on Joshua's shoulders was laid the task of leadership. He had crossed the Jordan and cut off his retreat. Swollen by

floods, the river ran at his back, and yonder were
the frowning walls of Jericho, against which he
was to lead his empty-handed army. In such an
hour Joshua's greatest necessity was God. No one
else could advise him and guide him. The pillar
of cloud which had led them by day, and the pillar
of fire which had preceded them by night, had
gone. The heavenly manna had ceased to fall.
In this solemn hour, with enemies upon every side
of him, and no human forces with which to contend
against them, the heart of Joshua must have cried
out for the leadership of God, for communion and
fellowship with him. Nothing else could give him
peace. And it was at such an hour that God revealed himself in this interesting and remarkable
way. The courage of Joshua stands out splendidly
in the incident. When he sees the Man in the
vision, he marches directly to him with the question, ''Art thou for us, or for our adversaries?''
His brave soul was ever ready to dare his fate,
trusting in God.

I

We need to find in this interesting story a pro-
found lesson for ourselves. Contact with God is
always the soul's supreme necessity. The story is
told of how Dante, wandering one day over the

mountains, drew nigh to a lone secluded monastery. It was at a time when his mind was racked
with internal conflicts and was seeking refuge from
the strife. So he knocked loudly at the monastery
gate. It was opened by a monk, who in a single
glance at the wan, pale face read its pathetic message of misery and wo. "What do you seek
here?" said he. And with a gesture of despair
the poet replied, "Peace." Ah, it was the same
old craving, followed by the same old search; but
neither the solitary places nor the monk's cell ever
brought true peace to the afflicted heart. It comes
not from without, but from within. We can have
it in the winter of age or in the spring of youth; in
the lowly cottage or in the stately mansion; in dis-
tressing pain or in buoyant health. The secret of
the soul's satisfaction, of its perfect peace, comes
in comradeship with God. Christ said to his disciples that tho in the world they should have
tribulation they should still have peace in him.
Joshua found it true under the walls of Jericho,
and you may find it true to-day under the frowning difficulties which face your to-morrow.

II

We learn from this theme that God ofttimes
meets men unexpectedly. Tho Joshua's need was

so great, the revelation of God which came to him in this vision came without any expectation or forethought on his part. The woman of Samaria who gave Jesus a drink at the well of Sychar came carelessly down with her water-pot, having no thought that the great sunrise of her life was at hand. And so it is that God often comes unexpectedly to meet us in great and wonderful revelation of himself. A Christian poetess of our time has told us in one of her poems that at a public reception, among many pictures on the walls of the palace, there was one which specially looked out on her, and held her spellbound all the evening. It was a picture of Christ as a King, treading the wine-press alone. Amid the hundred lights that gleamed on the faces of the guests, and the pictures on which scenes of beauty had been prisoned for their pleasure, and the sweet tide of music that rolled through the room, she tells us:

> "Suddenly face to face with Him I stood
> Who is not very far at any time
> From those who love Him."

She had no eyes during the rest of the evening for anything or any one save the Christ who, amid the crowds that came and went with the music, and that knew him not, seemed alone, terribly alone. So God comes to men and women to-day. Sometimes in sorrow, sometimes in joy, sometimes in the midst of gayety, and again in the hush of the house of prayer. My brother, if he comes, meet him as Joshua did, with brave and worshipful welcome.

III

I think we ought learn from our theme that God is most likely to come to the soul when life is hushed and quiet, in the hour of meditation, when the heart may listen. Joshua seems to have been alone, contemplating the frowning walls of the great city, which stood over against him, wondering how he should bring them to the ground. And it was in the midst of this meditation, when his life was hushed into stillness, that God appeared to him. If we would meet with God and have communion with him, we must have our times of meditation and secret fellowship with our Heavenly Father. The greatest workers and the most powerful thinkers that the world has ever known have been men who every day had their set hour for secret fellowship with God. Such times furnish the life-blood of all true greatness and true goodness. There is no doubt in my mind that the rush and hurry of modern life have not stabbed the church of Christ anywhere so deeply as in the tempting of thousands of Christians from the old-fashioned habit of secret prayer, a habit as old-fashioned as Jesus's talk about the closet and the shut door, and the prayer in secret that should be rewarded openly. I never speak on this subject but my heart grows tender and warm. My mother had a large family of children, and in the midst of the care for them all maintained great calm and sweetness of spirit. I was the eldest, and I used to wonder how she did it. My two sisters next in age to me, and myself, had noticed that every afternoon she went for an hour into a thicket not far from the house, and that a little later we heard her talking to some one, and that she always came out of that thicket singing, with her face shining like the sun. And so one day we followed her and crept under the trees until, ourselves unnoticed, we could see what she was doing. First she opened her Bible and read two or three chapters, and then she kneeled on the ground and began to pray. She prayed for her children by name, one after another, and all our faults, and all her love, and all her hope in God for us, were poured forth in petition and tears. Before she was through we were all crying. But she prayed on until evidently the captain of the Lord's host met her, for when she came out again her face was all aglow with joy, and she sang with the gladness of a bird in spring-time. God had spoken to her. It is in these secret, still places of meditation and prayer that strength is renewed. Some one sings a song of that prophet's chamber which the Shunammite woman had built for Elisha. It was only a

> " 'Little chamber' built 'upon the wall,'
>> With stool and table, candlestick and bed,
>> Where he might sit, or kneel, or lay his head,
> At night or sultry noontide; this was all
> A prophet's need: but in that chamber small
>> What mighty prayers arose, what grace was shed;
>> What gifts were given, potent to wake the dead,
> And from its viewless flight a soul recall!

> "And still what miracles of grace are wrought
>> In many a lonely chamber with shut door,
> Where God our Father is in secret sought,
>> And shows himself in mercy more and more!
> Dim upper rooms with God's own glory shine,
> And souls are lifted to the life divine."

IV

I think we should emphasize in our hearts the fact illustrated by this remarkable story, that God always comes when we need him, if our hearts are ready to respond in reverent obedience. Joshua soon found that the man with the drawn sword had not come to fight as a private in the ranks, but as captain of the Lord's host. He also learned that God demands our reverence. The call to put off

his shoes from his feet, because the place whereon
he was standing was holy ground, suggests the
very important truth that worship comes before
service. We shall never be strong to do God's will
until with reverence and love we worship God and
come into perfect harmony with the spirit and
purposes of God. One great reason why so much
of the work of the Christian church to-day is a
comparative failure and seems to produce little
effect for good, is that it is often service without
worship. Service, however humble, tho it be no
more than a cup of cold water to the thirsty, when
rendered in a tender, reverent, worshipful spirit
toward God and Christ, has about it a heavenly
magic, a divine electricity that is irresistible.

But the greatest lesson of all, still left for us
to learn, is that obedience to any message or vision
which comes to us from God is necessary to insure
the blessing which God seeks to bring to us. Many
people have wonderful dreams and visions and
opportunities, and yet nothing ever comes of them
for lack of obedience. Dr. Hillis says that many
years ago, in Paris, he made the round of the
studios. One day an artist friend took him into a
garret. Going up the steps the artist told him
that he would show him the most glorious dreamer
in France. He found the low ceiling of that

attic covered with pencil sketches; every inch of
the walls and the very floor were plastered over
with outlines. Every morning found the artist at
his canvas. In one ceaseless procession the visions
passed before him—angels, seraphs, sunsets, trees,
castles, scarred cliffs, golden clouds, palace, hut,
canoe, ocean steamer, mound, volcano, peasant,
prince, tropic luxuries—ten thousand sketches—
not one of them complete. A thousand dreams and
faces in the air, but no power to pin them down
to a canvas and fix them there forever. No artist
had more glorious visions of beauty, but men with
one-tenth the imaginative power painted ten times
the number of pictures and had a hundred times
the income. The artist who indulged in his dreams
and lived on his reveries was like multitudes of
people, inside the church as well as out, who dream
their dreams of ideal perfection and plan noble
schemes of helpfulness, but do practically almost
nothing. Some of you who hear this message have
been thinking for years of joining the church of
Christ and putting yourself into open fellowship
with Jesus, but you have taken it all out in reveries,
and up to this moment you have done nothing to
bring yourself into line with the forces of righteousness. Some of you who are in the church have had
wonderful visions of duty presented to you, and

again and again have had reveries in which you
planned fine things you were going to do to help
the church, to strengthen the poor and the weak,
and charm the sinful to the Savior, but all these
are only vague clouds, like those of the artist in
his attic, and your heart is not so easily stirred
to-day to such aspiration and desire as it was years
ago.   Obedience is the only key which will unlock
the storehouse of God's blessings.   The man who
obeys God, about whom it can be said, as is said
of Joshua in this record, ''Joshua did so,'' is the
man who is brought so into fellowship with God
that something of God's majesty seems to attend
him.   Hudson Taylor, the great Chinese missionary, was a man of that sort.   He did not impress
people by a commanding stature, by flights of
imagination, or by thrilling eloquence.   And yet
an audience would be spellbound by his unas-
suming, earnest talks, and the effects of his utterances were very powerful.   ''I am always very
glad when Mr. Hudson Taylor is out of the place,''
said a mother to a certain minister on one occasion.   ''Why?'' he asked, with astonishment.   The
reply revealed the influence which the missionary
carried with him: ''Because I am afraid he will
run off with my child for China.''   The fact is, she
felt she had to do with God when he was there.

V

When Joshua in reverent obedience accepted the
leadership of the captain of the Lord's host, he
went forward with the assurance that he had the
cooperation of Almighty God. He became a man
allied with the Supreme Power in the universe.
He became God's agent for accomplishing the purpose dearest to the heart of God, and was therefore
triumphant in the end over all opposition. The
whole history of mankind is filled with illustrations
of impossible things that have been wrought in and
through individuals, many of them common men,
who have been made uncommon in power and influence by their obedience to God and their alliance
with his will. Everything is possible to the man
who enters into a partnership with God and yields
perfect obedience to him.

The story of Christianity is rich in instances
which prove this true, and we need not fall back
on the story of the Master or the romantic and
marvelous success of the early Christians under the
leadership of Paul and Peter and John for our
proof. There never has been an age so dark, there
never has been a race so weak, but there have been
bright and shining lights, and brave and obedient
heroes whose alliance with God has given them a
power and an influence which no merely human

forces could possibly have supplied. You may see our truth in Martin Luther as he faces the Pope, and Emperor, and, indeed, every worldly and ecclesiastical power of his day. He was stronger than all of his foes because he was obedient unto God. You may see it in John Bunyan, an ignorant and profane tinker at Bedford; but brought into alliance with Heaven, obedient to the heavenly vision, he becomes the greatest moral influence of his age. You may see it in John Wesley, a humble youth whose father was often in jail for debt, but who after many wanderings to and fro across the ocean and the continent without success, and falling into many foolish blunders, at last met the captain of the Lord's host, in reverence put off his shoes from his feet, and gave himself with marvelous surrender to be God's man, and for more than half a century poured his life out as an oblation before God. Branch after branch of his natural life was withered. Men thought, Now he will be cast down and destroyed; but every time the new life rushed through all the dead fibers and they blossomed again in a nobler beauty. He started the whole church of Christ in all denominations and in all lands on a new career. Historians agree that he saved England from the deluge of blood that had swept over France. He started forces into action that have belted the globe, and millions upon millions of men and women in all parts of the world love and revere his name. All things were possible with him because of his alliance with God.

Brothers, sisters, let us enter into partnership with Almighty God. No matter how weak we are in ourselves, surrendered to him in reverent obedience to do his will, nothing can stand against us. Joshua became the wonder and the marvel of the nations because God was with him. The giants of Anak were as nothing before this humble Hebrew but yesterday a slave, because he went forth not in his own strength, but in the power of God. Again and again in the years that followed, when the odds against him were tremendous, God would meet with Joshua in the stillness of the night and tell him to have good courage, to be of good cheer, to fear not, for he would be with him and nothing would be able to stand against him all the days of his life. God kept his promise.

Now, my friends, I would never have courage to come into this pulpit again if I did not believe with all my heart and soul that God loves me as much as he did Joshua, that the people of Denver are as dear to the heart of God as were the children of Israel, and that if we are reverent, seeking to know God's purpose with open heart, and ready with quick obedience to do his will, he will lead us as surely and as manifestly as Joshua was led by him.

This wicked city needs that we shall be devout and earnest, and, above all, obedient to God. Multitudes of young men and young women, far away from home, strangers in a strange land, pursued and lured by many new and unusual temptations, need above everything else to find in the church of Jesus Christ a place where the power, and the mercy, and the love of God abound in manifestations of helpfulness, and in heavenly charm, to hold them back from evil ways and win them to the help which is in God. Let us with all our hearts and souls enter into partnership with God for the blessing and salvation of humanity in our city.

Some months after the death of Mr. D. L. Moody his son-in-law was turning over the leaves of Mr. Moody's Bible, when at the fifth and sixth chapters of the Gospel by John he found these words written by Mr. Moody in the margin: "If God be your partner, make your plans large." It is a very striking and significant sentence. Dr. John Robertson, the Scotch evangelist, was so imprest with the sentence that he wrote a strong poem about it in which he says:

"If God be your partner, burning stars are wheeling
   Worlds of help and hope to reinforce your strength;
If God be your partner, God's own hand is sealing
   Treasure-trains of years gold-laden all their length!
      You need not hesitate upon the marge,
      Make your plans large!

"If God be your partner, angel-swords are flashing
   Ranks of foes to drive back on their fleeing heel;
If God be your partner, never heed the clashing
   Spears that threaten blood to drink with stooping steel.
      What need have you of man's poor shield and targe?
      Make your plans large!

"If God be your partner, ocean waves are bearing
   Sail-filled fleets of rescue and of sure supply.
If God be your partner, deeps with deeps are sharing
   Glad response to your now haven-seeking cry;
      For you is chartered not a coasting barge—
      Make your plans large!

"If God be your partner, dawns soon day of reckoning—
   Day when God divides with faithfulness his own;
If God be your partner, heaven's on tip-toe beckoning.
   Race redouble then, go on, and take your throne,
      For God his partnership will fair discharge.
      Make your plans large!"

THE SUPREMACY
OF HUMILITY

THE SUPREMACY OF HUMILITY

"Whosoever will be chief among you, let him be your servant: Even as the Son of man came not to be ministered unto, but to minister, and to give his life a ransom for many."—Matthew XX: 27-28.

PHILLIPS BROOKS says that the word "humility" itself and its history are interesting. He recalls what Coleridge said, that "There are cases in which more knowledge, of more value, may be conveyed by the history of a word than by the history of a campaign." The story of this word is one in point. It was not a new word when the New Testament was written. It had been used for many years. Only it is striking that almost without exception the word "humility," used before the time of Christ, is used contemptuously and rebukingly. It always meant meanness of spirit. To be humble was to be a coward. Where could we find a more striking instance of the change that the Christian religion brought into the world than in the way in which it took this disgraceful word and made it honorable? To be humble is to have a low estimation of one's self. That was considered shameful in

365

the olden times. Christ came and made the despised quality the crowning grace of the culture that he inaugurated. Lo! the disgraceful word became the key-word of his fullest gospel. He redeemed the quality, and straightway the name became honorable. Think what the change must have been. Think with what indignation and contempt men of the old school in Rome and Athens must have seen mean-spiritedness, as they called it, taken up, inculcated and honored, proclaimed as the salvation of the world, and him in whom it was most singularly embodied made the Savior and King of men.

This wonderful miracle was wrought by giving men a new comparison for themselves. If in estimating his own value a man compares himself with personalities essentially lower and meaner than he is, then he becomes proud; but if he compares himself with the pure and matchless life of Jesus Christ, it ministers to humility. No sane man can be proud of himself as he matches his character against that of Jesus. So it comes about that a man grows greater, becomes of nobler quality and more splendidly useful to the world, and at the same time becomes more genuinely humble, because of the loftier personality with which he brings himself into comparison.

I

Humility is the key to the highest service. Christ sets us the example. It begins with the cross. Christ humbled himself to the death of the cross. He died as tho he were a malefactor under the curse of God. He who was rich, yet for our sakes became poor, in the Garden of Gethsemane wrestled in anguish until the agony wrung from him great drops of bloody sweat. Christ was humbling himself to be the ransom for the world. The burden of our sins he carried with a breaking heart. No wonder the apostle says, "Herein is love, not that we loved God, but that he loved us, and sent his Son to be the propitiation for our sins." We ought to get this picture of God into our hearts. There is infinite comfort in it. We ought never to forget that the great satisfaction, the delight of God's heart is in loving and serving his children. This truth is very strikingly set out in George Macdonald's "Robert Falconer." I will not attempt the Scotch dialect, but translate the substance into plain English. Robert is talking with his grandmother about the character of God, and says: "God is not like a proud man to take offense, Grannie. There is nothing pleases him like the truth, and there is nothing displeases him like lying, particularly when it is by way of upholding him. He wants no such upholding. Now you say things about him which sound to me fearsome." "What kind of things are they, laddie?" asked the old lady, with offense glooming in the background. "Such like as when ye speak about him as if he was a poor, proud, bailie-like body, full of his own importance, and ready to come down upon anybody that did not call him by the name of his office. Aye, think, thinking about his own glory, in place of the quiet, mighty, grand, self-forgetting, all-creating, all-upholding, eternal being, who took the form of man in Christ Jesus, just that he might have our sins to bear and be humbled for our sakes. Oh, Grannie, think of the face of that man of sorrow, that never said a hard word to a sinful woman or a despised publican. Was he thinking about his own glory, think ye? And we have no right to say we know God save in the face of Christ Jesus. Whatever is not like Christ is not like God."

Now it is only as we come into fellowship with Christ, and get his spirit of loving devotion to humanity, humbling ourselves to the cross of burden-bearing for others, that we become of the greatest usefulness to the world. At the Winona Bible Conference last summer Dr. F. W. Gunsaulus told the story of a boy in Vermont whose father was in jail. He had been sent to the jail for a long term when the boy was too young to remember him; and when the careless children jeered at him in school because of his disgrace, he went to his mother for the reason, and she had no answer but her tears.

But at length the father came home, and the growing boy entered into the bitterness of the grown man's soul as the ex-convict sought through the community in vain for employment. From his own little bedroom the lad heard his father and mother at night praying out of the anguish of poverty for God to send work by which the husband could earn a living for his loved ones. And slipping from his bed to his knees the boy vowed before God that if his father was given work now, he would devote his life in seeing that other men from prison got a chance to earn a living.

The boy grew up and went in his young manhood to Chicago. He prospered and grew very rich. But as his wealth increased his religious faith seemed to slip from him, and he was greatly troubled by his doubts of the doctrines of the church. Especially was the atonement a puzzle to him, and for years he made it a point to attend conferences and religious assemblages where the atonement was to be discust by eminent men.

At length Dr. Gunsaulus, counseling him as his pastor, said to the man: "Is there not some particular in which you have made less sacrifice for your fellow men than you should have done? You will never have a faith in the atonement that is vital until you have yourself imitated in some way the sacrifice of Christ."

Then of a sudden there rolled back over the rich man's heart the memory of the vow of his boyish days, unkept till then. This vision of remembrance came to him at midnight. He got up and drest himself, and went to the house of his pastor and told him the story of his boyhood and his vow, and with heart stirred to its profoundest depths and eyes wet with tears he said: "I'll do it. I'll begin in the morning."

Next morning he wrote to the warden of a great penitentiary, asking to have a released convict sent to him. The man came and met the clasp of a hand of honest brotherhood. The manufacturer sent him far into the West to nail up advertising signs, and gave him good wages. Then he got another man from another penitentiary and sent him out in the same way. One after another he set on their feet such ex-prisoners as he could find, until there were seventeen of them that walked through his private office to a clean, true life. And he told

no one of them of any of the others. But they ran
across one another as they traveled, and when they
told each other how they had been lifted up out
of their common pit of perdition by the same loving
hand, they could not help forming a brotherhood.
They wrote circle letters which went the rounds
among themselves, and the rich manufacturer in
Chicago was one of the circle.

Then an awful, ravenous disease laid hold on
the philanthropist and month after month led him
nearer the jaws of death. But he had no more
doubts about the atonement to confuse him. He
trusted One who had done for him more than he
had done for his fellow men. And he died in the
calmest of trust—a triumph of spiritual peace.

Dr. Gunsaulus said that as he was rushing to
catch the suburban train to go out to the dead
man's home for the funeral, a touch on his arm
stopt him. "May I go out to the funeral with
you—the wife and the boy and I?"

The man who spoke was tall and rugged, drest
in the rough garb of a ranchman. "Who are
you?" said the minister. "Oh, I was from Jackson, Michigan. I live out in South Dakota now.
I came for the boys—came to be at the funeral.
This is my wife. This is my boy, named after
him. Six of us have got boys with his name now."

"Of course he went to the funeral," said Dr. Gunsaulus. "And he went to the grave. After the coffin was lowered the big man in the coarse leather clothes brought seventeen white carnations and dropt them into the grave—seventeen white flowers for seventeen white souls. And the wife and boy came and dropt in flowers, too; that was for their home and all the other homes which this man had made possible."

II

Humility, only, can give to service its true dignity. Christ sets the standard of Christian dignity. That only has dignity which serves, in his order. How jealous some men are of their dignity! You hear men speaking together of another and they say, "You will have to be careful, for he stands on his dignity." It is a poor pedestal; a pitiful perch; often only a laughing stock. How different the dignity of Jesus. Christ says, "I am among you as one that serveth;" and to-day he is the highest in the universe.

At the great Presbyterian National Assembly a few years ago, when they were about to elect a moderator, and various names were being presented, Dr. Charles L. Thompson of New York came forward to present his candidate. Said he:

Brethren, I had a dream to-day, which was not all a dream. In my vision I saw a corridor reaching from this platform back and upward to the first century. Out of a door in that century came a man of small stature; bronzed, scarred, and weather-beaten; a dim halo of glory was about him, and while he wore the panoply of a soldier of the cross, he carried above him a tattered flag, like those of veteran soldiers returning from war. Upon it I read the name of Corinth, Ephesus, Philippi, and Rome, and as he reached this platform I said to myself, Surely I cannot be mistaken, this is none other than the Apostle Paul, the great missionary to the Gentiles. I ventured to inform him as to the character of our Assembly, and to assure him that the system of theology in which we believed was that which he had outlined as being in conformity with the Word of God. He seemed deeply interested, and after speaking to him of the growth of our church and of our missionary work, I offered to introduce him to some of the distinguished members of this Assembly. "Here, for instance," said I, "is Benjamin Harrison." "Yes," he replied, "a worthy successor of Washington—a Christian statesman, and an elder beloved. I would like to meet him, but not now, I will see him later." I said, "Here is also General

Wanamaker.'' ''Yes,'' he answered, ''I know his record from that of a poor boy to wealth and high public position. I know his evangelical spirit, his liberality, his personal worth; and that he hath built us a grand synagog where Christ only is preached. I long to meet him—but wait awhile, I will see him later.'' I said, ''Here also is James A. Mount.'' ''Yes,'' he answered, ''he is governor of the great State of Indiana. An elder in a little country church, has ordered his household in the fear of God, has a daughter in the foreign field and a son a home missionary. I long to meet him—but not now, I will see him later.'' ''Who, then,'' said I, ''do you first wish to see?'' He looked carefully over the Assembly and answered: ''Is there not a little bronzed missionary from Alaska here—a man about my size—a man of weak eyes and insignificant bodily presence—a man in whom the apostolic zeal of ancient times has found expression in the New World, and who has had the care of all the churches in the regions beyond?'' ''Ah!'' I cried, ''I know who you mean,'' and not waiting to hear another word I sought, found, and presented Sheldon Jackson. ''True yoke-fellow and brother beloved,'' said Paul, ''we are physically small—God made us short that we might accommodate ourselves to circumstances and magnify his grace. I rejoice that primitive zeal still flames in the church, and that here and in foreign lands are thousands of standard-bearers of the cross who may not rest until the nations that sit in darkness have seen a great light, and the world is filled with the knowledge of God as the waters cover the sea; 'be thou faithful unto death and let no man take thy crown.'"

And so Sheldon Jackson, the humble Indian missionary, was lifted to the highest dignity that his church had to give because they esteemed him to have humbled himself the most, and served the most laboriously the cause of humanity and of his Lord.

III

Humility makes all service glorious. Humble, reverent, loving service glorifies common life and makes it sacred. Sir Walter Scott says that the most beautiful scenery in Scotland is where the Highlands and the Lowlands meet. Not in the Highlands, nor yet in the Lowlands, but at the meeting of the two. And it is as true in the spiritual kingdom, when the beaten track becomes the highway of God, and the heavenly places in Christ Jesus are connected with the common duties and everyday business of life. How beautifully

Christ brings them together in the Lord's Prayer: "Thy will be done on earth as it is in heaven. Give us this day our daily bread." There you have the meeting of the Highlands and the Low-lands.

I was reading recently the story of a young fellow in one of the Northern backwoods districts who was a bright boy, a genuinely religious boy, and who had attracted the attention of the neighbors. They all said he ought to be a minister, and they persuaded his hard-working father, who had a farm not fertile, and whose resources were limited, to sacrifice himself further that the boy might be educated. The boy did well, his professors were proud of him, he had gone through two years at college; and it seemed as if he had a great future.

One morning, however, he opened a letter; it was from his mother. "Your father," she said, "died last night; we must leave everything to God."

The boy went to the president of the college to tell him about it. "We cannot let you go," said the president. "As you cannot now pay your own expenses, you must have help; we will see what we can do."

"Ah!" said the boy, "mother is at home; there

are three little children; and they cannot do anything on the farm. I must go home.''

''Oh,'' said the president, ''do you love your mother more than you love God? Don't you remember him saying, 'He that hateth father and mother for my sake and the gospel's?' ''

''Stop,'' said the young fellow. ''It cannot mean that. Don't you remember when he was in his agony on the cross he said to John, 'Behold thy mother!' The gospel cannot mean that.''

And the boy went back to the farm. He did not complete his education; he never became a minister, or any hero, or saint, as the people thought. But he plowed a straight furrow, did an honest day's work, paid his debts, and helped his mother rear the three children to a noble life. Do not God and angels looking down on such a man as that see that all the heroes are not to be found on the battle-fields? that the greatest saints are not those in pictures with a halo about their heads? My brothers! my sisters! what the world needs most is heroism, sainthood, in common life; Christian men and women who with humble hearts will do everyday duties without noise or show or advertisement, because the heart and the conscience, living in sweet fellowship with Jesus Christ, says, ''This is the way, walk ye in it.'' Believe me, it is

the life that stoops the lowest in service that will
soar the highest.

"The bird that soars on highest wing
    Builds on the ground her lowly nest;
And she that doth most sweetly sing
    Sings in the shade when all things rest;
        In lark and nightingale we see
        What honor hath humility.

"The saint that wears heaven's brightest crown
    In deepest adoration bends;
The weight of glory bows him down
    The most when most his soul ascends;
        Nearest the throne itself must be
        The footstool of humility."

THE SANCTUARIES OF LIFE

THE SANCTUARIES OF LIFE

"A glorious high throne from the beginning is the place of our sanctuary."—Jeremiah XVII: 12.

THE idea of sanctuary was originally a refuge. It suggested some one pursued escaping from his pursuer into a sanctuary such as the houses of refuge provided for the innocent slayer under the old Jewish economy. It was always true if a man reached the altar of the temple he for the present was safe. While he was in that sacred place he could not be molested. But while the thought of sanctuary is usually connected with escape from punishment or persecution, or public reprobation in some great sin or sorrow, the conception may well be enlarged to a much ampler sphere. The thought of sanctuary may well apply to the longing of the soul for shelter from the wear and strain and fret of life, the trivial and vexatious, and where the consolation needed is temporary rather than permanent.

No one lives very long in the world without coming to know the need of some sanctuary for the soul, some place of retreat where the inner self

shall be comforted and revived and renewed for
the struggle of life. One of the biographers of
Charles Dickens declares that the basal weakness
of the great novelist's character was in this, that
"There was for him no city of the mind against
outward ills for inner consolation and shelter."
Commenting on this another literary man says:
"Dickens depended more than most men on the
stimulus which outer things provided for him."
And Robertson Nicoll well says that this is the
analysis of a temper which can spoil religious character and service as well as literary. To the life
which prefers to work ever in the open, glittering
and noticed, indifferent to any law or love above
itself, and indisposed to retirement, there can be
no true sanctuary. And without a sanctuary there
cannot be that contemplativeness, that sense of proportion in things, that habit of rising above material standards and aims, that power of with-
drawal for a time from the ordinary ambitions and
entanglements of life, which form at once a man's
true consolation in adversity and his source of new
courage for the tasks and trials awaiting him.

Our text declares that in the last analysis the
throne of God is the place where man finds the
answer to his desire for quietness, to his passion
for peace, to his search for a sanctuary. If this

be true, then there is sanctuary only in something that shall recall us to God—something that shall bring God's nearness and protection to our consciousness so that in it we may find rest.

I

Nature is to many people a blest sanctuary. There are those who cannot look upon the sea, or look upward on the lofty mountains, or stand in the midst of the mountains, or walk in the great forests without it becoming a sacrament to them, bringing to them a spirit of worship and reverence that refreshes the soul and renews the strength of mind and heart. Many of us could join with the poet who sings:

> "A haze on the far horizon,
>   The infinite, tender sky,
> The ripe, rich tint of the cornfields,
>   And the wild geese sailing high,—
> And all over upland and lowland
>   The charm of the goldenrod,—
> Some of us call it Autumn,
>   And others call it God.
>
> "Like tides on a crescent sea-beach,
>   When the moon is new and thin,
> Into our hearts high yearnings
>   Come welling and surging in,—
> Come from the mystic ocean,
>   Whose rim no foot has trod,—
> Some of us call it Longing,
>   And others call it God."

II

Communion with noble souls in literature and in art is a sanctuary to multitudes of people. Mr. Bryce tells us that one day in the lobby of the House of Commons he saw Mr. Gladstone with his face white and drawn with sorrow about a threatened defeat of a great cause on which his heart was set. Mr. Bryce attempted to divert his mind by telling him how Dante in his last years had obtained a lectureship at Ravenna which raised him above the sufferings of poverty. Mr. Gladstone's face immediately lit up, and he said: "How strange it is to think that these great souls, whose words are a beacon light to all the generations, should have had cares and anxieties to vex them in their daily life just like the rest of us common mortals." The glimpse of noble human fellowship opened at once a sanctuary into which the great Christian statesman entered and was comforted.

To many of us the poet is the greatest of all teachers in bringing the hidden things of God to light. He is the great interpreter of nature as well as human nature, and brings the immanent, present God to our consciousness. To others the artist makes even nature more wonderful and inspiring than it seems to the eye at first glance.

Sylvester Horne, in discussing "The Influence of Art," quotes the saying of John Ruskin: "You may think, perhaps, that a bird's nest painted by William Hunt is better than a real bird's nest. We, indeed, pay a large sum for the one, and scarcely care to look at or save the other. But it would be better for us that all the pictures in the world should perish than that the birds should cease to build their nests." That is very true, and yet nobody could tell us better than Ruskin the other side of that question. The true artist is in his sphere and through his medium what the true poet is in his, and the true preacher in his—that is, an interpreter. He is, like the poet and the preacher, a seer with a certain God-given talent of letting others know what he sees. In the biography of a great artist there is the narrative of how he saw the beauty of a simple pastoral scene near some English village. He painted it, and when it was finished he showed it to an old inhabitant of the place. The man was amazed to perceive that he had lived eighty years in that very village and had never seen before how beautiful it was. The artist had come to him as Christ to the blind, and opened his eyes. He had opened a sanctuary to the man's soul where he found God and was encouraged.

So it is that not only the great masters of the older day, like Michael Angelo, and Tintoretto, and Fra Angelico, and Raphael, but many of the modern artists, like Watts, and Hunt, and Millais, and others too numerous to mention, have raised sanctuaries along the dusty paths of life into which men and women have gone, tired and worn, to be comforted and refreshed, and have had their hearts lifted up to the "glorious throne" where the soul finds peace.

III

The church, with its Sabbaths, its open Bible, its inspiring music, and its preaching of God, and Christ, and the soul, and the immortal career, is a sanctuary which not only rests the weary heart, but stills the fever in man's spirit, and reveals to the world-worn nature the superiority of spiritual things, and brings God close and makes him real. The shame of our generation is the perpetual attempt made to more and more override the Sabbath and make all days alike secular. No man has language eloquent enough to properly pay tribute to what the Christian Sabbath has meant to the world. The Sabbath—with its quiet, with its surcease of toil, with its opportunity to worship, with its communion and fellowships of home, with its perpetual reminder of God and the spiritual nature —what a sanctuary it has been through all the struggles of the ages. The church building itself and the church service are sanctuaries where weary souls find peace. Here, in the church, dominating everything, is the Bible. It is a book for all men, and it is our glory that it is free and unfettered; and it is gloriously true that it is so full of simple teaching that the wayfaring man, tho a fool, may read it as he runs and get great good; but that does not mean that there is no great, important, God-appointed office for the preacher. He is the interpreter. If he is called of God to do this work, his study of the Bible will discover meanings, beauties, and treasures in it that a superficial examination will not disclose. And who of us who have sought the church as the sanctuary of God through these years does not recall as among the happiest and most precious of experiences the hours when God has revealed himself to us in the sermon until we have been exalted and our spiritual power renewed?

So the music of the church is the greatest music in the world. The great composers have been men whose hearts God has touched. Souls that have looked upon the face of the Christ in Bethlehem, or on Calvary, or on the resurrection day have given to the world the greatest music that the human ear ever heard. The hymns in the church are high-water mark of joyous and saintly feeling, and to multitudes of tried and troubled men and women Christian music is the sanctuary where most frequently they find God. So it is that the church in our day is the source of new impulse in spiritual life as surely as in any age of the past.

The Christian life may be likened to the flight of a bird. The Duke of Argyle, in "The Reign of Law," has detailed the mechanism of flight. He tells us that the bird is led to flight by its inward impulse. You can never calculate that. He mounts upward, and he hovers there in mid-air; he drops heavily down to the earth; he spreads his wings out and recovers himself. He soars up at a new angle; he wheels round and round. As he circles there he is not afraid of the tempest; he plays with the lightning; and yet, so nicely adjusted are his wings to the environment of the surrounding atmosphere, the slightest change in the force or in the direction of the wind requires a new adjustment on his part. Now, the Bible likens the life of the child of God to the flight of an eagle. "They that wait upon the Lord shall renew their strength; they shall mount up with wings as eagles." And it is proved by all observation that those who wait upon God in the church services with sincere hearts find it a sanctuary where new impulses to righteousness of life and nobility of service are certain to be found.

IV

Secret prayer to God is one of the great sanctuaries of the Christian life. Shakespeare says, "At their wits' end, all men pray." It is the greatest folly that men go on till they get to the end of their wits before they think of prayer, because those who begin with prayer do not get to the end of their wits.

Dr. Gunsaulus preaches one of his great sermons on secret prayer from those words of Jesus when he tells of the pilgrimage we should make to our closets—"Shut the door." And he emphasizes the fact that the one thing Jesus seems most intent about, that you and I should enjoy the privilege of prayer and receive its benefits, is all explained and emphasized in those words: "Shut the door." Any man or woman among us who will have a secret place where daily we shall go into sanctuary and "shut the door," shall not lose the heavenly path, but if it is to be the true sanctuary we must shut out everything else and really pray to God. For, as Gunsaulus says, it was not an easy task

Christ set us when he said, "Shut the door."
"Why, surely," you say, "that is something I can
do with one hand, while I grasp other things with
the other hand." No, both hands must be inside.
There must be no effort to grasp things without.
"Well," you say, "what shall I shut the door
against? There are so many things with which I
must keep in touch. There is my church, my
family, my relatives, my dear friends." Oh, poor
soul! It seems such ordinary talk, does it not, in
the presence of the great, sweet Being who is saying, "Shut the door?" I must be alone with God;
I must feel again my personal relationship to my
Father; I must realize again that if there was only
one being in the world, and I were that being, while
the moral universe subsisted, still there must be a
cross, still a Christ, still a Gethsemane, still the
morning of the resurrection, still the open sepul-
cher. The only way to get rid of our enemies is
to "Shut the door." The real truth is that, when
the real crises of life come, the only enemy is
myself. This is the one I need to conquer. Here
are passions, prejudices, hates, lusts. Oh, my
friends, whatever your gain or loss, realize this,
that never until you shut the door will you go into
the presence of God; never until in secret prayer
you are alone with yourself will you be delivered

from your enemies. What can any man do to harm
me, unless I harm myself? If ever you are tossed
about upon seas of darkness, it will be because you
neglected to put the anchor on board and your ship
is at the mercy of the waves. "Shut the door."

V

All that we have said leads to this conclusion,
that loyal devotion to the personal Christ as our
Savior and Lord is our supreme sanctuary. Nothing else will ever supply our need. We need a
sanctuary, every one of us, from our sins. We shall
only find it in Christ. A minister said to a sick
man one day as he was about to go away after
calling on him, "Is there anything you want, anything you would like to have to make you comfortable?" The preacher had in his mind little
things for the sick-room, dainties and luxuries,
that are supposed to be desired by an invalid.
Turning earnest and longing eyes upon him, the
sick man said: "Yes, sir, I want the forgiveness
of my sins; I want that." Brothers, sisters, that
is the bed-rock want in your life and in mine.
There is not a man or a woman among you, I do
not care how moral and right-living you are, but
what if you were to speak out with the true conviction of your soul you would say to your inmost

self, "I need the forgiveness of my sins, and I want it, and must have it." We do not dare to lay our lives alongside the spotless holiness of Almighty God. We must have sanctuary, and we can only find it in the atonement of Jesus Christ on the cross, and daily and hourly we must have that sanctuary in him.

If we thus give ourselves up to Christ as our Savior, we shall appreciate the sanctuary that is in the thought that we are not our own, that we are bought with a price, even the precious blood of Christ. This will be a precious sanctuary to us in time of bereavement and sorrow. "Who took this rose?" cried a head-gardener, in anger, when he missed a certain rose he had, with very great care, brought to perfection. "Oh!" said his helper, "the master was here a little time ago, and he took it, and he told me to tell you he wanted it." The head-gardener was satisfied; the rose was not his. It belonged to the master. So sometimes in our great sorrows we are tempted to ask, "Why was he, why was she, taken? Why have I lost that? Why are my hopes dashed to the ground just as they were being realized?" Brother, the Master, the great owner of you and of yours, and of me and of mine, has come and done it. He wanted that beautiful flower and has taken it to his own bosom.

He has seen your danger in worldliness and prosperity and has pruned away the branch for which you grieve. You are not your own, and your divine Lord and Savior, watching over you with infinite tenderness, will do right. Is there not sanctuary for your soul in that blest confidence?

It is a precious thought that in communion with Jesus Christ we may always have sanctuary for our souls. I cannot always fly to the solitudes of nature that they may tell me of God; I cannot always have leisure for books or pictures that they may lift me into noble communion; I cannot always be in the sacred precincts of the church, or listen to inspiring music, or illuminating preaching of the word of God; it cannot be always Sabbath to my soul, the week-day calls to me for service and for toil; I cannot always have opportunity for my closet and the shut door; but there can come to me no day of trial when I may not in the midst of the hardest struggle find sanctuary in the consciousness of Christ, and his love, and his presence in my soul. F. B. Meyer gives a very beautiful interpretation of those great words in the One Hundred and Thirty-ninth Psalm, where David says, "If I take the wings of the morning, and dwell in the uttermost parts of the sea; even there shall thy hand lead me, and thy right hand shall hold me."

Father, mother, have you never helped your little baby to walk? Have you never taken the child's two hands clasped in your left and said, "Now, walk, baby; walk, darling; lean upon this hand and come." And the child has tried to put this foot and then that forward; but you know you have your right hand behind, holding his dress. "Even there thy hand shall lead me, and thy right hand shall hold me." We want the two. We want leading and we want holding. We want to be told our path, and we want to be kept from falling. How close this brings God to us. We do not have to deal with an incomprehensible spirit who broods in all spaces and tenants all ages, but we have to do with a tender hand; in fact, with two hands. I cannot see his face; I shall not see my Pilot face to face till I have crossed the bar; but meanwhile, tho I cannot see the face of Him who loves me, the face that was once wet with tears and blood for my redemption, I am conscious, hour by hour, that there is a divine hand leading and another holding, and that I am safe in their care.

THE SOUL'S MASTER, LEADER, AND RESTORER

THE SOUL'S MASTER, LEADER, AND RESTORER

"He maketh me to lie down in green pastures: He leadeth me beside the still waters. He restoreth my soul."
—Psalm XXIII: 2, 3.

CHRIST, by assuming to be the Good Shepherd of our souls, has absorbed all the teaching of this shepherd psalm of David into himself, and when we think of David's shepherd we have a vision of Jesus Christ.

I

There is first of all a thought of *mastery* in our text, "He maketh me to lie down in green pastures." The sheep does not lie down where he pleases, but where the shepherd sees fit. The first supreme characteristic of Christianity is this recognition of Christ as the soul's Master. There are those who boast their independence even of Jesus, but it is a lonely and hazardous undertaking.

I have read the story of a young man who when a friend tried to dissuade him from an enterprise he had on hand exclaimed proudly, "I am my own master." "Did you ever consider what a responsible post that is?'' asked his friend. ''Responsible! What do you mean?'' ''A master must lay out the work which he wants done, and see that it is done right. He should try to secure the best ends by the best means. He must keep on the lookout against obstacles and accidents, and watch that everything goes straight, or else he must fail. To be master of yourself you have your conscience to keep clear, your heart to cultivate, your temper to govern, your will to direct, and your judgment to instruct. You are master over many servants, and, if you don't master them, they will master you.'' ''That is so,'' said the young man. ''Now I could undertake no such thing,'' continued his friend; ''I should fail if I did. Saul wanted to be his own master and failed. Herod failed. Judas failed. No man is fit to be his own master. 'One is your Master, even Christ.' I work under his direction.''

I know of nothing more pitiful in the history of mankind than the story of some earnest, noble souls who have been so hedged about by prejudice that they have seen Christ and Christianity through colored glasses, and while they have sought to live good lives, have tried to live them alone, without divine help. The position of such a soul is graphically exprest by the little song of William Ernest Henley:

"Out of the night that covers me,
　　Black as the pit from pole to pole,
I thank whatever gods may be
　　For my unconquerable soul.

"In the fell clutch of circumstance,
　　I have not winced or cried aloud;
Under the bludgeonings of chance
　　My head is bloody but not bowed.

"It matters not how strait the gate,
　　How charged with punishments the scroll;
I am the master of my fate,
　　I am the captain of my soul."

How sad and lonely is such a soul compared to a man like Paul who exults in the consciousness that Christ is his Master, and that nothing can separate his life from that of his Lord. Put over against these lonely verses the wonderful words of Paul: "For I am persuaded that neither death nor life, nor angels, nor principalities, nor powers, nor things present, nor things to come, nor height, nor depth, nor any other creature, shall be able to separate us from the love of God, which is Christ Jesus our Lord."

There is a thought of mastery, of course, which is brutal and causes the man who is mastered to have a sense of degradation and a spirit which is servile. But to be mastered by the divine love is to be exalted and lifted up into a holy fellowship until we become heirs of God and joint-heirs with

Jesus Christ. Henry Ward Beecher was once crossing Fulton Ferry in company with a friend. It was a stormy morning, and Beecher stood on the prow of the boat rapt in meditation. His friend called his attention to a sea-gull that was bravely facing the wind and the snow. Beecher, with the reverie still unbroken, said, ''He is mine,'' and then added with dimmed eyes and flushed face, ''I am joint-heir.'' So long as we think of our limitations we lose sight of our great inheritance, but when we yield our souls completely to the mastery of Jesus Christ, we come to exult in the consciousness that Jesus cannot occupy the highest throne in heaven without sharing it with the humblest of his disciples. ''All things are yours, for ye are Christ's, and Christ is God's.''

II

We have also a thought of leadership. ''He leadeth me beside the still waters.'' Christ is the only leader of the human soul who always leads to peace. Life is a tragedy always to a thoughtful man who looks at it without hope in Christ. George Eliot once said: ''I hardly ever look at a bent old man, or wizened old woman, but I see also with my mind's eye that part of which they are the shrunken remnant, the drama of hope and love which has long since reached its catastrophe and left the poor soul like a dim and dusty stage with all its sweet garden scenes and fair perspectives overturned and thrown out of sight.'' That is, this woman thought every human life lived out to its natural close is a tragedy. Let me put over against that a visit I made the other day to an old man, a member of this church. He has been in his room in the hospital for three years. I found him in bed, as he is most of the time now. But he was cheerful and happy, and in the course of my conversation I asked him how long he had been a Christian. A smile came into his eyes as he said: ''Well, take seventeen from ninety, and there you are.'' And then he went on to tell me how seventy-three years ago, in a distant land, in his father's house, there had come to him one day the great call from God. He was all alone, but the Master called him to yield his heart to him, and then there came the other voice of the enemy, saying to him that his young friend who was not a Christian would have to be given up. But the Master speaking in his heart said to him, ''Why not bring your friend to Christ too?'' And so this young seventeen-year-old lad went out and found the other boy, and said to him, ''I feel that I ought to be a Christian. I have made up my mind that I will

follow Christ and try to do what he wants me
to do." And his friend thought for a few minutes
and looked up with wet eyes and said, "Then if
you do that I will go with you and we will become
Christians together." And as the old man told the
story his face glowed and the happy tears filled his
eyes as he said with great emotion, "From that day
to this Christ has been my leader. I began to be
a Christian that day, and I am a Christian now.
He has led me all the way." There is no tragedy
about a life like that.

Only this divine leadership can give us strength
for the noblest service. There is an old legend of
the Middle Ages concerning a knight who had vowed
himself to the service of humanity for the sake of
Christ. This man had taken the usual vow, and it
seemed a great and easy thing to be a warrior in
the cause of right, shoulder to shoulder with men
who were of the same mind with him. Presently
a task came to this warrior from which his whole
soul shrank. Some one had to discharge it. Why
not he? He hesitated, he questioned with himself,
he took advice from others, and all who knew and
loved him sought to persuade him from attempting
the seemingly impossible. He entered upon a vigil
in the church one night that he might consult with
God and his own soul as to what way he should

take. It seemed to him as tho the Master himself
appeared and addrest him somewhat in this wise:
"Turn back, my son, turn back, spare yourself; the
task is too great. Why should you leave all your
fellows behind, and undertake something in which
you may fail, and in which even if you succeed the
world will never know?" It seemed the Master's
voice, but there was another voice which spoke
within, and made him answer: "No, tho thou
comest with the voice of Jesus, I will not believe
that this is the voice of the Highest; it is not Jesus-
like," and when he had so said, the Master reached
out his arms to him and said, "Come, thou blest of
my Father, enter thou into the joy of thy Lord."
When we are completely surrendered to the leadership of Jesus Christ, we know the voice of Christ
which speaks in our inner soul and gives us courage
for heroic service. Under that leadership nothing
can affright us. Under the leadership of Jesus
Paul was able to make converts, and develop saints
in the palace of the bloodthirsty Nero. It was a
hell on earth, but men and women grew to be saints
there, because they were led by Christ. Are you
working in some shop, or factory, or store, where
Christ is blasphemed, and do you ask me to-day,
"Is it possible for me to be a Christian when my
fellow workers are gamblers and profane?" I re-

ply without hesitation, "Yes! you can if you will let Jesus Christ lead you." Does another young man say, "Can I be a Christian when all my fellow clerks scoff at Christianity and poison the very air I breathe all day long with vulgar and evil speech?" Yes, indeed, you can if you let Jesus Christ take you by the hand and lead you. "Can I be a Christian?" asks a woman whose husband sneers at religion, or who it may be is a drunkard and shames her by his degradation. My answer is, "Indeed you can." There is no situation this side of perdition so terrible that a man or a woman under the leadership of Jesus Christ may not find in the midst of all the storms and dangers of life the still waters of heavenly peace. There is not one of us but may be able to sing at the last:

"He leads us on
Through all the unquiet years;
Past all our dreamland hopes, and doubts, and fears,
He guides our steps. Through all the tangled maze
Of sin, of sorrow, and o'erclouded days
We know his will is done;
And still he leads us on."

III

There is a thought of restoration. "He restoreth my soul." David knew by personal experience what that meant. I think there must be some

deep meaning in the order of our text. First the
soul is mastered by the divine love. Then it is
surrendered to the heavenly leadership. Then
comes restoration. Mastery, leadership, restoration,
that is God's order. But it is only in Jesus Christ
that the sinner finds any promise or hope of restoration. The man who closes the Bible has no hope
for the sinner. Professor Huxley says: "Nature
never overlooks a mistake, and never makes the
slightest allowance for ignorance." It is the God
who gave his Son to save a world of sinners who
"restoreth the soul." The greatest thing David
ever said of God was, "Thy gentleness hath made
me great." Dr. Watkinson says: Great is the
efficacy of kindness. It may often look absurd;
love looks absurd when it attempts with soft words
to tame wild beasts. Love looks absurd when it
attempts to fetter madness with silver strands of
affection. Love looks absurd when it enters the
arena of strife, and seeks to reconcile contending
factions by the wave of an olive branch. But, mind
you, love is the sovereign conquerer that fills all the
world. Christ helps men by recognizing what is
good in them. He encourages us. His sympathy
means our salvation. He restores us through sympathy and gentleness and love. He saves us by forgiveness.

Some men sneer at Christianity because of its gentleness and spirit of mildness. They deal in blood and iron, thunder and lightning. They do not like the mildness of Christ, they have no faith in anything but force. Yet Faraday, the great scientist, told us that there was more energy stored up in a dewdrop than there is liberated by a thunder storm. It is said that a bank of snow six feet thick will stop a bullet shot at a distance of fifty yards. The bullet will not penetrate that downy bank of snow, but it will go through the solid embankment when fired at three times the distance. The bullet shatters the steel, penetrates the solid bank; but the soft feathery snow has a way all its own, and it takes in that murderous lead and loves it, and, as it were, soothes it. God dealt like that with David when he sinned, and Christ dealt like that with Peter when he denied him. Infinite gentleness, patience, clemency, long-suffering—these were the qualities by which their souls were restored when they were in danger of eternal disaster. So God restores us, and we must learn the secret of soul restoration in our attempts to share with Jesus Christ in restoring those about us. It is gentleness and love that are all-powerful.

Christ restores our souls through communion and fellowship with himself. Are there any here who are conscious of sin and are ashamed and grieved at the lack of harmony which you feel there must be between your soul and Him who is "altogether lovely" in all His thoughts and deeds? Yield your heart to Christ, let him lead your thoughts, and you shall become like him. If we do this, our friendship shall result in likeness to Christ. As has been well said, it is only the submissive soul that he can mold with the gentleness that gives the finest spiritual results. He will not force us. He is no Cæsar, but a Christ. We must yield our wills to cooperate with his. There intimacy shall result in likeness. Some of you have heard the legend of the *stigmata* of St. Francis. Men said concerning that sweet and gentle soul that he was so much with the Christ that even his body took on the likeness to his blest Master, and when his brethren undrest him to put his grave-clothes on him, they found in his hands the print of the nails of Calvary, in his feet the unhealed scars of crucifixion, and in his side a wound still bleeding from the spear-thrust. This is only a legend, and yet the story has a suggestion of truth. The miracle that is worked by intimacy with Christ is a miracle not of similitude of body, but of likeness of soul. Yield yourself here and now and always, plastic of soul and willing of spirit, to the influences of the Master, and your soul shall be restored so completely that the Christ tenderness, the Christ dignity, the Christ gentleness, and the Christ power shall be yours.

We are told by mariners who sail on the Indian seas that many times they are able to tell their approach to certain islands long before they can see them by the sweet fragrance of the sandal-wood that is wafted far out upon the deep. And so it is true that when the soul of a man or a woman is completely mastered by Jesus Christ, until all its thoughts and purposes are under his leadership, and the soul is so restored to its son-ship to God that man talks face to face with God as in the beginning, a subtle, silent force goes out from the personality which all feel and are in-fluenced by. So it is that the saintly man or woman carries an inspiration and continually sheds a benediction; so that his friends and all who meet him say, "His coming brings peace and joy into our homes; welcome his coming." Even Peter, the man of blundering sword and blunder-ing speech, was so restored through the tenderness of Jesus Christ that his shadow, as he passed by on deeds of mercy intent, had healing in it.

Surely the hope of a restoration like this is the noblest ambition that can inspire any human soul.

It is worth any struggle, however severe or however lengthy it may be. Repentance may be the work of a moment. Forgiveness is the work of an instant. But restoration takes time, and may be gradual. Let us not be discouraged with ourselves, if our faces are toward Christ, and with earnest hearts we are seeking to be like him. Somebody asked Paganini, "How long does it take to learn the violin?" And this was his grim answer: "Twelve hours a day for twenty-five years." It is simple. How long does it take to make a Christian? How long does it take to restore a soul into the likeness of Jesus Christ? Paul had been at it twenty-five years, during which time he had fought with beasts, had been stoned until he was left for dead, had been whipt at the whipping-post, had been imprisoned with his feet in the stocks, had been shipwrecked, all the while carrying his life in his hand, for Christ's sake, and tho all his world saw in him wondrous transformation, ever growing more wonderful and beautiful, yet Paul himself was compelled to voice his supreme longing in these words: "That I may know him." "What!" you exclaim, "Paul, don't you know him yet?" He shakes his gray head and says, "No, not as he is to be known. I know a little of him; I love him; his name is in my heart. I want to know him in the fellowship of his sufferings, that I may be made conformable unto his death; if by any means I might attain the resurrection of the dead." But Paul presses forward steadfastly with his eye on the prize, and day by day his soul is changed into the likeness of his Lord, until at last in Nero's dungeon they tell him that the ax is being whetted with which the tyrant is to take off his head. With a smile of ineffable peace he sits down to write his last letter to Timothy, his son in the Gospel, and the words leap from his pen: "I am now ready to be offered, and the time of my departure is at hand. I have fought a good fight, I have finished my course, I have kept the faith: Henceforth there is laid up for me a crown of righteousness, which the Lord, the righteous judge, shall give me at that day: And not to me only, but unto all them also that love his appearing."

FELLOWSHIP WITH CHRIST IN TEMPTA-TION AND TRIUMPH

FELLOWSHIP WITH CHRIST IN TEMPTATION AND TRIUMPH

"Then was Jesus led up of the Spirit into the wilderness to be tempted of the devil."—Matthew IV: 1.

THE temptation of Christ brings him close to us. It is the sure proof to us of his incarnation, of the reality of his human life. God cannot be tempted of evil, and it is only because Jesus became incarnate that he came within the possibility of temptation and was tempted in all points like as we are, yet was without sin. We must not make the mistake of imagining that there was anything unreal about this temptation of Christ. The reality of it is beyond question. His conflict in the wilderness, and his agony in the garden of Gethsemane, were not dramas acted on the stage of life by one who assumed our *rôle*, but facts in the real experience of Jesus.

We lose a vast deal of the blessing which the life of Christ can bring to us when we fail to appreciate the fact that the life of Christ was a typical human life, which shows what every human life may be in its essential essence, when completely given up to God and entirely obedient to the divine will. The possibility of the Christ-life, with all its beauty and glory, is in every human heart which is really surrendered to God. That is the hope of our humanity. Desperate, indeed, would be the outlook for the human race but for that inspiring truth. Christ conquered in temptation by the power and presence of God. We must share the same temptations with him, but if we go with Christ into our temptations, living in his spirit of obedience and faith, we, too, shall share his triumphs.

Let us study together some of the phases of temptations which, in the very nature of things, are certain to come to us, as they did to Christ.

I

As we study this story of the temptation of Christ we are imprest with the fact that one of the common temptations of our own lives is to *an unholy use of our power*. The tempter says to Jesus, "Command that these stones be made bread." There is in this an insinuation of lack of power. It is like the dare of one boy to another to jump off a precipice or to try to swim a swift current. As you read it you see the sneer in it. "If thou be the Son of God, command that these

stones be made bread." This temptation of Christ
was to use the power which God had given to
him to make himself comfortable—to take this
strange and wonderful power over nature by which
Jesus stilled the waves and saved poor men from
shipwreck, by which he fed the multitudes with the
little lad's loaves and fishes, by which he healed
lepers, and opened deaf ears and blind eyes; to
take this power to make bread to feed his hungry
stomach, and give material comfort to himself.
What a common temptation. But Christ gained
his great victory by refusing. He could go
hungry, but he would not prostitute his divine
power for selfish uses. Phillips Brooks, in his
great sermon on "The Food of Man," said: If
Christ had yielded, can we not picture him as he
descends the mountain? He has tasted bread.
His knees are strong. His famished body has
received new vigor; but what a weight is on his
soul! How he loathes the bread that he has
eaten! How beautiful seems the chance that he
has cast away! What a terrible defeat! And so we
are being tempted in the most commonplace experiences of life to satisfy our hunger for material comfort by bringing our souls to beggary. Christ conquered the world when he denied himself the lower
gratification that he might have the peace of God.

There are many men about us whom the world regards as successful who are really defeated. People looking on envy them, and call them successes, but from every high point of view they are failures. Here is a man who has made a success of everything he attempted in business. Everything his fingers touch seems to change to gold, and he congratulates himself, and his friends congratulate him, that he has conquered the world. But is it true? Has he conquered the world, or has the world conquered him? How has it been with his successes? Have they helped him to see God? Have they deepened his faith and his hope and his love? Have they made him a better citizen, a truer husband, a wiser, kinder father, a simpler, sweeter Christian? Or have his success and his conquest of material things hid God from him, and turned him into a mere money-bag or a safe-deposit vault? Such life victories are the worst defeats. They are like the story about the soldier, who shouted to his comrades through the darkness that he had caught a prisoner. His officer shouted back to him, "Bring him in." And the soldier answered, "But he won't come." "Then come yourself." And the answer was, "He won't let me." There are many men who count themselves victors who are the prisoners of their very successes. The world has chained them and clipt their wings, and made mere human moles of them.

II

We are tempted as Christ was to treat our faith in God as an experiment rather than what it is, an experience. Take the story as it is given us here, "The devil taketh him up into the holy city, and setteth him on a pinnacle of the temple, and saith unto him, If thou be the Son of God, cast thyself down." This is a temptation to presume upon God's mercy to us. Professor A. Morris Stewart, in his illuminating book on "The Temptation of Jesus," says that in this view we see our Lord tempted to indulge in a spectacular effect which he would have none of. His lowly, natural, human birth was the entrance God chose for Jesus to the world. His baptism, along with those who sought to "fulfil righteousness," was the entry he himself chose to his ministry. These have given us the Savior who is near to us, while close to God; round them gather countless reverent associations of faith's endearment. Compare with them the tempter's gaudy project! He would have annulled the holy simplicity, and would have led Jesus forth as a supernatural acrobat. Christ's reply, "Thou shalt not tempt the Lord thy God," is his distinct refusal to prostitute his divine power to a use which is merely theatrical. All the miracles of Jesus served a purpose of mercy, or were instructive as large object-lessons; and he never stooped to the performance of a merely impressive work of wonder.

There should be for us in this a warning against rashness and presumption and prideful display. Satan often appears as an angel of light to lead us out of the paths of duty and safety, under the pretext of trust in God. This wile may invite us to recklessness of any sort and to the abuse of divine care by trying to make it serve foolhardiness. We may rush into danger, praying for preservation, when our first need is pardon. Such snares beset religious life. Experience abounds in spiritual precipices, and we need to walk cautiously. We say that we are sons of God in Christ, and the tempter says, "Yes, and as sons ye may have much liberty; go where you will, do what you will, God will keep you from harm." Many souls have gone to ruin on that road. Instead of seeking circumstances of difficulty that grace and power may abound, we must avoid danger whenever we seek our Father's care; and his answer may come in successful avoidance rather than in rescue. If you are where God puts you, he will meet you where you are. And if he sends you or beckons you across a rough and discouraging way, you may go forward in faith to the place he has appointed, and he will guard your way. It is not for us to tempt God; but trust him and obey.

III

We are often tempted as Jesus was to make conquest without bearing the cross. As we follow this story of Christ in the wilderness, we read, "The devil taketh him up into an exceeding high mountain, and showeth him all the kingdoms of the world, and the glory of them; and saith unto him, All these things will I give thee, if thou wilt fall down and worship me." This was a temptation to the conquest of the world without suffering and without sacrifice. Mr. F. B. Meyer says that this seems to have been a continual temptation with Jesus. Again and again Satan returned to the onset, seeking to tempt Christ to evade the cross. Apparently all through his life that was the one great temptation suggested to him, because some months before he died on the cross, when Peter said in substance, answering Jesus, who had spoken of the death that was to come, "Spare thyself, spare thyself, do not do it, do not think of it," Christ turned sharply to him and said in substance, "That

is what Satan is saying to me all the time. Get
thee behind me, thou who speakest with his voice.
I will not listen to thee, for this temptation is the
one above all things that cuts me to the heart.''
At this time Christ was very successful. Crowds
flocked about him to hear him preach, and multitudes came to be healed of their sickness. And
looking at it from human standards it seemed a
pity to stop doing so much good and throw away
his life on the cross. So Satan seems to have kept
suggesting to him, ''Keep on doing as thou art
doing; go on teaching; go on healing; go on
blessing men.'' And that is the temptation that
is coming to men all the time now. Satan is
always trying to get us to save ourselves when
the duty of Christlike service is calling to us. He
comes to the young missionary with the same suggestion of the danger about risk in foreign lands.
He is forever appealing to us to take our ease and
save our strength when the call of human need is
stirring in our hearts and consciences. My brothers, Christ could not save the world except by way
of the cross. It cost the life-blood of the Son of
God to make our pardon possible, and we cannot
do the work which God has for us to do in the
world without the cross. We must not choose the
easy path. We must not take the broad road. We

must walk with Jesus. We must bear our burdens as he did. We must keep close to God in the path of duty if we would share his eternal triumph.

IV

Christ conquered and we must conquer by outspoken loyalty in our relation to God. Hear these ringing answers of Jesus, "Man shall not live by bread alone, but by every word that proceedeth out of the mouth of God." And again, "Thou shalt not tempt the Lord thy God." And yet again, "Get thee hence, Satan: for it is written, thou shalt worship the Lord thy God, and him only shalt thou serve." Christ shows us the way to victory by straight-out, open loyalty to God. The man who does that has no perplexity about what is right. Shakespeare tells us that when we begin to quibble and hesitate, "The native hue of resolution" may become "sicklied o'er with the pale cast of thought." But if we steadfastly take the straight line, "as the crow flies," in loyalty to God, we have no such trouble. Once recognize a duty clearly and plainly, and you may know that it will claim its due; it is not to be bullied, or wheedled, or cajoled; it cannot be adapted, or softened, or relaxed. There is no way out of duty but the way through it, and Christ has pointed the way for us.

See **how** Christ clings to the Scriptures. It is an example for us. I have heard of a humble but holy Christian who once went about his village repeating sentences of Scripture, and saying after each, ''Measure yourself against that.'' '' 'Honor thy father and thy mother;' measure yourself against that.'' '' 'Thou shalt not covet;' measure yourself against that.'' '' 'Blessed are the pure in heart;' measure yourself against that.'' Many of you remember David Copperfield, the wonderful creation of Charles Dickens. At an early age he became an outcast, and was thrown out upon the streets, and into the vortex of temptation, but in all his wanderings he carried in his mind a picture of his mother. It was with him as he trudged through the hop country. It was with him as he lay down to sleep at night. It was with him as he awoke in the morning. Before him at all times, as he walked through the dingy streets of London, and as he gazed at the strange people, was this picture of his mother. It kept him pure. My friends, let us firmly establish in our hearts a picture of Jesus Christ, and when temptations come to us from base companions or evil thoughts, the picture of Jesus dwelling there in our hearts will furnish us a standard against which we may measure ourselves and stand strong for God.

V

If we are faithful under temptation, as Jesus was, we, too, shall have the divine comfort which came to him. We read in the issue of this wonderful story of temptation, that after the devil left Jesus, "Angels came and ministered unto him," and later that he returned to his work in "the power of the Spirit." To the sincere and faithful Christian no trial shall be without its fellowship, and it is the loneliness of the fight that is the hardest to bear.

Donald Sage Mackay tells how he once crossed the Atlantic in winter. He had been shut down in the cabin for several days, but one afternoon, just before nightfall, when the wet, wintry sunset smeared the southern sky, he crawled up to the slippery, solitary decks. Around him was the great waste of waters, heaving like a fevered bosom, and already black with the shadows of approaching night. There was not a human being that he could see on deck, and he never felt more acutely the sense of absolute loneliness. On every hand were the tumbling, chasing, foam-streaked waves; underneath the creaking, laboring ship, but not a sign of life in the darkening day. Just as he was about to go down to the warmly-lighted cabin, suddenly upon the ragged edge of the horizon he saw the

flashing of a light. Nearer and nearer it drew, and
in a few minutes he picked out the lines of a gaily-
lighted ship upon its voyage. Signals were ex-
changed, and in its presence there came into that
wintry night a sense of fellowship which destroyed
the loneliness that a few moments before had been
so oppressive.

Now is it not like that when some great trial,
some fierce temptation, sweeps over the soul? Is
it not this sense of utter loneliness which is the
hardest thing to bear? There is a solitariness in
many great sorrows and trials which seems to cut
us off from the ordinary friendships of life. Again
and again men and women say to me, "No one can
realize how much I have to bear, or how much I
have come through." And it is that sense of loneliness that makes so many people desperate—makes
them lose faith and courage, lose all interest in life,
so that they are ready to turn anywhere, go anywhere, do anything but the right thing, so as to
forget the intolerable loneliness of their hearts.
And thus discouragement becomes so often the vestibule of temptation and defeat. But, my dear
friends, if we are faithful to God in resistance to
evil, and loyal as Christ was, his angels shall come
and minister to us. We shall not go alone through
the fiery furnace, but "the form of the fourth"

shall be with us. We shall not go alone into the
den of lions, for the angel that guarded Daniel
shall be with us. God's angels are still ministers
of mercy to his children, and consoled and comforted by them we shall, as did Christ, return to
our work "in the power of the Spirit."

Christ comes back from the wilderness of temptation with a new note of power, and goes forth to
his ministry with a strong, courageous joy we have
not noted before. So if we will bear our trials and
endure our temptations in like spirit, they will
enrich us with new beauty and strength.

"Perhaps you have heard of the method strange,
    Of violin makers in distant lands.
    Who by breaking and mending with skilful hands,
Make instruments having a wider range
        Than ever was possible for them, so long
        As they were new, unshattered and strong.

"Have you ever thought when the heart was sad,
    When the days seemed dark and the nights unending,
    That the broken heart by the Father's mending
Was made through sorrow a helper glad,
        Whose service should lighten more and more
        The worried one's burdens as never before?

"Then take this simple lesson to heart
    When sorrows crowd and you cannot sing,
    To the truth of the Father's goodness cling;
Believe that the sorrow is only a part
        Of the wondrous plan that gives through pain,
        The power to sing a more glad refrain."

THE THRONE OF LOVE

THE THRONE OF LOVE

"God is love."—I. John IV: 8.

THE old Greeks, whose civilization developed along the line of architecture, and painting, and the decorative arts, said, "God is beauty." The Romans, led by the Cæsars on a hundred battle-fields to victory, until they boasted that the Roman eagles never turned backward, said, "God is strength." The Jew, inheriting from Moses, the great law-giver, said, "God is law." It was not until John had laid his head upon the Savior's bosom and communed with Jesus Christ that any man was able to say with confident heart, "God is love."

I

Love is the link between man and God. If we had to make God love us, we should give up in despair. It is the fact that God does love us, even in our unworthiness, that gives us hope. Mark Guy Pearse says that one of his boys said to the other, in his hearing, and in a threatening tone, "You must be good, you know, or father won't love you." The father who was listening called the son who had spoken and said, gravely and tenderly, "Do you know what you have said? It is not true, my boy, not a bit true; you never made a bigger mistake, my son. I don't love you because you are good. There are lots of boys, but I love you, just because you are my own little son. If you grow up to become the worst man, I shall love you with a love that will break my heart, but I shall love you still. I don't love you only when you are good. I love you because I cannot help loving you. When you are good I love you with a love that makes me glad, and when you are not good I love you with a love that makes me sad." "Is that it?" said the boy. "Then I will be good, father." God's love is not conditioned. Nothing you can ever do, nothing you can ever feel or believe, nothing you can ever be, will make God love you more than he does. When we really get this into our hearts and stay our hearts on it, it banishes all real loneliness from the world for us. How tender are some of these illustrations used in the Bible to express this love of God. Take the one which says "As one whom his mother comforteth, so will I comfort you." How many of us who are getting on in life love to let our thoughts run back into the sweet old days of childhood, days that live only in our memories. And the center of every picture which memory and imagination paint of those rare old days is the loving figure of mother. We remember in times of trouble how natural it was to go to her for comfort, and how we never went in vain. And now since we are men and women, and have children of our own, and possibly grandchildren, still there are hard days, and trying times, and cruel disappointments and heartaches, which come to us sometimes, when we find ourselves wishing that we could go back to mother as we did when we were children, and put the aching head between her knees, and feel her caressing hand upon our hair, and her kiss on the hot cheek. But those days will never come back to us. The mother is separated from us by a thousand miles perhaps, or perchance by the river of death. Her comfort is only that which memory holds. But there is One who is the same yesterday, to-day, and forever; whose very essence is love, and whose comfort is like a mother's; and tho our sorrow and trouble may be our own fault, the mother-heart of God will not turn us away because of that.

I saw a story the other day of a little boy who said to his mother, "If I could say anything to God, I would say, 'God, love me when I am naughty.'" And is not this the cry of every one of our hearts, that God may love us when we are naughty? And this is what God does, for God is love. As Dr. Strayer says: The sun cannot shine upon the just, and not upon the unjust, for the sun is light, and it cannot help shining. God cannot love one and withhold his love from another, for God is love, and he cannot help loving. He loves us when we are good; and when we are bad he loves us still. He loves some with the love of pity, and others with the love of pride; he loves some with the love of compassion, and others with the love of complacency. But he loves us all, and will never cease from loving us, no matter how far we stray from him. If some are lost, it is because they will become so estranged from good, so loveless, that God's love no longer affects them; but it will still be theirs, and will follow them even down to doom.

II

The paragraph connected with out text brings out very clearly that it was God's love that gave Jesus to be our Savior. The life and death and resurrection of Jesus Christ are true manifestations of the love of God. John says: "He that loveth not, knoweth not God; for God is love. In this was manifested the love of God toward us, because that God sent his only begotten Son into the world, that we might live through him. Herein is love, not that we loved God, but that he loved us, and sent his Son to be the propitiation for our sins.'' We have here manifested the harmony between God's justice and God's love. In this scripture we see how love and righteousness are each vindicated and satisfied. God puts away the condemnation of our sins by laying it on his own dear Son. Christ, as pure and spotless as the Eternal Father himself, took our place: "He hath borne our griefs, and carried our sorrows: . . . He was wounded for our transgressions, he was bruised for our iniquities: the chastisement of our peace was upon him; and with his stripes we are healed. All we like sheep have gone astray: we have turned every one to his own way; and the Lord hath laid on him the iniquity of us all.'' As has been well said by another, the death of Jesus was more than the sacrifice of Christ: It was the sacrifice of God. The blood of Jesus, an apostle says, was the blood of God. "God commendeth his love toward us, in that, while we were yet sinners, Christ died for us.''

No gospel is worth preaching to sinning men and women that leaves out the stupendous fact that Jesus Christ died on the cross as a sacrifice for sin—a propitiation for us. Dr. Denney, the English scholar, tells this story: A friend of his was a convert of Mr. Moody's and has himself become very useful as an evangelist and greatly blest in the conversion of souls. This man is "a fishing-tackle maker," and an enthusiastic fisherman, and he told Dr. Denney once of losing his bait in a mysterious way without catching anything. The explanation was that by some accident or other the barb had been broken from the hook. And then the evangelist said, "This is exactly what happens when people preach the love of God to men, but leave out of their gospel the essential truth that it is Christ on the cross, the substitute for sinners, in whom that love is revealed. The condemnation of our sins in Christ upon the cross is the barb on the hook. If you leave that out of your gospel, I do not deny that the bait will be taken; men are pleased rather than not to think that God regards them with good-will: Your bait will be taken, but you will not catch men." There is no doubt that this is true. No preaching of Christ is "the power of God unto salvation" that leaves out the secret of that power. Theories of the atonement may change, and doubtless will change from age to age, and the water of life will alter its shape with the vessel that holds it, but the water itself never changes. And that river of life only flows from the cross of Christ.

III

The consciousness that God is love robs death of its power to frighten, and makes the "King of Shadows" our servant. It has been often said that death makes pagans of us all, and that in our views of death we come nearer reverting to heathenism than anywhere else. It is undoubtedly due to the frailty of human nature that the most pagan ceremony in Christian lands is a funeral, and many of our artists have only deepened this gloom by their pictures. But George Frederick Watts, who was himself a most devout Christian, did much to Christianize death by his art. Dr. Thomas Phillips, describing the works of Watts in the Tate Gallery in London, says that more than any other artist he has helped us to think of death as Jesus thought of it, as the sleep which the Father gives to his beloved. He speaks of death as the kindly nurse which puts the tired children to bed. In his "Court of Death" he represents it as a queenly figure sitting on a throne, to which the people of the world draw near. The old king comes, yielding up his crown, as if he were glad to get rid of what had caused him vexation and sorrow. The strong soldier lays down his sword in the prime of his days, and surrenders his life in the glory of his strength. The suffering cripple draws near for relief, and an old matron waits for rest with an appealing look for Death to take her. An invalid places her head wearily to rest on the knee of Death, and a little child plays unconsciously with the folds of her dress, dying without knowing it, dying almost in play. Behind stand the figures of Silence and Mystery, watching the threshold of the unknown and the unseen. In the lap of Death there is a little child, to suggest that death itself is but a birth to the larger life beyond. In the background of the picture there is the suggestion of the dawn, and it is a significant fact that, as the years rolled on and the painter perfected his picture, he made the background brighter and brighter. We all know something about the ambition of wealthy and famous people to be presented at court in lands where there is a king or a queen. That was Watts' idea of death—presentation at court.

The same artist has another picture called "Death and Love." Death is represented as a fine, graceful, womanly figure entering into a house whose door is embowered with roses, the emblems of happiness and youthfulness and joy. On the doorstep is the figure of Cupid, the young god of love, endeavoring with unavailing agony to push Death away. His wings are wounded in the effort, and the fair roses fall withered at the touch of

Death. Death herself goes forward with bowed head, as if sorry for her work, and with outstretched arms, as if not to be averted. As you look at the figure you say: How beautiful, and yet what a stern beauty! How gentle, and yet what an inexorable gentleness! The back of Death is illumined by a light that comes from beyond, and is transfigured by the light that comes from eternity. The painter seems to desire to suggest that death looked at from behind is often beautiful with a hallowed light.

Watts contradicts the popular view of death in another respect. We are accustomed to think that death is most cruel when it snatches away the life of a little child, or smites down a youth in the blossom of his days; but Watts pictures this as the most beautiful aspect of death. In one of his paintings he represents it as "Death Crowning Innocence." Death is represented as a gentle mother encircling the brow of a young child with ineffable tenderness. The artist's thought is that to a child death means play and coronation.

Now all these pictures are supremely Christian. They are simply putting on the canvas the wonderful revelation of our text that "God is love." When we yield our hearts to him, and are cleansed from our sins through Jesus Christ, and live in the consciousness of God's love, death ceases to be an enemy.

IV

As God is love, it naturally follows that it is our love, and our love only, which can give value to our service to God. Some people have thought that there was an incongruity between "the fear of God," that has been called the master-phrase of the Old Testament, and "God is love," the dominant phrase of the New Testament. But the fear of God is perfectly in harmony with the love of God. The young man who resists temptation to evil, not because he is afraid of being found out, but because he reverences the loving prayers of his distant mother, acts in the fear of his mother; and that is the best analogy one can possibly have of the fear of God which is taught in the Bible. Lord Roberts, the famous English general, speaking to a company of boys in London, recently, said: "You will find it very helpful in your struggle if you can bring home to yourselves the absolute truth of two great sayings, 'Thou God seest me' and 'God is love.' If you can realize that in all times and in all places you are ever in the sight of God who loves you, it will help you to fight against doing before him what you would be ashamed to do in the sight of those you love here on earth."

There is a very precious comfort in the assurance that if we bring the best service we can to God, however humble it may seem, in the light of God's love it will be glorified. There is a simple old Eastern legend which very beautifully illustrates this thought. This Oriental legend tells of a king who, on his birthday, sat on his throne among his subjects, while his subjects brought their presents to him, to show how much they loved him. The merchant brought his pearls from the sea, and the man who had great possessions brought tithes of his possessions and laid them at his feet. The rich came to bring him their wealth, and the scholar came and brought the first-fruits of his learning. And all made their tribute-offering to the king. But there was one poor woman who had nothing in the world to give. All she had was but a farthing, and she said: "I cannot take him that." Then she thought, "Yes, I will take him that, for he is wise. He will not think I only love him a farthing's worth." So she went to the king, sitting on his throne, and he held out his hand, and she dropt her farthing in, and turned her head away and went on. But she had not gone far before she felt a hand on her shoulder; and she saw it was the king who held out his hand. There was a gold coin in it, and he said, "You gave me this?"

"No," she said, "I did not give you that; I have not seen one of those for ever so long." "Oh," he said, "but you did; I have held it in my hand ever since." "No," she answered, "I did not give you that." "Well, take it in your hand." And she took it in her hand, and it was nothing but a farthing. And she put it in the king's hand, and it was a gold coin again!

That old legend is full of beautiful meaning as illustrating our theme. Our lives sometimes seem very valueless when we keep them for ourselves selfishly; but when we put them in the King's hand and see what he does with them, and how they are transfigured and transformed, we are amazed at what we behold. Let us put ourselves completely in the hand of God. If we will do that, he will multiply us a hundredfold. Let us not hold back that which it is within our power to give to carry the Gospel to the heathen, or lift the burden from the shoulders of God's poor. Tho it seems little in our hands, if with loving purpose we put it in the hands of God it shall be multiplied under his touch of infinite love. The word of sympathy it is our chance to speak, tho it be as humble as the "cup of cold water" that Jesus blesses, becomes a great thing when the loving countenance of God shines upon it.

And there must be some of you here who need another phase of this message. You have held yourself back from God's guidance. You have gone your own way, and, it may be, hardened your heart against God's love. My friend, no one can make so much out of you as God. Give yourself to him. Open your heart to his love, and a nobler character, a holier personality, a diviner career shall open to you than any that you have ever dreamed of. Some poet making this consecration has sung what should inspire your heart:

> "I launch my bark upon thy sea,
>   Dear Lord of all,
> Knowing thou wilt be near to me
>   Whate'er befall,
> And that thro' all life's mystery
>   Naught can appal.
>
> "I launch my bark upon thy sea,
>   Most blessed Lord,
> For thine own voice has called to me,
>   And I have heard
> Thy love-song sung so pleadingly
>   My soul has stirred.
>
> "I launch my bark upon thy sea,
>   And now away!
> My hopes and help are all from thee;
>   And rising day
> Doth scatter myriad lights so free
>   That gem the spray.

"My bark *is* launched upon thy sea!
　　Sea, bark—both thine!
Blow with thy breeze, where'er it be
　　Across the brine:
This is my cry—'Send me, send me,
　　O Love Divine.'"

THE INDWELLING CHRIST

THE INDWELLING CHRIST

"Christ in you, the hope of glory."—Colossians I: 27.

SPURGEON says that when Christ once enters into a soul, by degrees he occupies the whole of it. And he illustrates it with the legend of a man whose garden produced nothing but weeds, till at last he met with a strange foreign flower of singular vitality. The story is that he sowed a handful of this seed in his overgrown garden, and left it to work its own sweet way. He slept and rose, and knew not how the seed was growing, till one day he opened the gate and saw a sight which much astonished him. He knew that the seed would produce a dainty flower, and he looked for it; but he had little dreamed that the plant would cover the whole garden. But so it was: the flower had exterminated every weed, till as he looked, from one end to the other, from wall to wall, he could see nothing but the fair colors of that rare plant and smell nothing but its delicious perfume. Christ is that plant of renown. If he be sown in the soil of your soul, he will gradually eat out the roots of all ill weeds and poisonous plants, till over all your

445

nature there shall be Christ in you, the hope of glory.

I

Christ in us awakens hope of a glorious personality. When a man is conscious that he has opened his heart to the coming of Christ, and that his Savior is influencing his life, it enlarges his idea of his own possibilities. Dr. Jowett says that once an old villager who lived in a little hamlet situated on a high hill said to him concerning the air of his town: "Ay, sir, it's a fine air is this westerly breeze; I like to think of it as having traveled from the distant fields of the Atlantic!" And so to the apostle Paul, with the quickening wind of redemption blowing about him, in vitalizing, strengthening influence, it seemed to him to have had its birth in the distant fields of eternity! To Paul's thinking, redemption was no after-thought, no patched-up expedient to meet an unforeseen emergency. Paul saw in it "The eternal purpose which he purposed in Christ Jesus our Lord." Christ was dwelling in him, so that he could say that it was no more Paul that was living, but Christ living within him. This is the source of Paul's triumphant optimism which breathes through all his writings. To Paul's idea human life was glorified by this wonderful presence of Jesus in the heart. Recall some of his sentences which indicate this feeling. Listen to him as he says: "The unsearchable riches of Christ;" "Riches in glory in Christ Jesus;" "The riches of his goodness and forbearance and long suffering." There is the atmosphere of the spiritual millionaire glowing in such utterances. This presence of Jesus in the heart gave Paul a consciousness of freedom from the guilt and power of sin. Hear him as he says, "But now being made free from sin, and become servants to God;" again "But now in Christ Jesus ye that once were far off are made nigh in the blood of Christ." Again ' ear him say, "There is therefore now no condemnation to them that are in Christ Jesus." These reveal to us what a wonderful thing this new Christian life was to Paul. For him a new day had dawned, and the birds began to sing, and the flowers to bloom, and a sunny optimism took possession of his heart. We have only to give Christ the right of way in our hearts, as Paul did in his, to put to work all those dynamic spiritual forces of which Paul is always talking in his letters. You take up these letters of Paul to the different churches, and you will read of the wonderful spiritual ministries at work in hearts surrendered to Christ: "The Holy Spirit worketh!" "Grace worketh!" "Faith worketh!"

"Love worketh!" "Hope worketh!" "Prayer worketh!" Yes, and other things that we are likely to count as our enemies are drafted into our service when we are really Christ's. Hear Paul as he speaks of them: "Tribulation worketh." "This light affliction worketh." "Godly sorrow worketh." Paul sees everything working together for good to them that love God. But we must not forget that the source of all this wonderful spiritual chemistry which brings everything to our aid comes from the dominance of Jesus Christ in us. I have seen some apt lines that go back through the centuries and are attributed to St. Patrick, the old Irish patron saint, whether rightly or not I do not know, but they express what ought to be the inmost sentiment of the Christian heart in the daily journey through life:

"Christ with me, Christ before me,
  Christ behind me, Christ within me,
  Christ beneath me, Christ above me,
  Christ at my right, Christ at my left,
  Christ in the fort,
  Christ in the chariot seat,
  Christ in the poop,
  Christ : the heart of every man who thinks of me,
  Christ in the mouth of every man who speaks to me,
  Christ in every eye that sees me,
  Christ in every ear that hears me."

II

Christ in us assures glorious service on our part. Christianity lacks the credentials of genuineness when faith and joy do not issue into service. We are the disciples of Him who went about doing good. I have seen this legend, which is told in the Greek Church. It is related of two of its favorite saints, St. Cassianus and St. Nicholas. Cassianus, in beautiful robes, entered heaven. "What hast thou seen on earth, Cassianus?" asked the Lord. "I saw," he answered, "a peasant floundering with his wagon in the marsh." "Didst thou help him?" "No." "Why not?" "I was coming before thee," said St. Cassianus, "and I was afraid of soiling my white robes." Just then St. Nicholas entered heaven, all covered with mud and mire. "Why so stained and so soiled, St. Nicholas?" said the Lord. "I saw a peasant floundering in the marsh," said St. Nicholas, "and I put my shoulder to the wheel and helped him out." "Blest art thou," answered the Lord. "Thou didst well; thou didst better than St. Cassianus." And the Lord blest St. Nicholas with a fourfold blessing.

The glory of Christian service, that which gives it its dignity, its romance, and its supreme beauty, is that we do it out of love for Christ and a consciousness that we are sharing with him. I have

been reading recently an address by Dr. Horton,
the English preacher, on that wonderful man,
Francis of Assisi.   Under Francis there grew up a
wonderful revival of real Christianity.   To him
Christ meant love, and love meant self-giving.   To
have attained to Christ meant to have found out
that life, to be true life, consists in love of others.
If God so love the world, if God has made the
world, and is lavishing his love upon it, then the
Christian whose life is hid with Christ in God
must let his heart go out in love and sacrifice to
all creation.   Francis simply let the Christ-life
that was in him energize.   He allowed it to come
out, and that meant love.   As he moved about it
was like some magic influence producing flowers
and sunshine in a gloomy desert.   The weary world
stretched itself and woke to fresh life in the morning breeze of his breath of love and hope.   Men
felt that God was still alive and at work; that the
Lord Jesus was at hand;   that the Spirit was
brooding yet. They were not forgotten; not alone;
they were cared for.   Love was still an active force
that could heal, and tend, and succor.   Francis
showed men that he believed in the possibility of
their complete recovery and restoration into the
image of God.   He never despaired of any, or despised any.   No action of love was too small to be

worth doing, and worth doing well. He aimed at creating in others a sense of their own dignity as children of God, and their own power as members of the body of Christ. When we read of such a life we are likely to lose the great benefit that we might receive from it by a feeling that it is the life of a genius, impossible to ordinary mortals; but we cheat ourselves in that way. There is no genius here save the genius of complete obedience to God and perfect welcome to Jesus Christ. The secret of Francis's power was in this, that he was in love with Jesus Christ, and his love infected other men with love of Jesus, too. As we study such a life it ought to make us ashamed of the poor result of religion in our lives; it should send us back to the Gospel to catch once more the Spirit of the Lord. Oh, the world needs so much men and women of this type, not here and there a genius, but multitudes of them who shall be the incarnation of Him who went about doing good. Such a personality is sustained by bread from heaven. Matthew Arnold once, in the heat of the summer, met a minister whom he knew in the East London slums, and was so imprest with the tremendous burdens the man carried, and the great joy and comfort he saw in his face, that he went away and wrote these verses:

" 'Twas August, and the fierce sun overhead
    Smote on the squalid streets of Bethnal-green,
    And the pale weaver, through his windows seen
    In Spitalfields, look'd thrice dispirited.

"I met a preacher there I knew, and said:
    'Ill and o'erworked, how fare you in this scene?'
    'Bravely,' said he; 'for I of late have been
    Much cheer'd with thoughts of Christ—*the living Bread.*'

"O human soul! as long as thou canst so
    Set up a mail of everlasting light,
    Above the howling senses' ebb and flow,

"To cheer thee, and to right thee if thou roam,
    Not with lost toil thou laborest through the night,
    Thou mak'st the heaven thou hop'st indeed thy home."

You never hear of men who are giving themselves for others like that asking whether life is
worth living or not. You never hear of such people
committing suicide. No, indeed; it is the bored
sensualist; it is the man with jaded passions; it is
the man given over to selfishness, who loses the
zest and the enthusiasm of living. It is the life of
service, glorified by the fellowship of Christ, that
is the most glorious and virile life in the world.

III

Christ in us insures true happiness. Happiness
is the prize toward which millions of men and
women turn their faces. It is one of the things

that cannot be bought for gold. If it were to be had in the market what a millionaire's auction there would be over it in our day. But great wealth is no security for happiness. Stephen Girard, who gathered together immense wealth, wrote toward the end of his life to a friend: "I toil like a galley slave, and often I cannot sleep at night. I set no value upon fortune. My chiefest emotion is simply to work." Nathan Rothschild, one of the richest men who has ever lived on the earth, acknowledged the perfect failure of his life so far as happiness was concerned. When some one was speaking about his palatial home and its marvelous adornment, as making him happy, he sneered with great bitterness, "Happy! me happy?" It takes something more than money, or earthly goods of any sort to make men happy. There is a story of a man who so loved his gold that he hid it in a hole in the earth, and used to uncover the hole, take out the gold, and run it through his fingers, and feel that there, indeed, was life, and, there indeed, was happiness, and yet he had no rest. One day chance called him out, and when he came back his hoard of gold was gone, and in its place there lay a little child. Unwelcome was the exchange. But the trustful eyes of the child looked into the eyes of the man, gained on him, led him back from his sordid love of gold to be a gentle lover of men—trusted, revered, and loved. So great was the power of the child's love that it made a miserly man a gracious son of humanity, and in doing so awoke the soul to far nobler happiness.

Sylvester Horne recalls the famous lines in Omar Khayyam:—

> "A book of verses underneath the bough,
> A jug of wine, a loaf of bread—and thou
> Beside me singing in the wilderness,
> Oh! wilderness were Paradise enow,—"

and declares that that is the philosophy of the epicure—an attractive materialism at the most. But when we think of Christ, and his coming into our human hearts and lives, bringing heaven's love and fellowship down to earth's scenes, there is a thought in these lines of Khayyam that thrills through one with a suggestion very far from the imagination of the Persian:

> "Thou
> Beside me, singing in the wilderness,
> Oh! wilderness were paradise enow."

Christ beside me singing his psalm of life: "Be of good cheer, I have overcome. Ye believe in God, believe also in me. He that believeth in me hath everlasting life. He that cometh unto me shall never hunger. Come unto me, and I will give you rest. These things have I spoken unto you that your joy may be full. In the world ye shall have tribulation, but be of good cheer, I have overcome the world." It is when Christ is talking to us by the way, in words like that, that our burning hearts are ready to exclaim to him who is the Lover of our souls:

"O thou
Beside me, singing in the wilderness,
Oh! wilderness were Paradise enow."

IV

Christ in us gives hope of glory in heaven. David asks, "Who shall ascend into the hill of the Lord? or who shall stand in his holy place?" And the answer comes back clear and plain, "He that hath clean hands and pure heart; who hath not lifted up his soul unto vanity, nor sworn deceitfully. He shall receive the blessing from the Lord, and righteousness from the God of his salvation. This is the generation of them that seek him, that seek thy face, O Jacob." That is very straightforward and plain direction. If we are to go up the hill to heaven it is our own life that is the first matter to be taken into hand. Our dealings with men, are they clean? Are they straight? Will they bear the light? Could we bring them here on Sunday morning and justify them in God's house? Our business—is it done honestly, without deceit? Is there no advantage taken by deceiving our fellows? It is that kind of a man to whom the door is open. It is of no use to put on a bold front and go up the hill in train with Christ's followers unless the Master himself dwells in our hearts, purifying our motives, cleansing our hands from every evil thing. But when Jesus dwells in us, giving to our words and actions the beauty and charm of his own goodness and unselfishness, then the gates of heaven open, and we have no doubt of the glory that is to be. To such a man life's trials are only steps by which he climbs upward.

Theodore Cuyler tells how he once ascended Mount Washington by the old trail over the slippery rocks. A weary, disappointed company they were when they reached the cabin on the summit, and found it shut in by the clouds. But toward evening a mighty wind swept away the banks of mist, the body of the blue heavens stood out in its clearness, and before them was revealed the magnificent landscape, stretching away to the Atlantic Ocean. So faith's stairways are often over steep and slippery rocks; often through blinding storms; but if Christ dwell in the heart, God never loses his hold on us, and in due time he brings us out into the clear shining after rain. To such a career

the growing years only bring nearer the triumph,
the supreme victory of our lives.

"They call it 'going down the hill,'
 When we are growing old,
 And speak with mournful accents
 When our tale is nearly told.

"But it is not 'going down,'
 'Tis climbing high and higher,
 Until we almost see the mountain
 That our souls desire.

"For, if the natural eye grows dim,
 It is but dim to earth;
 While the eye of faith grows keener
 To discern the Savior's worth."

THE CHRISTIAN'S
DELIVERANCE FROM SIN

THE CHRISTIAN'S
DELIVERANCE FROM SIN

"O wretched man that I am! Who shall deliver me from the body of this death? I thank God through Jesus Christ our Lord."—Romans VII: 24, 25.

I

SIN is one of the terrible, vital facts in human life. No man can slumber long to the awful truth that he must deal with this question of sin. The libraries of the world are full of discussions of the nature of sin. The poets, and the philosophers, as well as the teachers, have often pondered over it. Dr. Jowett, the famous English preacher, refers to Matthew Arnold's assertion that sin is not a monster, but an infirmity. But Jowett says that when he takes Matthew Arnold's statement into his own soul, into his own secret consciousness, it will not stand the test. If sin were only an infirmity, there would be no sense of guilt or burdensome shame. If your eyes have an infirmity, you have no sense of responsibility for it; but when you sin, you are conscious of more than infirmity. When we seek to label our sin as infirmity, our souls re-

ject the term in a consuming sense of their own
shame.

Edgar Allan Poe, whose own brilliant, but un-
controlled and undisciplined, personality had surrendered the citadel of the heart to troops of evil
passions, writes of sin as tho it were an evil spirit
that overruns and captures the soul, something
that man cannot help. In "The Haunted Palace"
he voices this thought with brilliant phrase:

> "In the greenest of our valleys
>   By good angels tenanted,
> Once a fair and stately palace—
>   Radiant palace—reared its head.
> In the monarch Thought's dominion—
>   It stood there!
> Never seraph spread a pinion
>   Over fabric half so fair!
>
> "Banners yellow, glorious, golden,
>   On its roof did float and flow,
> (This—all this—was in the olden
>   Time, long ago),
> And every gentle air that dallied,
>   In that sweet day,
> Along the ramparts plumed and pallid,
>   A winged odor went away.
>
> "Wanderers in that happy valley,
>   Through two luminous windows, saw
> Spirits moving musically,
>   To a lute's well-tuned law,
> Round about a throne where, sitting
>   (Prophyrogene!)

In state his glory well befitting,
 The ruler of the realm was seen.

"And all with pearl and ruby glowing
 Was the fair palace door,
Through which came flowing, flowing, flowing,
 And sparkling evermore,
A troop of Echoes, whose sweet duty
 Was but to sing,
In voices of surpassing beauty,
 The wit and wisdom of their king.

"But evil things, in robes of sorrow,
 Assailed the monarch's high estate.
(Ah, let us mourn!—for never morrow
 Shall dawn upon him desolate!)
And round about his home the glory
 That blushed and bloomed,
Is but a dim-remembered story
 Of the old-time entombed.

"And travelers, now, within that valley,
 Through the red-litten windows see
Vast forms, that move fantastically
 To a discordant melody,
While, like a ghastly rapid river,
 Through the pale door
A hideous throng rush out forever
 And laugh—but smile no more."

Beautiful and pathetic as are these lines, we
know in our own consciousness that the "evil
things, in robes of sorrow" which "assailed the
monarch's high estate," never could have captured
it if there had not been treachery within the castle.
It was because the monarch yielded to the invasion

that he was overthrown, and his fair estate ravished. It is impossible that we can be despoiled by sin unless our own souls surrender to it. There is no more popular verse in the Bible than one of the last wonderful declarations of the New Testament which says: "Whosoever will may come!" One of our earnest evangelists recently said that he was afraid we had emphasized the word "Whosoever" more than we had emphasized the word "*will*," and yet salvation depends upon the will. And he goes on to declare that no man is ever beaten by sin without being a party to it. Take the poem quoted a moment ago. The brilliant Poe was a victim of strong drink. His life was utterly enslaved and ruined by drunkenness. But he was a party to it. That vicious habit never could have handcuffed him without his consent. If passion holds you in its grip, and leaves you bankrupt of purity and strength; if you are crippled and paralyzed by sin, it is because you have consented to it. The devil said to Jesus when he was on the pinnacle of the temple, "Cast thyself down." Satan had no power to cast Jesus down. He could not be overthrown unless he consented, and Christ refused to consent, and came off victorious. So the devil comes to you and tempts you to cast yourself down, because he has no power to cast you down.

The whole thing rests in our own souls. The power of choice, of decision, is there.

II

Our text suggests to us that there is no possible escape from the sorrow and misery and sense of defilement which sin brings into the heart save by deliverance from sin itself. Punishment for sin is not an arbitrary thing. Sin carries the necessity for punishment within itself. Sin is rebellion against God, and separates from God. Jowett, to whose comment on the nature of sin I referred a moment ago, recalls that saying of the Scripture: "Your sins have separated between you and your God," and goes on to emphasize the suggestion that sin is a kind of knife, which gets into the joint, and pries the limb asunder. You were intended to live and move and have your being in God, but your sins have disjointed you. But sin is not the separation; the separation is the consequence of the sin. When I sin, God is not away. I am painfully conscious that he is near. "I hear his voice, and even while I hear I revolt. I have sinned when God's voice was calling to me like an alarm bell in the dead of night. My sin is not an ignorant quest of God. My sin is an illumined and fully conscious departure from God. He is there. I

turn my back upon him.'' And no man in that
condition is happy. He is forever haunted, and
the specter of his sin is liable at any moment to
rise before him and condemn him.

There is a Buddhist story which tells of a man
who had lived wickedly and who became very ill
and nigh unto death. In the fever he had a dream,
and in this dream he was conducted through the
under-world to the hall of justice in which the
judges sat in curtained alcoves. He came opposite his judge, and was told to write his mis-
deeds upon a slate provided for that purpose.
Sentence was then passed that he should be thrice
struck by lightning for his sins. The curtain was
then drawn back, and he faced his judge, to find
there seated the very image of himself, and he
realized that he had pronounced the verdict. He
had unconsciously judged himself. And this is
going on all the while. ''Be sure your sin will
find you out,'' some people seem to think
means that you are always in danger of being
found out. But that is a very small thing compared to what it really does mean, that your sin
is a thing so personal to yourself that you can never
escape it. There is another passage which says,
''He that sinneth against me wrongeth his own
soul.'' The poet writes truly:

"Tho no mortal e'er accused you,
Tho no witness e'er confused you,
Tho the darkness came and fell
Over even deeds of hell;

"Tho no sign nor any token
Spake of one commandment broken,
Tho the world should praise and bless
And love add the fond caress;

"Still your secret sin would find you,
Pass before your eyes to blind you,
Burns your heart with hidden shame,
Scar your cheek with guilty flame.

"Sin was never sinned in vain,
It could always count its slain;
You yourself must witness be
To your own soul's treachery."

III

If we had to stop there, this would be a sad and
hopeless sermon which no man would have a right
to preach. But, thank God, there is deliverance.
This chapter in Romans is a sad, dirge-like story
clear through till we get past the first verse in the
text, where Paul reaches the climax of his anguish
in the exclamation, "O wretched man that I am!
Who shall deliver me from the body of this death?"
But how different is the next verse: "I thank
God through Jesus Christ our Lord." Deliverance
comes through Jesus Christ. How does it come?

It comes through complete surrender on the part of the sinner—a surrender of his sin, a giving it up. And on the part of Jesus Christ a giving up of his divine nature to strengthen and bless his weak and suffering brother. But there can be no salvation without surrender to God through Jesus Christ.

That most successful evangelist known as "Gipsy Smith" told recently how he was holding a series of meetings on one occasion in England when he received a letter asking for prayer, and telling a story of sorrow and tears. There was no name attached. The letter, however, awakened his interest so much that he waited for half an hour after the close of the meeting the next night, hoping the writer would make himself known, but he did not. On the Sunday, however, he came to the church and talked with the evangelist in a private room. He was a fine-looking man. He said, "I am the writer of that letter; I am the father of nine children, all of whom are living. My wife is very delicate. I have held a position of trust for thirty years, and am looked upon as a respectable citizen. I am a fraud." He then went on to relate that twenty-five years before he was a gambler, and stole five hundred dollars from his employer, and so covered it up in his books that the theft was never known. He had never been able to get the five hundred dollars to repay it, but had never gambled again, and continued: "You don't know the hell I have been carrying about ever since. Three times I have presented myself to a church for membership, for I wanted to be a good man, but when I got to the church I dared not enter. It seemed as if that five hundred dollars stood up and said, 'You dare not enter. The sheep will bleat, the oxen will low, and will be heard.' The only way to silence them is death. In your sermon you said 'Slay utterly.'"

"Yes."

"That means confession?"

"It does."

"That may mean exposure?"

"Yes."

"It may mean prison?"

"Yes, it may."

He then spoke of his wife and children, and Mr. Smith said: "Don't you see, you don't sin alone. It is not what you do for yourself only. It is what you do for other people, too."

He said, "See what it means for my wife and children? Oh, have pity!"

"Stop a minute," said the evangelist. "The sin was not against your wife. First of all, it was

against God, and you have got to put God in his
right place. What are you going to do with him
over this business? You will have to get right with
God. You have to set everybody else aside, and
begin with God, prison or no prison, exposure or
no exposure, disgrace or no disgrace. God, God
first.''

The broken man trembled like a leaf in the
storm, and then with the tears streaming down his
face he cried, ''Thou God of my mother, have
mercy on me!''

The evangelist dropt on his knees at his side
and put his arms about him and tried to help him
to pray.

At last he got his feet on the Rock and said,
''Prison or no prison, Christ for me.''

Presently he got up from his knees, and Mr.
Smith inquired, ''Have you the same employer
you had thirty years ago?''

''Yes,'' he said.

''Does he still go to business?''

''Yes, every morning.''

''Then,'' said Gipsy Smith, ''ask for an interview to-morrow morning, and I will pray for you.
He has kept you for thirty years, and you have
been a valuable servant. Tell him all your story—
how you gambled, how you got into the tight fix;

tell him everything; and then say, 'Sir, if you can have pity on my wife and children, take so much off my salary each week; but if you cannot, then send me to jail. God stands for the man who stands for the right.'"

The next morning, from nine to eleven o'clock, the time when the interview was to take place, Smith shut himself up to pray for that man and his employer. It seemed as if God was listening and was going to answer. At five o'clock in the afternoon he was looking for the man and saw him coming up the street looking for the number of the house. The evangelist could not wait, but rushed to the door and called him. He stumbled up the steps and threw his arms around the preacher's neck and they stood and wept together, and when they got inside he said, "God is good. I told my story. My master listened. He wept with me, and when I had told him all he crossed the office floor and got hold of my hand—the hand that did the deed—and said, 'Herbert, from to-day you are my friend. I will not only forgive you, but from this hour I will raise your salary.'"

Now that man was saved from his sin, as every man must be saved, through complete and perfect surrender to God through Jesus Christ. I am sure that in this great company there must be many who need to hear this heart-searching message. The stain of sin is upon you. The fever of it is in your blood. This old battle which Paul tells about so clearly is one you know. This body of death which often disgusts you and humiliates you and shames you is nevertheless chained to your very self. My friend, there is only one deliverance, and that is in Jesus Christ our Savior. It is only of Jesus that it can be written,—

> "He breaks the power of canceled sin,
>   He sets the prisoner free."

And, thank God, there are many here who like Paul have felt that they were the chief of sinners, but, having been redeemed from their sins through the blood of Christ, are ready with joyous hearts to complete the hymn with the lines that follow,—

> "His blood can make the foulest clean;
>   His blood availed for me."

THE VOICE OF THE
GOOD SHEPHERD

THE VOICE OF THE GOOD SHEPHERD

"My sheep hear my voice."—John X: 27.

THE most fascinating and charming voice in all history is the voice of Jesus Christ. On one occasion a number of men, hard-headed, stern officers of the law, who had been sent to arrest Jesus, came back without him, not having even spoken to him concerning their mission, and they made as their excuse, "Never man spake like this man." They could not withstand the charm of his voice and his message. He came to Jericho and looked into the eyes of a dishonest customs officer, and spoke to him with cheerful, masterful tone, "Come, Zacchæus, this day I must abide at thy house." And his voice stirred the man of greed to the depths of his hungry soul, and transformed him into a good man and generous. At his voice the raging waters were quieted, the wind ceased, and whitecaps faded into calm. His voice charmed Mary Magdalene from her sins, and made her immortal in her new life of love and sweet devotion to her Master. His voice tamed the wild man of Gadara—banished the devils

from his soul—clothed him in his right mind, and
sent him forth an obedient minister to proclaim the
gospel of the Prince of Peace. At the sound of his
voice the fishermen deserted their nets and their
boats, and followed him through poverty and hard-
ship and abuse and persecution, and counted it all
joy to be martyrs in loyalty to his name. At the
sound of his voice blind Bartimæus shook off his
blindness and his beggary together and became a
new man in Christ Jesus. Saul listened to that
voice on the way to Damascus, and lost his bigotry
and his hatred, became a man of prayer, and was
transformed into Paul, the great missionary to the
Gentiles. That voice has not lost its power or its
charm. Charles Wesley sings:

> "He speaks, and, listening to his voice,
>   New life the dead receive;
> The mournful, broken hearts rejoice;
>   The humble poor believe.
>
> "Hear him, ye deaf; his praise, ye dumb,
>   Your loosened tongues employ;
> Ye blind, behold your Savior come;
>   And leap, ye lame, for joy."

I

The fact that the Good Shepherd is still living
and speaking to the souls of men is the center and
the glory of Christianity. Often we are so ab-

sorbed in worldly things, so deafened by the noise
of the earth, so blinded by the dust and turmoil
of the street, that we do not clearly see or hear
him who speaks to us. If we fail to listen to him
as the supreme voice, all our conceptions of living
go astray. He stands in the midst of the business
world, where we are straining for success in our
career, and says to us: "Blest are the poor in
spirit: for theirs is the kingdom of heaven. Blest
are they that mourn; for they shall be comforted.
Blest are the meek: for they shall inherit the
earth. Blest are they which do hunger and thirst
after righteousness: for they shall be filled. Blest
are the merciful: for they shall obtain mercy.
Blest are the pure in heart: for they shall see
God. Blest are the peacemakers: for they shall
be called the children of God. Blest are ye, when
men shall revile you, and persecute you, and shall
say all manner of evil against you falsely, for my
sake. Rejoice, and be exceeding glad: for great is
your reward in heaven." Are we listening to this
voice and heeding it? Or are we so given up to
worldliness that the beatitudes by which we live
sound an altogether different note? Are these the
beatitudes that stand above the desk in your office,
or your bank, or your store, or hang in your home,
the message of which is treasured in your heart?

Or are they something like this?—"Blest are the proud-spirited: for theirs is the kingdom of this world. Blest are the greedy, and the shrewd, and the cunning: for they shall get the earth. Blest are the bold, and the unscrupulous, and the daring: for they shall sit in the seats of the mighty. Blest are ye when all men shall speak well of you, and ye shall be popular and famous on every hand." My friends, which class of these beatitudes is really yours? Let us search our own hearts! Let us in the sanctuary of God be honest with ourselves. In our everyday thinking and living and doing are we listening to the voice of the Good Shepherd?

The late Joseph Parker, of London, once preached a significant sermon on "The Religion of Wakefulness." His theme was taken from Luke's description of the transfiguration of Christ, which tells how the disciples, overcome by the tremendous occasion, had fallen asleep, but on waking saw his glory and heard the voice from heaven. The Revised Version reads, "When they were fully awake they saw his glory." Dr. Parker lays the emphasis on the necessity for Christians to be wide awake to the great facts of the spiritual life. This is an alert age. Never has there been an age so intellectually awake—awake to scientific investigations, awake to invention, awake to methods of gaining control over nature and the wonderful forces with which the storehouses of the earth are filled. But because of this very wakefulness on the intellectual and physical sides we are in danger of becoming sleepy and heavy and lethargic on the side of the Spirit, and we must confess that multitudes in the churches are half asleep. Perhaps none of us are clear of guilt in this matter: May God arouse us that we may be fully awake to the right things! Many people are busy doing the wrong things, or things in which there is no gift of peace or joy in doing. They are busy at the wrong places, greatly occupied with things that are not worthy of their occupation; they are busy here and there, busy enough, too busy, and they let the King pass by.

On the Mount of Transfiguration, when the disciples were fully awake, they learned infinitely more of Christ than they had ever known before. Years afterward Peter wrote, "We were eye-witnesses of his majesty." And it was then that they heard the voice from heaven, "This is my Son, my chosen: Hear ye him." Are there not those who listen to me this morning who need to awake out of sleep, and with clear eyes gaze anew on the transfigured Christ, and give intent hearing to the voice of the Good Shepherd?

II

The voice of the Good Shepherd is heard seeking after the lost. Christ's story of the shepherd leaving the ninety and nine folded, and going forth through the darkness of the night seeking after the lost sheep, is realized to-day in every land. Humanity is lost until it comes under the care of the Good Shepherd.

I once had a father call upon me in a city where I was pastor to ask my assistance in getting his son released from prison. And he told me the sad story, how the boy had gone away from home, where he was loved and protected, and became lost to his family. Without father or mother, and without sufficient maturity or wisdom to guide his steps, he was a failure from the start. Things grew worse with him. He got into bad company, and, more sinned against than sinning, had been thrust into prison. The father, who had lost track of him, heard of him only through his shame and disgrace, and as fast as the trains could carry him he had come to his rescue. We got him out of prison. The father clothed him in respectable garments and took him home to his mother. Years afterward he told me that he had become entirely restored to goodness and to manhood. Now it is just like that in the spiritual realm when we turn away from God, when we reject the Christ who has redeemed us, and go our own way. When we do that spiritually, we become homeless and outcast. Then it is that Christ comes through the darkness and night of our sin, calling after the lost. Is he not seeking some of you here to-day? Ah, if you will but listen to the voice of the Good Shepherd you will know the caressing tenderness of his tone, the loving mercy of his arms, and the joy and the glory and the power of feeling that you are in the care and ownership of the Good Shepherd.

III

The voice of the Good Shepherd speaks in comfort and assurance to his flock. Christ speaks of those who love him and listen to him and follow him as "Mine own." What a wonderful thing it is to feel that Christ speaks that way of us. These words seek to give us some glimpse of the mystic fellowship of the Son of God with his own disciples, the inner knowledge of kinship, fellowship, and love. Christ in his prayer for all who love him says, "And this is life eternal, that they should know thee the only true God, and him whom thou didst send, even Jesus Christ." There is no life so brave, so noble, or so peaceful as the life that is consciously under such care of Jesus.

There is an old story of Fletcher, who was the great preacher of his day. At Madeley Wood there is a cottage, still standing, which contained a great baker's oven. The wife who lived in that house in Fletcher's time was a devout Christian, and used to go to hear Fletcher every Sunday morning, much to the annoyance of her ungodly husband. One Saturday night, in a drunken mood, he vowed that, if she dared to leave home the next day, he would heat the big baking-oven for her by the time she returned, and put her inside. In face of such a threat the woman hesitated a moment; but at length decided that she would go to Madeley as usual and at all cost! But she purposed in her heart not to return home at once; she would remain at Madeley that whole day, and the next, till her husband's fury had passed.

But Fletcher's sermon that morning changed her plans. The sermon was on Nebuchadnezzar, the burning fiery furnace, and God's marvelous deliverance of his chosen servants from the flames. For one hearer, at least, that sermon had special applicability. As this woman from Madeley Wood listened to it, the spirit within her was changed. Her timorous resolutions vanished; she prayed more earnestly for the conversion of her husband, and resolved to go back immediately, and to brave, if need be, a sevenfold heated fire. In this spirit she returned home.

As she drew near to the house, sure enough she saw the oven heating, and hotter than she had ever known it, and her heart for the moment almost failed her. But bravely she lifted the latch, and prepared to face her infuriated husband. To her amazement, he did not spring to the door to seize her! But there, yonder, in the far corner of the cottage, he was upon his knees. Instead of curses and vile imprecations, he was actually in prayer! The lion had become a lamb! In one short hour, by the finger of God, to this brutal blasphemer had been given the heart of a little child!

It may be that I speak to some of you who face trial and difficulty in the path of loyalty to Jesus Christ. If so, I want to say to you, with all the earnestness possible, that Jesus is able to care for his own, and if you will listen to the voice of the Good Shepherd this morning, he will speak to you with comfort and assurance that he is able to keep what you will commit to him against every day of adversity and trial.

IV

The voice of the Good Shepherd always leads the Christian toward the highest power and the noblest career. All who have studied the career of Moody, the greatest evangelist of the last generation, have noted how slowly he came to his remarkable power. His first visit to England, in 1867, attracted almost no attention whatever. But it was on that visit that Moody heard these words: "The world has yet to see what God will do with, and for, and through, and in, and by the man who is fully and wholly consecrated to him." On his return to America from that visit he came under the influence of Henry Moorehouse, who preached for Moody several days in Chicago; and it was through the preaching of Henry Moorehouse that Moody reversed the order of his preaching: He discovered, as tho it were an entirely new discovery, that God is love; he saw that the great appeal to the human heart is not the threatening of the law, but the love of God, and after listening to Henry Moorehouse night after night, that became the great predominant note, that God loves men.

From that day Moody came into closer touch with Christ. He saw with clearer eyes, and the voice of the Good Shepherd led him onward. In 1871 his church was burned to the ground in Chicago. He started out to try to get money for a new church. He tells the story of what happened: "My heart was not in the begging. I could not appeal. I was crying all the time that

God would fill me with his Spirit. Well, one day in the city of New York—oh, what a day! I cannot describe it, I seldom refer to it. It is almost too sacred an experience to name. Paul had an experience of which he never spoke for fourteen years. I can only say that God revealed himself to me, and I had such an experience of his love that I had to ask him to stay his hand. I went to preaching again. The sermons were not different. I did not present any new truths, yet hundreds were converted. I would not now be placed back where I was before that blest experience if you should give me all the world.'' And from that day on Moody was the greatest personal religious factor in the world while he lived. What was the secret? He had given unreserved hearing and obedience to the voice of the Good Shepherd. My friends, my heart longs that such divine hungering and thirsting after righteousness may possess our souls today that we shall be filled with that spirit of perfect obedience to Christ. Is it not true that this is our great need? The fields are white for the harvest all about us. Multitudes of men and women brought up in Christian homes, taught in Christian Sunday-schools, are in this great city, wandering from God, going farther and farther into sin, while we do little to gather them for our Lord. What we need above everything to do this great work is a closer fellowship with Christ, a keener, more sensitive ear to hear his voice, and a heart that will yield in complete surrender to do his bidding in seeking and saving the lost.

We must not forget to give a moment's thought to the great goal toward which the Good Shepherd is seeking to lead all his flock. Christ says, ''My sheep hear my voice, and I know them, and they follow me: and I give unto them eternal life; and they shall never perish, and no one shall snatch them out of my hand.'' That makes not only the present, but the future, safe and glorious.

"I cannot see the distant shady trail
    That winds among the gnarlèd oaks and ferns;
  And yet I know that, on beyond the blue,
    For me a quenchless love-light burns.

"And so I climb and feast among the flowers,
    And at the midnoon dream beneath the pine;
  While, at the flaming sundown-red, I sip
    My own eve-star's ambrosial wine.

"And when at last I mount the far-off crag,
  I know that, on the happy, wind-blown crest,
  The wished-for hand shall flash the long-sought light,
    And in the splendor I shall rest."

THE END.